WHAT YOUR COLLEA
ARE SAYING . . .

"I will admit, when I first began reading, I was thinking, 'Here we go again, another book on differentiation.' As I read, my feelings quickly changed. I believe this book provides different information than previous books I've read on the subject. It is very easy to read, and most teachers could make substantive changes in their instruction immediately. This may be the quickest way to improve math learning and understanding I've seen. I am anxious to incorporate the strategies in this book in my planning for all students to enhance their ability to know, understand, and do math while loving it!"

—Marcia Carlson
Classroom Teacher
Crestview School of Inquiry
West Des Moines, IA

"While we know that the importance of differentiation is the key to student engagement and success, implementing key differentiation practices remains elusive to us as we balance competing curriculum, student, and administrative demands. Smith's book seamlessly unpacks what differentiation is and is not and provides explicit and, dare I say, beautiful examples of what this can look like in the classroom. You will be hooked from the first page and be inspired and empowered to transform your classroom, your teaching, and your students' mathematical learning experiences through and with this practical, realistic, and meaningful differentiation system."

—Beth Kobett, EdD
Assistant Professor
Stevenson University

"I believe Dr. Nanci Smith's *Every Math Learner: A Doable Approach to Teaching With Learning Differences in Mind* is arguably the best book now available for math teachers. In my conversations with math teachers and observations of classrooms, there is generally good-to-great expertise in math content knowledge. Problems occur, however, when there is lock-step reliance (perhaps with minor variations) on the math textbook or when there are beliefs and practices that all students predominately learn in the same way. Dr. Smith—a master teacher and trainer—flips the paradigm from teaching to learning. I've personally seen Dr. Smith's work with teachers, and know that she creates tremendous excitement within the teaching profession for practically and substantively moving from teacher-centered classrooms to learning-centered classrooms that support the needs and interests of *all* students."

—*Mark Boyer*
Retired Assistant Superintendent for Learning
Singapore American School

"For years I have searched for a book that had practical tips and ideas of how to differentiate instruction for secondary mathematics. That book has FINALLY arrived! While reading the book, I felt like I was having a conversation with someone who understands students and what helps them make sense of their learning in the mathematics classroom. This book provides teachers with 'common sense' ideas and activities to help engage students in their own learning."

—*Cathy Battles*
Consultant, University of Missouri
Kansas City and Regional Professional Development Center

"*Every Math Learner* is a powerful tool for educators serious about meeting the needs of all learners in their mathematics classrooms. Nanci Smith balances philosophy with practicality while providing a glimpse into real classrooms with real students. Teachers will ultimately learn how to lift students up to their greatest potential in learning."

—*Eileen Hogan*
District Mathematics Facilitator
Winnetka District #36

"*Every Math Learner* continuously invites the reader to interact with the content through the Watch It!, Try It!, and Consider It! processes. The immediate application of the book's content, the mathematics examples, and the videos of real secondary classrooms are helpful for all educators who want to learn more about their students, differentiate instruction, and plan and implement units or lessons that deepen students' mathematical interest, understanding, and learning."

—*Nora G. Ramirez*
President, Arizona Association of Teachers of Mathematics

"As a New York State public school administrator, I have observed Nanci Smith work with middle and high school teachers across disciplines. She is engaging and interactive! Her ability to respond spontaneously to questions in all disciplines is remarkable. So excited to see these books coming out!"

—*Ellen Shields*
Retired Curriculum Director
North Shore Public Schools

"This book is an excellent resource for teachers and administrators alike. It clearly explains key tenants of effective differentiation and through an interactive approach offers numerous practical examples of secondary mathematics differentiation. This book is a must read for any educator looking to reach all students."

—*Brad Weinhold, EdD*
Assistant Principal
Overland High School

"As a Professor of Mathematics highly involved in K–12 education I look for two major things in teaching resources. There must be solid, rigorous mathematics and there must be attention paid to varying the delivery system to allow learners to access the mathematics in appropriate ways. Nanci Smith has done both things admirably in this valuable and unique addition to our teaching resources."

—*Billie Earl Sparks, PhD*
Professor of Mathematics, Emeritus
University of Wisconsin – Eau Claire

"Dr. Smith provided a clear and well-structured solution to truly making math 'doable' for all students. As our society continues to move towards a more technology based economy the importance of math concepts becomes more essential for all our students. Dr. Smith, provides clear understandable solutions for educators to reach all students to assure they meet the demands of 21st Century."

—*James Scott*
Director of Educational Services Nadaburg School District

*This book is dedicated to Marianne Boyer, the best
big sister anyone could have. You taught me
to subtract with regrouping in your bedroom,
and more importantly about life.
You have always believed, and continue to believe in me.
Thank you.*

*This book is also dedicated to Cathy Battles.
You are one of the most generous, patient, and kind
people on the planet. I am constantly thankful
that I came to your district for work and
that you became my friend.
I am glad that you didn't really retire
and that now the teachers and students
of Missouri can all benefit from your wisdom.*

EVERY MATH LEARNER

A DOABLE APPROACH TO TEACHING
WITH LEARNING DIFFERENCES
IN MIND
GRADES 6-12

NANCI N. SMITH

FOREWORD BY CAROL ANN TOMLINSON

CM CORWIN
MATHEMATICS

FOR INFORMATION:

Corwin

A SAGE Company

2455 Teller Road

Thousand Oaks, California 91320

(800) 233-9936

Fax: (800) 417-2466

www.corwin.com

SAGE Ltd.

1 Oliver's Yard

55 City Road

London EC1Y 1SP

United Kingdom

SAGE India Pvt. Ltd.

B 1/I 1 Mohan Cooperative Industrial Area

Mathura Road, New Delhi 110 044

India

SAGE Asia-Pacific Pte. Ltd.

33 Pekin Street #02-01

Far East Square

Singapore 048763

Acquisitions Editor: Erin Null

Editorial Development Manager: Julie Nemer

Editorial Assistant: Nicole Shade

Production Editor: Libby Larson

Copy Editor: Gillian Dickens

Typesetter: C&M Digitals (P) Ltd.

Proofreader: Ellen Brink

Indexer: Robie Grant

Cover Designer: Scott Van Atta

Marketing Managers: Rebecca Eaton and
                                    Margaret O'Connor

Printed in the United States of America.

ISBN: 978-1-5063-4074-6

This book is printed on acid-free paper.

Certified Chain of Custody
SUSTAINABLE   Promoting Sustainable Forestry
FORESTRY
INITIATIVE   www.sfiprogram.org
SFI-01268

SFI label applies to text stock

17 18 19 20 21 10 9 8 7 6 5 4 3 2 1

DISCLAIMER: This book may direct you to access third-party content via Web links, QR codes, or other scannable technologies, which are provided for your reference by the author(s). Corwin makes no guarantee that such third-party content will be available for your use and encourages you to review the terms and conditions of such third-party content. Corwin takes no responsibility and assumes no liability for your use of any third-party content, nor does Corwin approve, sponsor, endorse, verify, or certify such third-party content.

CONTENTS

Downloadable at resources.corwin.com/everymathlearner6-12

Chapter 2: Tools and Templates for Find Out

Chapter 3: Tools and Templates for Teach Up

Chapter 4: Tools and Templates for Step Up

Chapter 6: Tools and Templates for Power On

Chapter 7: Tools and Templates for Step Back

Chapter 8: Tools and Templates for Close Up

VIDEO CONTENTS

CHAPTER 4: STEP UP

CHAPTER 5: SET IT UP

CHAPTER 6: POWER ON

CHAPTER 7: STEP BACK

CHAPTER 8: CLOSE UP

With special thanks to the teachers and principals from Skyline Ranch Elementary School and Grandview High School. Skyline Ranch Elementary is a public K–8 school in the Florence School district in Arizona. Grandview High School is a public 9–12 high school in the Grandview C-4 School District in Missouri.

Additional thanks to the University of Missouri Kansas City Regional Professional Development Center (UMKC RPDC) for connecting us with Jennifer Price, principal, and the teachers of Grandview High School.

Grade	Teacher
Grade Six	Kimberly Farless has been teaching for 14 years and currently teaches fifth through eighth grade math. She loves seeing her students' faces light up when they finally understand the topic. She enjoys inspiring students to love math.
Grade Nine, Algebra	Charles Criniere is a high school math teacher at Grandview Senior High. He is currently teaching Algebra 1 and Math Plus. He has taught every math class from pre-algebra through College Algebra in his ten year career. He is devoted to educating and inspiring all students to apply algebraic models and situations into real life situations.
Grade Ten, Geometry	Kaitlyn Ritts is a third year teacher teaching high school geometry this school year. She especially loves seeing the expressions on her students' faces when they finally solve a tricky problem.

Grade 11, Algebra 2 	Cathy Battles is currently a math consultant. Prior to this she was a high school math teacher for more than 30 years and taught almost every class from pre-algebra, At Risk Math, AP Calculus and IB SL mathematics. She loves to see the expression on students faces when they have successfully worked through a challenging problem or understand a challenging concept.

FOREWORD

When I began my career as a high school teacher, my general hallmark
was unpreparedness. I think it's unlikely that any novice teacher ever set
foot in a classroom with less of a sense of what teaching meant than I did. I
began teaching at the end of the first marking period—Halloween week, which
has always seemed an appropriate metaphor somehow. I had not majored in
education, had not been a student-teacher, and had no idea how to write a
lesson plan. My three chief concerns were how to figure out what to teach next;
how to "manage" my adolescent students who, during the first marking period,
apparently had comported themselves with the abandonment of dervishes; and
how to find time to sleep.

My students came from economically "modest" homes at best. Most were
poor. Their experiences with the wider world were limited. (My eleventh-grade
history students had never heard the country called the USA and had no idea
what that stood for.) In time, I would understand that "their" world had as
much to teach me as "my" world had to teach them, but in the beginning, I
was absorbed with how to help them make sense (and maybe even meaning) of
the content I was assigned to teach them.

Of course, I saw quickly that some of the students read fluently and
comprehended thoroughly while others were unable to make their way
through simple text with even the most fundamental idea of what they had
read. Certainly I realized that some students completed homework proficiently

and even elegantly, while others turned in incomplete and incorrect work, and still others seemed generally to give up along the way and brought nothing to represent themselves. I saw also that some students had parents who closely monitored their children's schoolwork, some whose parents had no personal models for that kind of monitoring, some whose parents were too exhausted by life's demands to dig deeply into school matters, and some whose home lives seemed frightening to me—and draining to them.

Those patterns of difference were evident in class discussions, in group activities, on tests, and even in private conversations. Yet, if I concluded anything from the student differences I saw, it was not much more than that some kids had a steeper hill to climb than others. Perhaps it was just how I thought life was.

Interestingly, I really liked the students. In the limited way I knew how to do it, I cared deeply about them. I thought about them through most of my time away from the classroom. I valued what I learned from them on a daily basis. I celebrated with them when they did well and felt sad for them when they did poorly.

As is always the case with young people, they knew I cared. They knew I was working hard for them to make our time together meaningful. They appreciated my attempts at creativity. They thought I was a good teacher, and they were sad when I moved away at the end of that year. I was sad as well.

It was not until about 4 years later, in my third teaching assignment, that I began to see student differences as they would come to shape my teaching. The transformation was not abrupt. In some ways, it's still in process over 40 years later. Nonetheless, I recall with impressive clarity some of the moments that were catalysts for change.

I was teaching then in the middle school where I taught for 20 years. As I stood in the hall during the class change between first and second periods during the second week of the school year, a very small middle schooler whom I had not noticed before came up to me and whispered something I couldn't hear. The hallway was predictably noisy. I was tall. He was short. It took three attempts before I could understand what he was trying to tell me. He was 15. He was about to join my second-period class. And what he was whispering to me was, "I can't read." He did not know the full alphabet.

I had no idea how to teach reading. I had no idea what materials I might use with him, how I would find time to work with him in class, what the other students would do while I worked with him, how I would grade him, or anything else that was a practical approach to what seemed an overwhelming challenge for both of us. The one thing I did know was that he had taken a huge risk in sharing his secret with me, and I couldn't let him down.

I also didn't know, of course, that this fragile-looking child named Golden had launched me on a 40-plus year journey to create classrooms that seek out and respond effectively to the varied learning needs of students in those classrooms. There were other catalyzing moments to follow.

There was the day in the spring of that year when I realized with painful clarity that there were students in my class who were as far ahead in their learning as Golden was behind. At that moment, it was clear to me that I was doing them a damaging disservice to provide them and their parents with messages that they were doing wonderfully in our class when, in fact, they were not growing, not stretching, at all.

There was the day when a student that I saw as "just a typical seventh grader" and for whom I was making the happy assumption was just fine with "the typical seventh-grade assignments" wrote in his journal, "I like it on the days when we get to pick what to do in class. I get to read things I care about because I don't have many books at home, and it makes me feel special that you gave me a choice." Truth is, he had a choice because my attention was turned to Golden and a few assorted peers that I was learning to teach at their entry points. The "choice" was just a default option that enabled me to focus on the kids whom I *was* seeing as "special" in terms of the ways they needed me. I understood, at least in a rudimentary way, at that moment that every student needed to feel that my attention was, at times, particularly focused on him or her—and that, in fact, every student had differences that mattered in their learning. My vision at that moment was more or less binary—"Golden" and "everybody else." I needed to expand my field of vision considerably.

And there was the day—after completing report cards for the first marking period the night before—when I stood at my classroom door to welcome students in first period as they entered the room. I involuntarily seemed to associate a report card grade with the first few students who entered, and I had a thought that was clear and blunt. I could go ahead and complete report cards for the rest of the year with 27 weeks left, and I'd be remarkably accurate. If that was the case, and I knew it was, then my teaching wasn't making much of a difference. It wasn't changing things for kids. Those who were doing poorly in class continued to do poorly for the most part. Those who were at the top of the heap nearly always remained there. And those in the middle, for the most part, remained "middling." When I saw the class as a unit, planned for the class as a unit, taught them as a unit, nothing much changed. Again, it would take me a while to unravel that insight, but I knew I needed to understand it more fully.

There were many of those moments in the "Year of Golden," probably because I was ready for them. In retrospect, they'd been all around me in my first 3 years of teaching, but I didn't process them. Now, that seemed important.

I began to ask myself questions. What would it mean to have a classroom that tried to respond to the varied learning needs of the students in it? How could I think about what the class as a whole needed to accomplish while, at the same time, taking into account the current status of each student in regard to the whole-class agenda? How could I think about class time differently? About use of space? About materials? When did it make sense for us to work as a whole group? When in small groups? When individually? How could I possibly know "who was where" at a given time when my classes nearly always had 35 to 40 students in them? How could I explain my thinking to early adolescents? How could I invite them to be my partners in creating this kind of classroom?

I was fortunate to work with some colleagues who were willing to explore these questions, and many others, with me. Over time, we developed a philosophy of teaching, a set of principles to guide our work, a curriculum that was both content and student driven, and a toolbox of instructional and management strategies that invited attention to student variance. When I look now at the work we were doing so many years ago, I am still struck by its core of logic and its freshness. There were holes in the fabric of our thinking, of course—always ways to improve. But the work was good. We were better teachers because of it. And our students were the primary beneficiaries.

The question around which our work centered was this: How do we know our students more fully as individuals and craft classrooms that respond to what we learn about them? In time, the approach came to be called "differentiated instruction." The ideas embodied in the approach are not new. They've been pursued by teachers at least since Confucius said, "People differ in their gifts and talents. To teach them, you have to start where they are."

Differentiation is, in my view, a way of thinking about teaching—a philosophy more than a particular set of instructional strategies. Its goal is to ensure that each learner grows as much as possible as a result of classroom experiences. That goal is rarely realized when we teach students by the "batch." We are nearly always better teachers when we balance our emphasis between what we want students to learn and the humans we're asking to learn it.

I'm delighted that Nanci Smith has written this book for secondary math teachers. I had the opportunity to work with her when she was a high school math teacher doing exemplary differentiation with her students in all levels of math. That she knows the secondary classroom (and its inhabitants) well, understands her content deeply, and understands differentiation comprehensively allows her to speak with the authority of experience. She has implemented for the long haul what she commends in this book.

Every Math Learner: A Doable Approach to Teaching With Learning Differences in Mind, Grades 6–12 is both comprehensive and approachable. It provides enough background and rationale to enable teachers to be thoughtful in their planning but always follows with clear guidelines, multiple mathematics examples, templates that provide structure for planning and implementation, and even videos created with the specific purpose of enabling readers to see what ideas look like when translated into action. The book guides readers in thinking through all aspects of responsive instruction in secondary mathematics classes—getting to know students as people and as emerging mathematicians, creating environments that support differentiation, developing routines that enable flexibility and stability, and using assessment to guide teaching and learning. An element in the book that is particularly compelling to me is a chapter on how to help students understand math—to think mathematically— rather than simply to "do" mathematics. This chapter, like all the others in the book, should help teachers extend their own mathematical strength as they work to help their students do the same.

I hope your experience with the book creates some epiphany moments for you—and serves as a catalyst for developing your own way forward in most effectively teaching each of the students in your care. That's the core goal of differentiation.

Carol Ann Tomlinson, EdD

William Clay Parrish Jr. Professor & Chair
Educational Leadership, Foundations, & Policy
Curry School of Education
University of Virginia

PREFACE

Imagine it with me. The teacher is standing at the front of the room and about to model division. She has a pile of beans in her hand that she is about to put on the overhead projector to model putting a certain number of beans into a certain number of piles. Division. Right? The students, for the most part, are watching and rolling their eyes. Some are working on other projects. Some are politely waiting. Some are *not* politely waiting. The teacher in frustration says, "Stop acting like elementary school children! There is a reason I chose to teach high school. Now we have to divide." You see, that was me and that is a true story. It was my first year of teaching, I was teaching a pre-algebra class, and the book said the lesson was on whole-number division. It never dawned on me to do anything other than to teach whole-number division that day. I have never wanted a "do-over" so badly as when I think of my first year of teaching and especially that class. Thankfully, there are rarely pre-algebra classes in high school any longer, and we usually do not teach long division with whole numbers in secondary mathematics, unless it is in sixth grade in the numbers and operations unit. Even so, this scenario plays out in classrooms regardless of the topic.

I began teaching in the age of self-esteem. That is what we talked about almost more than anything else—being careful to preserve students' self-esteem. One teacher quipped to me that we sure inherited a group of students who felt good about themselves. . . . They didn't know anything, but they felt good about themselves. I took this charge seriously and as a result tried to treat all students in my class the same, and I behaved as though all students were learning equally and doing equally well. I was, after all, preserving their self-esteem. If I recognized that a student didn't understand, wouldn't that damage him or her? If I recognized that a student was more advanced or learning more quickly than others, wouldn't that make the rest of the class feel bad? The equalizing of my students only communicated to them that I did not know them well or did not care. I quickly realized that it was not their self-esteem that I needed to guard but their self-efficacy that I wanted to build. Today we call that a growth mindset, which we will discuss more fully in Chapter 5. These thoughts and realizations became the foundation of my most basic beliefs in education, although they have been significantly defined and refined over the past 25 years as our field has grown in research and practice.

REFRESHING THE CALL FOR DIFFERENTIATION

I'm a math person. I still consider myself a classroom teacher even though I have had a journey in education that has given me a wide variety of opportunities. Truthfully, I usually assume everyone already knows anything I have to share. I have been working with states, districts, schools, and teachers for over 15 years. I have even had the opportunity to work with international schools and speak at international conferences. I find the same thing—we all *know* that students are different and learn differently. We just don't really know what to do about it. Especially in mathematics, and especially in secondary mathematics, where the curriculum is so vast and the stakes are so high.

So why write this book now? Several recent issues compel me to put my practice into text. In light of more rigorous mathematics standards and increasingly high-stakes testing throughout the county and even internationally, differentiation seems even more of a necessity now than ever. Yet at the same time, there are noted authors and speakers who malign differentiation as an impossible dream for teachers. This is understandable considering that at the height of differentiated instruction (DI) popularity, differentiation was almost seen as a magic wand: for any ill, "differentiate!" was the battle cry. This was certainly not realistic or ever the intent of differentiation. As impossible expectations and unrealistic implementations of differentiated instruction played out, it was easy to conclude that differentiation does not work and is unfair to ask of teachers. We know that we are to teach mathematics through engaging, sense-making work and provide access to rich tasks for *all* students. How, then, can we downplay the need to approach learning in various ways and through differentiated tasks? Differentiation is not only about helping struggling students, to which it is most often referred today. Differentiation is for all students, at *all* readiness levels, with different ways to make sense of learning, and with different interests. Differentiation enables us to allow access to rich and compelling mathematics for all students. The time is more necessary than ever for a practical approach to addressing real learning differences in our students.

WHY WRITE *EVERY MATH LEARNER*

Thank you for picking up this book and looking inside. This book is for you—the dedicated educator. You see, today we need to be more dedicated and more flexible than ever before. You would probably agree that it is difficult to be an educator today. We work in a time when standards are evolving and require different types of learning and reasoning (especially in mathematics) than we may be used to. With our best efforts, we still hear, and have heard for years, how poorly the United States does as a nation in international mathematics testing, and of the disappointing results of internal testing showing the low percentage of students who reach proficient levels on the National Assessment for Educational Progress (NAEP) test as well as state and local tests. All of this amid the confusion of the teacher evaluation process and parents unsure of just about everything mentioned. And still we recognize the awe and privilege of touching young lives every day. This book is designed to help you do just that in the area of mathematics.

I now travel for a living, working with schools and districts across the country and occasionally around the world. I find myself occasionally lying (or at least hedging the truth) to the person next to me on the airplane when he or she asks what I do. I sometimes just don't want to get into the "evils" of education, especially mathematics education. I really don't want to hear how they are not a "math person" or always hated mathematics. And yet, the majority of adults and parents I know want to go back to how mathematics was taught when they learned it. Does anyone else find this ironic?

It probably does not come as a surprise to you that many students—and, if we are honest, adults and teachers (other than secondary mathematics teachers, that is)—dislike math. Math doesn't appear to make sense. There is a belief that either you are or are not a math person. That math is all about whether answers are right or wrong. Most adults who admit to disliking mathematics or even being math-phobic can usually name the teacher and the event responsible for this attitude (Boaler, 2015). This is scary stuff. Mathematics instruction and classrooms cannot continue in the same ways they have been operating for the past 50 or more years. I remember as a young teacher in the late 1980s hearing a speaker say that we teach mathematics today as if we are preparing students to be 1940s shopkeepers. I look at classrooms today, and although there is some change in some classrooms, I wonder if the speaker would notice significant differences in the majority of classrooms today.

With that said, there are some differences in the mathematics classroom today. Largely due to the shift in emphasis of what it means to be proficient in mathematics from speed and getting correct answers to connections, reasoning, and representation while determining accurate answers, many mathematics classrooms are doing some things differently. Many teachers have begun requiring multiple representation and strategies for operations and problem solving. There are classrooms filled with discourse and collaborative learning. These are positive changes. However, too often mathematics is still often being taught as steps, formulas, and memorized facts, just like in the old days. The "smart kids" often dominate discourse, and that is just fine with other students who do not want to participate or feel stupid and are also fine with the teacher who wants to keep moving and who is only looking for correct answers. Students too often still do not really believe that math is supposed to make sense and apply to their lives. They still believe that a person is either good at math or isn't. And I truly believe that the reason for a lack of change is not a lack of desire but rather a lack of information. It is time for practical and specific examples to illuminate what mathematics learning can and should be for each and every student in every classroom.

MEETING *ALL* STUDENTS' MATHEMATICS NEEDS

If we are to help all students reach high expectations, given their diverse backgrounds, methods for learning, and gaps and accelerations in prior knowledge, differentiation is needed now more than ever. However, it has to be realistic and practical differentiation, not the "magic wand" approach. In the pages that follow, you will find how differentiation as a structure can help reach all students in mathematics (Chapter 1).

The second chapter will discuss how to determine who your students are as learners and how to use the information to design learning opportunities that excite and motivate your students. It gives concrete lesson examples and grouping strategies.

Next we will take a look at mathematics content and what it means to *understand* mathematics, not just to know and do mathematics. We will look at how to continuously "teach up," maintaining high expectations and rigor in planning units, lessons, and assessments (Chapter 3).

The fourth chapter looks at the purposefulness of differentiation—how to make proactive decisions during planning. Chapter 4 shows you how to choose tasks that will deepen mathematical understanding, offer multiple entry points, and be accessible to all students through differentiation. The chapter is full of strategies and the "how-to" of differentiation.

Chapters 5 and 6 address the "daily-ness" of the classroom. In Chapter 5, we look at how to set up expectations in your classroom and establish a healthy learning environment with a growth mindset. This chapter describes one area of the fine-tuning of differentiation and learning mathematics in general, starting with how to set up a collaborative learning community and environment and how to establish growth mindsets for all learners. The key is how to keep the learning environment operating effectively as the year goes on.

Chapter 6 addresses the management of the classroom and balancing differentiated tasks. Differentiating working conditions does not need to be difficult. The role of routines, such as how to move in and out of groups, how to respect others who are working on different things, turning in work, what to do when you are finished, and so on, is part of making differentiation work. This chapter gives advice on some of the subtleties of making differentiation a natural way to learn.

Following this, we address the role of assessment. What does assessment look like in a differentiated classroom? Can you differentiate tests or other assessments? How? Is that fair? What about feedback and grading? How do you get students to self-assess? This is addressed in Chapter 7.

Finally, we will look at a week in the life of a differentiated mathematics class in Chapter 8. We will look at the initial planning and how formative assessment each day informs adjustments to the plans. We will look at the decision-making process through a description of the week in the life of a seventh-grade teacher and an Algebra 1 teacher.

Every Math Learner provides detailed information for turning every aspect of your mathematics class into a differentiated mathematics class. With that said, special areas of expertise that benefit from differentiation were not able to be fully addressed in this book, including English language learners and special education students. All of the strategies in this book are appropriate for these identified learners, but the depth of these fields cannot be represented in this book. Appendixes A, B, and C provide further resources for reading in these areas and further reading on rigorous mathematical tasks.

THE DIFFERENCE OF *EVERY MATH LEARNER*

There have been many books on differentiation and even several on differentiating mathematics. *Every Math Learner* will complement the existing books by extending the structures, strategies, and examples of differentiation, but it will also be different in several ways.

GOALS

I see a greater sense of pressure, frustration, and disappointment among teachers today than ever before. I wish I could change that. This book does *not* change the testing pressure. It *does* offer concrete strategies, examples, and classroom stories that help students learn mathematics more effectively and maximize each student's learning potential, thus *leading* to improved test scores.

It is my goal that this book will provide you with specific and practical tools to design and implement rich and engaging mathematics instruction, tailored to your students' needs. Along the way, I will encourage you to think deeply about the mathematics content, reaching new and exciting "aha moments" to pass on to your students. Through this two-pronged approach, rich mathematical content, and engaging differentiated instruction, you and your students will experience new levels of learning and accomplishment. I sincerely hope that this book will equip you, the math teacher, to make mathematics understandable, doable, and enjoyable for you and all of our students.

FEATURES

Throughout the chapters of *Every Math Learner,* you will find features to facilitate your implementation of differentiation. Each chapter will include the following:

- Specific content across Grades 6 to 12 but primarily through Algebra 2
- Chances to pause and think about content through "Consider It!"
- Many strategy examples, including "Try It!" strategies that are immediately usable
- Balancing the "what" and the "why" of differentiation
- Frequently Asked Questions (FAQs) and answers pertaining to the chapter
- A chance for you, the reader, to reflect, summarize, and plan your next steps
- Templates and checklists to design and refine your instruction
- And the best part . . . video!

I am excited for you to use this book, especially because we have gone out in the field and captured real classrooms with real students for you to see differentiation in action. There is just nothing like seeing what is being explained, is there? Well, the best would be for you to try it in your own setting, but of course I couldn't capture that for you. I trust you will, though.

WHO IS THIS FOR?

This book is for anyone who teaches mathematics. It was primarily written with secondary classroom teachers in mind, but mathematics coaches and curriculum developers will also benefit from the structures of thought and practical examples and tasks. In addition, administrators will find the book helpful when determining what should be seen in mathematics classrooms.

USING *EVERY MATH LEARNER*

Corwin Publishing has a saying: Corwin books are not meant to be read. They are meant to be used. This book is being written with the idea of "using." With that in mind, the book can be used

- for individual teachers to design their own units, lessons, and activities;

- for teacher teams to help guide differentiated tasks and assessments;

- for coaches and mentors to guide teachers in their own growth and goal setting;

- as a professional development tool to focus on specific strategies;

- to adjust materials and program resources to better meet students' needs.

CONCLUSION
....

This book will help you, the teacher, understand your students as learners and why some things work with some of them and others don't. It is a practical guide to all aspects of the classroom and how to maintain order and sanity as you consider the students in your care and how to help them come to know, understand, and (dare I say) LOVE mathematics!

ACKNOWLEDGMENTS

If you think about giving a thank you speech for where you are right now in your life, whom would you acknowledge? You now understand the overwhelming sense I feel that I have gotten to this point only because of the love, friendship, and support of so many people.

Over the past 25 years or more, I have learned from and worked alongside many extraordinary educators. Thank you to Regina Newman for believing in and supporting me and to the Middle School Mathematics team at North Shore School District for working so hard to try new and strange things in order to do the best for your students. Thank you to the incredible teachers at Roslyn School District: Kristina Wood, Gabby Gizzi, Amy Fetters, Loretta Fonseca, Renee Huntley, and especially Orit Guriel. You helped me learn how to put experience and thought into words, stretched my thinking, and put ideas into action that I would not have foreseen. Working with you shaped all of my future work.

Judy Rex, you have been on this journey with me from the beginning and have talked me off the ledge more times and in more ways than I thought possible.

Mark Boyer taught me how to dream and believed in me when there was little in which to believe. He encouraged me and provided opportunities and gentle direction. Your retirement from education is a loss for us all, so I am very thankful to my sister for having married you so that I won't lose you from my life.

My learning and refined thinking on differentiation would be nothing without colleagues like Cathy Battles, Eileen Goodspeed, Marcia Embeau, Jessica Hockett, Cindy Strickland, and Sandra Page. Thank you for pushing, questioning, and sharing with me.

My life would not be the same without Lisa Fritz, Ellen Shields, and Betz Frederick. Everyone should have such unwavering love and support to get you through amazingly tough times.

Carol Tomlinson is my role model for graciousness, wisdom, encouragement, and gentleness. Your brilliant mind strikes awe in me, and I shudder to think that I am trying to write a book in your field. My words echo hollow to my ears in comparison to your voice in my head. Again, I thank you for all that you have done in my life these past 16 years.

To my family that has ridden the road with me—my husband and best friend Russ and children Josh, Abbi, and Chris and their spouses Tory, Jeff, and Jen—thank you for being there in all the ups, downs, and round-abouts. You encourage and tease equally . . . well maybe tease more . . . and I wouldn't have it any other way. Thank you for putting up with me and loving me and being proud of me. And thank you for giving me grandchildren: Maddi, Izzi, Lexi, Sophi, Judah, Landon, Elena, and Charlotte (at this writing—but I'm not pushing).

I would not have become involved in this project if not for Erin Null. Your perseverance, generosity, and helpfulness made my qualms go away and encouraged a vision beyond anything I thought possible. Then you made the vision reality. Thank you for being constantly available and quick to respond with sound ideas and feedback.

Above all, I give my praise to my Lord and Savior, Jesus Christ. You are the perfect model of a teacher who loves, reaches individuals in individual ways, and never gives up.

PUBLISHER'S ACKNOWLEDGMENTS

Corwin would like to thank the following individuals for their editorial insight and guidance:

Emily Bonner
Associate Professor of Curriculum and Instruction
University of Texas at San Antonio
San Antonio, TX

Marcia Carlson
Classroom Teacher
Crestview School of Inquiry
West Des Moines, IA

JoAnn Hiatt
Mathematics Instructor
Belton High School
Olathe, KS

Lyneille Meza
Director of Data and Assessment
Denton Independent School District
Denton, TX

Daniel Kikuji Rubenstein
Executive Director
Brooklyn Prospect Charter School
Brooklyn, NY

ABOUT THE AUTHOR

 **Dr. Nanci N. Smith** is currently a full-time national and international consultant and featured conference speaker in the areas of mathematics, curriculum and assessment, differentiated instruction, and collaborative teams. Her work includes professional development in 45 states and nine countries.

Nanci taught mathematics at the high school and university levels and differentiated instruction as a master's course.

Dr. Smith received her PhD in curriculum and instruction, mathematics education from Arizona State University. She is Nationally Board Certified in Adolescent and Young Adult Mathematics.

Nanci is author of *Every Math Learner: A Doable Approach to Teaching With Learning Differences in Mind, Grades K–5* and *A Mind for Mathematics: Meaningful Teaching and Learning in Elementary Classrooms,* as well as coauthor of *A Handbook for Unstoppable Learning.* She was the consultant, designer, and author of the *Meaningful Math: Leading Students Toward Understanding and Application* DVD series and developed an NSF-funded CD/DVD professional development series for middle school mathematics teachers. She has various published chapters in the areas of differentiation, effective mathematics instruction, curriculum design, and standards implementation and has given interviews for publications and NPR. She has been a featured speaker for the NCTM national conference as well as numerous other conferences in the United States and abroad.

Nanci lives in Phoenix, Arizona, with her husband Russ and three cats. Besides educating all students, her passions are her family—especially her eight grandchildren—travel, and knitting.

CHAPTER ONE

START UP

WHY KNOWING AND ADDRESSING STUDENTS' LEARNING DIFFERENCES IS CRITICAL

Undoubtedly you have heard of "differentiated instruction." Depending on your experience or background, you might associate learning styles or choices with the term. You may associate Tier 1 Response to Intervention (RTI). All of these have aspects of differentiation, but none are the complete picture. In this chapter, you will find the following:

Introduction	Frequently Asked Questions
What Differentiation Is and Is Not	Keepsakes and Plans
A Glance at a Differentiated Classroom	

INTRODUCTION

Welcome to school! There is something so very exciting about a new class of students, a new year of potential, and the fulfillment of touching the future. As teachers, we love getting to know our students. We love thinking about how much they will grow this year through another turbulent tween or teen year. We feel excitement to share our content that we love, and we hope our students will love it too.

And very quickly, as we get to know our students, we recognize who each student is as an individual human being and as an individual learner. We come to understand that Maddi already knows much of what is in our grade level or course content, and what she doesn't already know, she will learn in less than half the time it takes the rest of the class. There is outgoing Elena, who prefers to learn with others, asks for help freely, and offers help equally as freely. Judah is a constant bundle of energy and desires to follow directions, even if he usually forgets what the directions were and asks you to repeat them as soon as you finish giving them. There is Izzi, who prefers to draw and thinks in color and pictures, and Landon, who is shyly constant in his learning. There is Alexia, who reads thick novels voraciously but is less inclined to enjoy math. Sophia is extremely shy, bright, and capable but doesn't want to show it and does not like to do anything in front of the class. And there is Justin, who you didn't even realize was a special education student with an Individualized Education Plan (IEP) until the IEP showed up in your mailbox. Aamino just moved to this country from Somalia and hasn't been in a formal school for over a year and has very limited English. Nick is very bright but is slowly losing interest in school because he is tired from taking care of his little brother and sister after school, even though he could use some attention himself. And that is just a few of the students in class. When we consider all of the students and the overwhelming amount there is to learn this year, we don't lose our love for students and enthusiasm, but we begin to wonder just how to pull all of this off!

Let's face it. We didn't go into teaching for the prestige or money. We care about students. We care about the quiet and shy, the rowdy and rambunctious, the leaders and followers, the musicians, artists, athletes, cheerleaders, scholars, strugglers, and everyone in between. And in most classrooms, I have just described your student population. We want to forward our content and give a love of it to our students. Our kids come to us from a wide range of backgrounds and families, experiences, and mastery. And we need to reach and teach them all: to have high expectations for each student and help each one fulfill his or her potential and beyond. And that is where differentiation comes in.

WATCH IT!

As you watch Video 1.1, *Getting Started With Differentiation*, consider the following questions:

1. How is differentiation not individualization, yet about the individual?
2. What descriptions confirm your understanding of what differentiation is and is not?
3. What is new or surprises you in the description or definition of differentiation?

Video 1.1 Getting Started With Differentiation

WHAT DIFFERENTIATION IS AND IS NOT

If you ask a group of educators what is differentiation, you will undoubtedly hear it is about helping every student succeed to the best of his or her ability. That is true. However, if you dig deeper for details, explanations can vary drastically and have changed in emphasis over the years. I have heard everything from "it's just the old individualized instruction back again with a new name." Or, "this is just about multiple intelligences," or even "all you have to do is give choices." Today, largely due to a common description of Tier 1 of Response to Intervention (RTI) as quality core instruction for all students that is differentiated, many educators equate differentiation with interventions for struggling learners. Just like the story of the blind men describing an elephant based only on the part of the elephant they can feel, all of these explanations give a small sliver of the bigger picture of differentiation. Far too often a person's sliver of differentiation is taken as the whole, applied in ways that are neither appropriate nor purposeful, and the conclusion is that differentiation just does not work.

According to Carol Ann Tomlinson (2014), "Teachers in differentiated classrooms begin with a clear and solid sense of what constitutes powerful curriculum and engaging instruction. Then they ask what it will take to modify that curriculum and instruction so that each learner comes away with knowledge, understanding, and skills necessary to take on the next important phase of learning" (p. 4). In essence, differentiation is a teacher's decisions about instructional and assessment design to best equip his or her students for learning.

Sounds simple, and in some ways, it is. In some ways, it absolutely is not. The decisions teachers make need to be based on the foundation of explicitly clear standards and learning goals, knowledge of their students as learners, effective pedagogical strategies and task choices, and assessment data. When thinking about students as learners, there are three areas as defined by Tomlinson (2001) that provide a structure for decision making: Readiness, Interest, and Learning Profile. These three characteristics of learners will be the basis on which we discuss and develop how we can embrace and address the differences in our learners. What follows is a brief introduction to each characteristic that will be developed in detail with lesson examples in the following chapters.

READINESS

"This is easy." "This is too hard. I can't do this." Neither of these reactions from students is what we want to hear. If those are honest reactions from the students, then we have not addressed their readiness. In some ways, readiness differentiation is like the Three Little Bears of Education: We want "Just Right." The problem is that it is usually impossible to find just one "just right" for an entire class (Hattie, 2013).

Readiness differentiation begins with determining the entry point for each student on the learning trajectory for the activity, lesson, or unit. We tend to link readiness with "ability grouping." Yet there are significant differences in what we commonly think of with readiness grouping and ability grouping or tracking, no matter how flexible the ability grouping may be designed to be. Many areas affect readiness, including but not limited to life experiences, prior knowledge, ability to abstract and generalize, and home support.

We have all experienced the wide range of learners in our classrooms that can be based on a wide variety of factors. Certainly, a student's prior knowledge plays a major role in whether the student is perceived as advanced, typical, or struggling. In addition, there are factors that equally affect (or perhaps have a greater impact on) a student's alacrity with learning mathematics, such as the speed at which students process and learn new information, the help and attitudes about education that students experience at home, and past experiences in school. Add to this students who are from other countries and learning English as a second language, or are identified as gifted or with a form of learning disability, and the range of learners can seem overwhelming. To teach all students with the same strategies, at the same pace with the same expectations, does not make sense. This is the essence of readiness differentiation.

Please notice that readiness does not imply ability! In fact, we now know without a doubt that ability is based on effort and is not a fixed commodity. According to Carol Dweck (2006), "No matter what your current ability is, effort is what ignites that ability and turns it into accomplishment."

Readiness addresses that range of challenges where learning can happen for a student, being neither too easy nor too hard. One of the problems with considering readiness is that when looking at the students' actions, it is easy to associate readiness with what students can and can't do . . . *especially* what they cannot do.

I remember reading an article several years ago about the new superintendent my district had just hired. In it she stated that we would be committed to finding all of the holes and gaps our students had and filling them. At first this might sound noble and an appropriate endeavor. But think about it. The implication is that our education was to work from a deficit model—find what is wrong and fix it. Working from this negative frame of mind leaks out in our attitudes and speech too often, leaving students to feel unsuccessful, unable to learn, and, at worst, dumb.

Readiness, on the other hand, works from a position of strength on the part of the student. What is it the student does know and is able to do? This provides the entry point into the learning. When we consider the "next step" in the learning progression for a student, we are addressing readiness. Readiness differentiation offers all students appropriate challenge, a taste of success with effort, and a developing sense of efficacy and pride in learning.

Figure 1.1 illustrates readiness differentiation as determining entry points on the learning path.

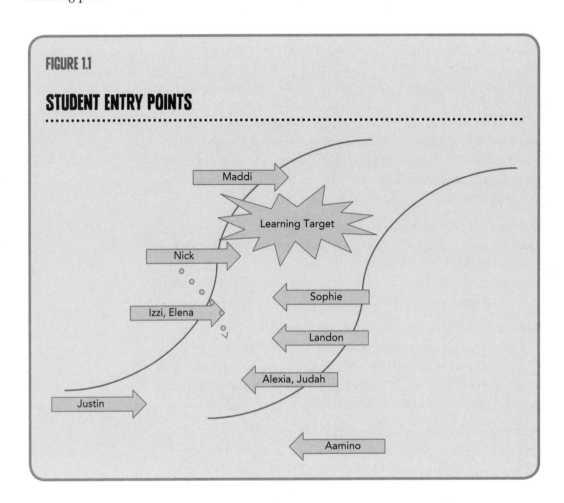

FIGURE 1.1

STUDENT ENTRY POINTS

Maddi

Learning Target

Nick

Izzi, Elena

Sophie

Landon

Alexia, Judah

Justin

Aamino

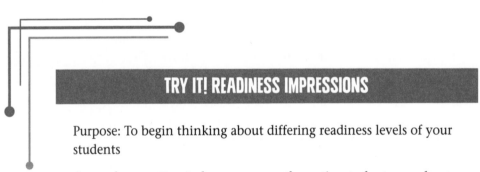

TRY IT! READINESS IMPRESSIONS

Purpose: To begin thinking about differing readiness levels of your students

As you have gotten to know your mathematics students, you have an instinct as to their readiness levels. At what readiness levels would you put each of your students for mathematics, recognizing that this is a general statement and that readiness certainly changes?

1. Make a list of readiness groupings for your classroom. Next to each student's name, explain why you placed that student in that group. For example, acquires new skills and concepts quickly or still struggles with basic facts.

This initial list is based on your current knowledge of your students. Detailed information on determining readiness is provided in Chapter 2, and further examples of designing for readiness is provided in Chapter 4.

INTEREST

We all know the power of interest—when students are really excited and hooked on what they are doing. The adage about time flying when you are having fun is never truer than when students are involved in learning and doing something they enjoy.

When I first considered differentiating by interest, I was largely stuck. For the most part, my students did not have hobbies and extracurricular activities that were mathematics related. No student came up to me and asked, "Is today the day we are going to learn slope? I've been waiting so long to learn all about slope. Please tell me it is today!" There are only so many shopping problems you can use with ratio or integers . . . and the boys didn't really care about shopping. Trying to print math problems on their favorite color of paper wasn't exactly doing it either! What a misunderstanding I had about differentiating by interest.

It is incredibly powerful when we can link our content learning to students' hobbies and passions. It is equally important to ignite new interests through our own modeling of interest and passion for our subject. Interest differentiation is about igniting intrinsic motivation for learning. Eric Jensen (1998) gives three criteria for increasing intrinsic motivation that fit perfectly with interest differentiation: providing choices, making content relevant to the learner, and using engaging and energetic learning activities. Figure 1.2 models Jensen's lesson factors that contrast increasing students' motivation versus apathy.

How we determine our students' interests can be easy—talk to them. Ask them. Beginning-of-the-year surveys are usually filled with interest items. We find out their hobbies, extracurricular activities, favorite movies and books, and hopes and dreams. We can also find out what are their favorite ways to learn mathematics, such as

FIGURE 1.2

MOTIVATION VS. APATHY LESSON FACTORS

Classroom Factors	Classroom Factors
Choices—access to content, process, product, grouping, resources, and environment	**Required**—no student voice, specific task or assignment for all
Relevance—what is being learned is meaningful in the eyes of the learner and connected to the learner's experiences. Content is developed at a conceptual and applicable level	**Irrelevant**—content appears out of context and disconnected from the student and is often learned only to pass a test
Engaging—emotional, energetic hands-on, and provides for the learner's input	**Passive**—learning activities have low interaction such as seatwork and note-taking
Results in	
Increased intrinsic motivation	Increased apathy and resentment

hands-on activities, games, and group work, and why. When we can make connections among personal interests, learning interests, and content, we have them hooked! All of these pieces of information begin to build a bank of interest differentiation possibilities.

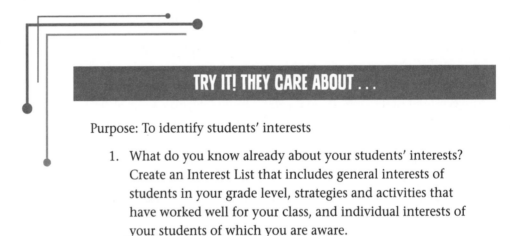

TRY IT! THEY CARE ABOUT . . .

Purpose: To identify students' interests

1. What do you know already about your students' interests? Create an Interest List that includes general interests of students in your grade level, strategies and activities that have worked well for your class, and individual interests of your students of which you are aware.

Strategies for assessing your students' interests are given in Chapter 2 and on the companion website at resources.corwin.com/everymathlearner6-12.

LEARNING PROFILE

Perhaps the most debated and questioned aspect of student differences is learning profile. In general, learning profile refers to the way brains best receive information, make sense of information, commit information to memory, and recall information from memory. I imagine that all of us have learning stories that exemplify when a lesson completely connected with us and when one completely did not. Sometimes it is a connection with the teacher. Other times it is dependent on the type of task. This could be a hint as to your preferences in learning. When I was a student, I struggled with teachers who primarily lectured. I still do not like listening to audiobooks and can get bored with long phone calls. I need visuals. When sitting in a lecture, I take extensive notes to make the talk visible. How about you? In what ways do you feel you learn best?

There are many different structures by which we can consider learning profile. Notice that the term is learning *profile*, which is an all-encompassing term for many different styles of learning. In fact, learning style has so many different meanings that it is wise to ask someone to clarify what he or she means when using the term.

Different authors and researchers have different opinions about learning profiles—whether we are born wired in certain ways, if these paths change over time, and if they vary subject to subject. For our purposes, we will have a more general conversation about learning profile and how we can use it to structure differentiated tasks in mathematics.

Learning profile includes four broad categories: Group Orientation, Cognitive Style, Learning Environment, and Intelligence Preference (Tomlinson, 2001). Figure 1.3 elaborates on each of these areas.

Certainly other factors can play into learning profile—there is plenty of research indicating learning differences between the genders as well as among cultural influences. While the learning profile structures are generalizable, none is true for every student. It is part of our job to be a student of our students—to determine what each student's combination of preferences will be as we teach mathematics. When considering learning profiles for your students, please be aware of two very important warnings.

- It is possible that some students learn in exactly the same ways that you do. You can also count on the fact that other students will not learn in the same way. Yet, it is completely natural for us

FIGURE 1.3

CATEGORIES OF LEARNING PROFILE

Group Orientation	How do students prefer to work? Alone or with a partner? Who likes to figure things out first and then share? Who likes to work through an activity with someone else? Which of your students work to please themselves, others, or the adults in their lives?
Cognitive Style	Which of your students need to see the big picture before they can make sense of the details, or do they need details in order to build to a big picture (whole-to-part or part-to-whole)? Who thinks very linearly and who is more global and nonlinear? Which students work better with collaboration and which work better with competition? Who are more reflective and who are more action oriented?
Learning Environment	Who needs a quiet and calm atmosphere to concentrate and who can concentrate in noise and activity? How does temperature and light (bright or dim, natural or fluorescent) affect the learning of different students? How are desks arranged? What about music playing?
Intelligence Preference	Students will come with different learning intelligence preferences such as the theory of multiple intelligences (Gardner) and triarchic theory (Sternberg), which includes analytical, practical, and/or creative orientation to learning.

Consider It!

Think about your own learning profile. What are your natural tendencies for preferred learning activities and instruction? How does this influence your lesson design? Who in your class learns in the same way? Who does not? Do you know how they might learn? Chapter 2 will explain how to recognize your students' learning profiles.

to teach in the ways we best learn. That will always be our most natural fallback option. Thus, it is important to be aware of and plan for the wide variety of learning profiles in your classroom.

- We need to be careful not to try to determine "what kind of learner" students are, lock them into that description, and then always assign them to tasks by what we assume is the student's "type." It is possible to use discussions about learning profile to help students understand differences in how people learn and their likely strengths and weaknesses, as discussed in Chapter 2. However, in differentiating by learning profile, it may be best to offer varied learning profile approaches to exploring and expressing learning, with the student making the choice of the specific task.

THREE CHARACTERISTICS OF DIFFERENCE

A friend and colleague, Cindy Strickland, uses an image of a three-legged stool to illustrate differentiation, with each leg labeled with one of the learning aspects of students. Figure 1.4 provides an illustration of the balance of the "differentiation legs."

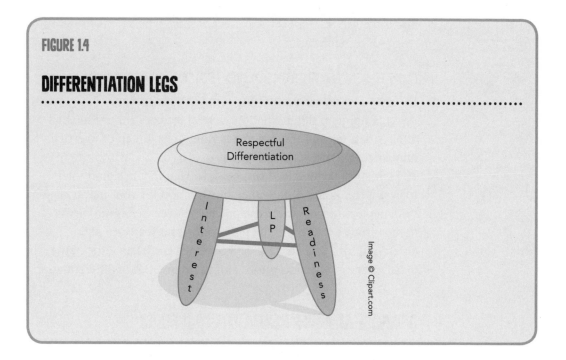

FIGURE 1.4

DIFFERENTIATION LEGS

Respectful Differentiation

Interest

LP

Readiness

Image © Clipart.com

Have you ever sat on a three-legged stool with uneven legs? I have. I can do it for a little while but soon am looking for a different place to sit. It wobbles and is uncomfortable. Worse would be sitting on a three-legged stool with only two legs . . . or what about one leg? That is a pogo stick, not a stool. This should be the picture of respectful differentiation: Decisions about differentiation need to be in balance according to students' learning needs. Just like a stool out of balance, differentiation out of balance may cause unanticipated consequences.

- When we differentiate only by **readiness,** we tend to track our classrooms without meaning to. Students begin to feel that they are always working with the same other students and can self-classify as smart or dumb, math person or not.

- When we differentiate only by **interest,** we can give the impression that learning for learning's sake is never necessary and that if a student isn't really interested, the learning can be skipped.

- When we differentiate only by **learning profile,** we can create learning cripples that are not flexible in their approaches to learning and not able to learn from a wide variety of tasks, opportunities, or teachers.

Consider It!

As you think about ways you currently differentiate in class, to which of the differentiation "legs" do you most naturally lean? Is there a "leg" that you do not address often or with which you feel uncomfortable?

The three-legged stool is the perfect balance when we consider the whole of differentiation.

DIFFERENTIATION IS AND ISN'T . . .

You may already be questioning some of your previous understanding of differentiation. Several misconceptions about differentiation can hinder teachers from investing in or effectually implementing differentiated instruction in their classrooms. The remaining chapters of this book will equip you step-by-step to be able to design differentiated instruction for your mathematics students. Before beginning the process, however, it is important to more fully understand the philosophy and structure of differentiation. Consider Figure 1.5, which contrasts some of the most common misconceptions and the actualities of differentiation.

A GLANCE AT A DIFFERENTIATED CLASSROOM

Most secondary mathematics classes run in a similar fashion. Students come in and usually have a warm-up of some kind on the board. Next, the previous night's homework is reviewed, followed by any new notes. Students then practice the type of problems the notes just covered, often with a worksheet or a practice set of problems in the text. If there is time, tonight's homework is begun at the end of class so the teacher can be sure students can finish at home. While there is nothing inherently wrong with any of these pieces, a steady diet of this type of learning is surely uninspiring at best and demotivating and disconnected at worst. Consider two examples of a slightly different way to design a differentiated mathematics class.

MIDDLE SCHOOL CLASSROOM

The teacher begins the lesson:

"Good morning! We have been working with adding and subtracting integers. We have talked about real-life examples of positives and negatives—can anyone give some ideas about that? (Students suggest spending money, going deep-sea diving, population growth or decrease, etc.) I am wondering if you and a partner could come up with one real-world situation that would be an addition or subtraction with integers—and one of the integers has to be a negative number. Write your situation on one of your white boards, and model and solve the situation with an equation on your other white board. We will have a class challenge in a few minutes."

FIGURE 1.5

DIFFERENTIATION IS AND ISN'T

Differentiation Isn't	Differentiation Is
A way to make struggling students pass the test	A way to address all students and all ranges of readiness. Readiness differentiation is one third of the total picture of differentiation and is not limited to struggling students.
Fluffy	A way for individual sense-making and connections by providing multiple methods for learning and demonstration of learning. It focuses on providing access to deep and rich content founded on standards.
The individualized instruction from the 1970s or personalized instruction	A way to address individual students and how they learn, but it does not endorse individual lessons for each student. Rather, it considers which groups of students will most benefit from which methods and tasks.
All about multiple intelligences	Inclusive of multiple intelligences, but a learning profile is one third of the total picture of differentiation, and multiple intelligences is one of many ways to address learning profiles. This is a small slice of the total picture of differentiation.
Just about giving choices to cover your bases	Inclusive of giving choices to increase motivation, but the design of the choices offered is significant. Again, interest differentiation is one third of the total picture of differentiation.
Instinctive	Not instinctive. Our instinct is to teach the way we learn or the way we were taught. Differentiation is based on assessment data and understanding our content as well as our students.
Untenable and not worth a teacher's time	Possible. No one differentiates every lesson every day. Choosing when and what to differentiate is part of a teacher's decision-making process. Designing effective differentiation does take time and planning, especially at first. It gets easier over time and is worth it when you see students engaged and excited to learn.

Students work with their partners and create scenarios and equations. Before the whole-class challenge, partners pair up to challenge each other and check their contexts and equations. Having three or four partners challenge the class with their contexts and show their solutions concludes the warm-up.

"Let's review what we have done so far with adding and subtracting integers. We began by using two-color counters and making zero pairs with addition. The counters got a little more complicated with subtraction, especially when we needed to add in zero pairs in order to subtract what we wanted. We also used what we already knew from modeling addition and subtraction of whole numbers in elementary school on number lines. We already knew that addition moves to the right on a number line, and subtraction moves to the left. This remains the same regardless of what is being added or subtracted because it is about addition and subtraction and not what is being added or subtracted. However, we needed to combine that with the idea that in mathematics, a negative sign means opposite. So, when we add or subtract a negative number, we move in the opposite direction on the number line."

"Yesterday you practiced using a number line to model addition and subtraction of integers. Some of you actually walked on our floor number line to make sense of moving in the opposite direction. Some of you drew hops on your table number lines, and some of you didn't need a physical number line but could imagine it in your mind to get to the correct answer. Everyone explained how to add or subtract integers in their own best method on their exit cards."

"Today we want to work some more with adding and subtracting integers and see if we can come up with ways to do this without needing a physical model. I am going to ask you to move to one of the corners of the room, based on your preference in adding and subtracting integers. The four corners are as follows:

1. I like to add and subtract with a number line.

2. I like to add and subtract with counters.

3. I don't like manipulatives and can use symbolic notation.

4. I would like some extra help in a small group, teacher-led discussion."

Students move to the four corners of room and form groups of two or three with others in their preferred work situation. The students are given a bank of problems to complete with their choice of solution method. The problems are all set up in related groups of four as follows:

$$3 + 5$$
$$3 + (-5)$$
$$-3 + 5$$
$$-3 + (-5)$$

The problem groups were chosen to lead into the closing whole-class discussion, which will formalize the patterns for adding integers.

Examples are available that model the first two problems on the sheet using the various methods for students who might need the extra support. Any student who realizes that he or she is not sure about how to do the practice problems will move to the teacher-led group.

In the teacher-led group, the same problems are modeled with number lines and counters to find solutions. The teacher has different students choose one of the methods and explain how they would solve the problems for the group, and the teacher only gets involved if needed. The number line method and counter method are used to check each other's answers. Once the teacher-led group is working well, the teacher is free to check in with the other three groups.

After work time, the teacher brings all the students back together to discuss the answers. For each problem, students are asked if anyone got any other answer, and models are put up showing how answers were found to determine the correct answer. Students run this part of the class as they are very familiar with sharing possible answers and defending their reasoning, which allows the teacher to check work and make any anecdotal records. She also monitors to be sure that all students are recording the correct answers to the problems in their groups of four.

$$3 + 5 = 8$$
$$3 + (-5) = -2$$
$$-3 + 5 = 2$$
$$-3 + (-5) = -8$$

Now that the problems have been correctly solved, students are asked to talk in their groups to see if they can see any patterns in the solutions. Students can immediately see that when the addends are the same sign, you "add the numbers without the sign on it and use whatever the sign was." When asked to explain why this makes sense, students are able to explain using both the number line and counters that adding two positives is just what they have always done. Adding two negatives is the same except with negative numbers: If you begin negative and add more negative, you are summing up negatives.

Students also can see that the pattern with adding a positive and negative number is like subtracting, but the signs are confusing. Discussion and modeling lead to the realization that if more negative is being added, the sum is negative after removing zero pairs or moving on the number line. If more positive is being added, the sum is positive. After recognizing the patterns and discussing why the pattern would always be true, integer addition "rules" are summarized and formalized.

- If the signs of the addends are the same, add the absolute values and keep the sign of the addends.

- If the signs of the addends are different, subtract the absolute values and use the sign of the integer with greater absolute value.

Finally, the subtraction problems are discussed in relation to their related addition problems.

$$3 + 5 \qquad\qquad 5 - 3$$
$$3 + (-5) \qquad\qquad 5 - (-3)$$
$$-3 + 5 \qquad\qquad 3 - 5$$
$$-3 + (-5) \qquad\qquad -3 - (-5)$$

Consider It!

- What learning beliefs and attitudes need to be in place for differentiation to be viable and for middle school students to work together?

- In what ways did this lesson incorporate readiness, interest, and/or learning profile differentiation?

- How did using manipulatives to model the mathematics lead to students "discovering" the rules? How do you think this approach would affect students' understanding of integer operations?

- What new ideas do you see in this example that you could replicate in your classroom?

Students are asked to draw lines from a subtraction problem to the related addition problem and why they chose the relationship. For homework, students are asked to find a general pattern relating subtraction of integers to addition of integers. They are also to create their own sets of eight related problems as shown above, with solutions.

HIGH SCHOOL CLASSROOM

The teacher begins:

"On the board you will find a choice of warm-up problems. Please choose the one that you feel is just right for you—not too hard or too easy. Once you have completed your problem, please find a partner with whom to compare your homework answers based on the homework assignment you did last night—red, purple, or green. Compare not only your answers but also the method you used to solve it. If you have different answers, try to convince each other of your work. You can also check with someone else who did the same assignment. Only ask for help if you cannot figure it out. You have 10 minutes."

Students compare their homework problems that were based on readiness. All problems were on the current topic of rates of change, but problems were tiered based on applications problems, representations, and whether examples and/or reminders were provided. All assignments had three common problems, which would be the basis for whole-class discussion following the independent review.

During the homework conversations, the teacher circulates among the students and notes which students chose and completed which of the warm-up problems and answers any pressing homework questions. As students finish their homework review, the class comes back together to discuss the problems that were in common on all assignments to reinforce the concepts of rate of change, unit rate of change, and slope.

"We have been working a lot with this idea of a rate of change. We began by connecting it to work you have done in middle school with unit rates and proportions. It is the same thing and can be determined in the same ways you have used in middle school, including bar models, tables, and solving a proportion. However, we have extended your understanding to include the role of a rate of change within a linear function. In a linear function, the rate of change remains constant, whereas the rate of change can vary in other functions, as we will see later this year. Before we begin, work with your small groups to discuss these questions:

1. In what numeric form does a slope come? (rational number)

2. What does a slope represent in a graph? (rise or change in y over run or change in x)

3. How can you estimate the value of the rate of change given a linear graph? (increasing is a positive slope, decreasing a negative slope; the more "steep" or the faster the rise or fall, the greater the absolute value of the slope)"

After discussing these questions, students are prepared to begin the new topic.

"Today we want to explore how the rate of change can be used to graph a linear function without needing to first create a table. You will have an option of three different explorations, but everyone will complete the same problems within their tasks:

- Color-code a graph: Given an initial point and a slope value, plot the initial point in green. Show the rise from the point in blue and the run in red. Plot the next point in black. Repeat the process four times until you can graph the line. Repeat the process with other points and slopes.

- Create a human graph: On the grid in the back of the room, one student draws a point out of the cards and stands on the point.

Consider It!

In this example, most of the mathematics lesson was differentiated. That is not always the case. Often one aspect of a lesson will be differentiated in some way, such as a choice of closure activities or a tiered practice.

- How do you respond to this lesson?

- What do you feel can be done with your students?

- Of what parts are you unsure?

- Make a list of pros and cons from this lesson as a baseline for your learning as you work through this book.

The next student draws a slope card and walks the slope from the first student to create a second point. Two more students will create additional points on the graph until all students can extend their arms to form a line. Repeat the process.

- Hands and brains: Students will work in pairs. Student A will be the "brain" and can only describe what to do. Student B will be the "hands" and can only complete exactly what the brain says to do. In this manner, they will graph a line given an initial point and a slope. Students complete several lines, switching roles each time. After they are confident on how to graph a line given a point and the slope, groups of four will create a short infomercial or skit on graphing a line given a point and a slope."

As students are working, the teacher circulates to monitor progress and answer any questions. As students are finishing, students number off within their task groups to form new groups of three made up of students from each task choice. They move into the mixed groups for the final discussion and closure activity.

To conclude the lesson, students are asked to share how they graphed a line in their respective activities and to conclude what was in common. They are challenged to come up with a simple list of steps on how to graph a line when given a point and a slope.

As a final closure activity, students are asked to graph a line from a given point and slope on an exit card. All students will do the same homework assignment tonight—linear graphs given a point and a slope.

WATCH IT!

As you watch Video 1.2, *Balanced Differentiation in the Classroom*, consider the following questions:

1. In what ways are different aspects of student differences addressed through differentiation?

2. Why a three-legged stool? Why balance the three legs of differentiation?

3. To what extent does a strategy (such as offering choice or designing stations) define or determine differentiation? In what ways could a strategy serve as a basis for differentiation?

Video 1.2 Balanced Differentiation in the Classroom

WHAT IS THE DIFFERENCE?

There are some foundational belief differences between a differentiated class and a more traditionally taught class. Figure 1.6 gives a summary list of some of these differences. All of the differentiated facets will be developed throughout the rest of the book and through the video clips.

FIGURE 1.6

TRADITIONAL VS. DIFFERENTIATED CLASSROOM

More Traditional Mathematics Classroom	Differentiated Mathematics Classroom
Student differences are ignored or avoided	Student differences form the basis of lesson design
Texts and resources are the basis for instruction	Standards and knowledge of students as learners are the basis for instruction
Predominantly teacher presentation	Teacher provides means for students to make connections through investigation, collaboration, and communication
Predominantly whole class	Students are arranged to work in a variety of ways, including whole class, pairs, small groups, and individual work. Pairs and groups are purposefully designed
A single pace is expected for all students	As much as possible, flexible time and due dates are used for students who require additional time or to provide meaningful challenge and extension for students who work more quickly
A single lesson or activity is used for all students	Different lessons or activities are designed to reach all learners, varying in design among readiness, interest, and learning profile addressing the same learning outcomes
A single assessment is used	A variety of assessments are used to allow students to demonstrate what they know, understand, and are able to do, with options available when appropriate
A single definition of success is expected, and it is most often speed and accuracy	Success is rooted in student growth and effort, risk taking, and perseverance

Consider It!

Think about your current classroom practice. No one is purely in one or another category. Where are your current classroom practices as you consider the two columns of "traditional" and "differentiated" classrooms? Are there any shifts you want to make at this point?

CONCLUSION

"Educators should be champions of every student who enters the schoolhouse doors" (Tomlinson, 2014). I don't know any educator who doesn't agree with this statement. And yet too often, there are students who feel incapable, unaccepted, and unappreciated—especially in mathematics. As teachers, we have incredible power to set the climate of our classrooms, as well as inspire and transform our students. We know from brain research now that there are no such things as "math people" or "non–math people." We know effort changes everything. And we know that designing engaging lessons and activities that fit our individual students can change their and our world.

FREQUENTLY ASKED QUESTIONS

Q: How can you differentiate when we have the same standards and give a high-stakes standardized test?

A: Differentiation is about maximizing learning for every student. The standards provide the content, or *what* we teach. Differentiation is how we craft the learning experiences for students so that they are able to reach the standards. If students can learn at deeper levels, make sense of what they are learning in ways that make the most sense to their brains, and store and retrieve from memory more effectively, they will have greater success on all assessments, including the high-stakes standardized tests.

Q: What about students who refuse to try?

A: I wish I had a foolproof answer. There isn't one. However, students who are in a class where they feel accepted, have some voice in their learning, and know that the teacher believes in them will almost always start to change their behavior. Usually the behavior comes from negative past experiences. Replacing those beliefs about school and how they associate school with positive experiences and a taste of success goes a long way. There is nothing like relationships to begin to heal students who are shut down.

Q: How do you find time to do all of this?

A: First remember that no one differentiates every lesson every day. The start of differentiation can be frustrating because you don't have activities and plans ready to go. Think about what you already have and gather ideas from colleagues and the Internet as you are able. Instead of choosing which activity you want to use, determine which students would best relate to which of the tasks. Then use them all and you have a differentiated lesson. The best advice comes from Carol Ann Tomlinson: Start slow, but start.

Keepsakes and Plans

What are the keepsake ideas from this chapter, those thoughts or ideas that resonated with you that you do not want to forget?

What Is Differentiation:

1.

2.

3.

The Learning Environment:

1.

2.

3.

A Glance at a Differentiated Classroom:

1.

2.

3.

Based on my keepsake ideas, I plan to:

1.

2.

3.

CHAPTER TWO

FIND OUT

STRATEGIES FOR DETERMINING WHO EACH OF YOUR STUDENTS IS AS A MATHEMATICS LEARNER

The key to differentiation is knowing who the students are whose learning you are entrusted with every day. The tools and techniques in this chapter will help you understand the differences in how your students learn and begin to look at how to address these differences. In this chapter, you will find the following:

Who Our Learners Are
Strategies to Determine:

    Readiness

    Interest

    Learning Profile

Frequently Asked
Questions

Keepsakes and Plans

Think about yourself for a minute. How do you best learn mathematics? Do you prefer to have a detailed list of steps given followed by repeated practice? Or do you prefer to see how the math applies to specific situations and then learn how to complete the skills? Would you rather have hands-on activities or talk it out with colleagues? Do you like to work with others in tackling open-ended tasks, or would you rather think on your own? Do you take a concept and imagine how you could use it in your own life or in new situations? Our learners are as complex in how they learn mathematics as you are. You can also count on them learning differently from you as well as from each other.

Students will differ in their learning preferences, their interests, and their entry points into the learning continuum. As teachers, we need to become students of our students in order to design effective differentiation. Just how we "study our students" can vary, but the importance of studying our students does not vary. It is only when we are armed with the knowledge of our students as learners and as human beings that we are able to form strong relationships and build learning opportunities that intrigue and challenge each of them.

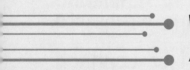

WATCH IT!

As you watch Video 2.1, *Getting to Know Your Students as Learners,* consider the following questions:

Video 2.1 Getting to Know Your Students as Learners

1. How can you get to know how your students learn differently?

2. How can you help students understand that everyone learns differently?

3. How is community built as students become aware of and share learning differences?

4. How can information about how your students learn be used to organize groups and design tasks?

WHO OUR LEARNERS ARE

Our students come to us from varied backgrounds and life experiences, and they bring varied messages about who they believe they are as learners in school, especially in mathematics. Spend 5 minutes in any mathematics classroom and you can see these differences in students. It helps to understand how our students view themselves as mathematics learners as well as to determine strategies that can help them best learn. Before looking at ideas of how to determine how your students best learn, reflect on what you already do to get to know them.

One method for finding out how your students feel about themselves as learners of mathematics is to have them write a mathematics autobiography. Often students have not thought about themselves as "math learners," and this activity will help them recognize their own strengths and weaknesses, attitudes, and likes and dislikes.

Consider It!

How do you currently get to know your students? Make a list of what you currently do to get to know your students and what you are currently finding out about your students. As you look at each activity you use, identify the type of information you have gained—is it about student readiness, interest, learning profile, personal beliefs, hobbies, other? Is there any missing information about your students as learners?

TRY IT! MY MATH AUTOBIOGRAPHY

Purpose: Find out your students' self-perceptions on learning mathematics

As one of your first assignments of the year, have your students describe their favorite math classes and learning activities as they reflect on their own mathematical experiences. Use the following guidelines:

1. How do you feel about learning mathematics? Do you enjoy learning mathematics? Why or why not? Are you a strong mathematics learner? Why or why not? What strategies do you use to learn mathematics? List or explain as many as you can.

2. Describe your favorite mathematics class that you have ever been in and why that particular mathematics class was best for you. Please do not mention any teacher's name. Include any specific learning activities that you enjoyed as well. Write about what works for you to learn mathematics the best.

3. Why did the class or activity work well for you? What did you learn from it?

4. What does not work well for you in learning mathematics? Why do you not like to learn that way?

5. If you could tell me one thing about how you would like to learn mathematics this year, what would it be? Okay . . . if you want to tell me two things, that would be okay as well.

Mathematics autobiographies will give you insight into your students' mathematical beliefs and attitudes. The importance of students' self-belief and self-talk is further developed in Chapter 5 with the discussion of growth mindset.

My Mathematical Autobiography is a strategy to find out about your students' beliefs as mathematics learners. As well as finding out how your students feel, you also need to find out how your students learn.

TIPS FOR ELL/SPECIAL EDUCATION STUDENTS

Students from other countries will want to share their own learning experiences and backgrounds. Encourage them to draw or write about their learning experiences. Provide a word bank and sentence starters to help them. Sentence starters could include the following:

- I like to learn by . . .
- I do not like to . . .
- I do/do not like to learn with other students.

Word bank ideas with picture support:

- Play games (picture of two students playing cards)
- Write problems (written mathematical problems)
- Talking in class (students talking to each other)
- Drawing (mathematical picture)

How you find this out depends on whether you are looking at students' readiness, interest, or learning profile. Interest and learning profile differentiation serve a slightly different purpose in learning than readiness. Interest and learning profile are used primarily to motivate and allow students access to learning opportunities that will meet their preferences. Readiness is about appropriate challenge, prior knowledge, extensions, and the content rather than the manner in which the content is learned. Because of this, the assessment for readiness is dependent on preassessment and formative assessment. Formative assessment is fully developed in Chapter 7.

STRATEGIES TO DETERMINE READINESS

Assessments, observation data, and surveys can provide a glimpse into our students as learners and be useful as tools to begin designing differentiated instruction. Perhaps the most glaring aspect of student differences in our classrooms is readiness. We often wonder what to do about Justin, Alexia, and Aamino (introduced in Chapter 1), who are behind the rest of the class in mathematics but for very different reasons, and worry that we aren't challenging Maddi at all. The same components in class that make readiness obvious, such as homework, assessments, discussions, and activities, are also the basis on which we differentiate by readiness. All of your assessment data, whether formal or informal, form the basis of determining a student's readiness. Before beginning any unit, and in fact most lessons, it is important to preassess.

There are many different ways by which you can preassess. Many teachers use a pretest that is an alternate version of the summative assessment that will be given. This is especially effective if you are gathering pre- and post data to document growth. Other options, however, are more student-friendly than giving a test on which they are not supposed to be able to do the work! No matter what form your preassessment takes, it needs to gain information about the following:

- Key vocabulary
- Essential prerequisite skills
- Skills that will be taught in the upcoming unit
- Key concepts and big ideas undergirding the unit
- Students' individual information, not collective or collaborative

Figure 2.1 provides a list of preassessment strategies and descriptions.

FIGURE 2.1

PREASSESSMENT STRATEGIES

Strategy

Concept Map

Students are challenged to create a concept map for the upcoming unit. Students can be provided any of the following information:

- Key vocabulary
- Graphs, tables, or other visuals
- Problem examples
- Lesson titles

Students create a linked concept map based on their prior knowledge and expectations of how ideas will fit together. In their maps, students provide definitions and explanations as to why they have grouped, joined, or connected any areas. As a readiness differentiation, templates of maps or graphic organizers can be given to students to fill in.

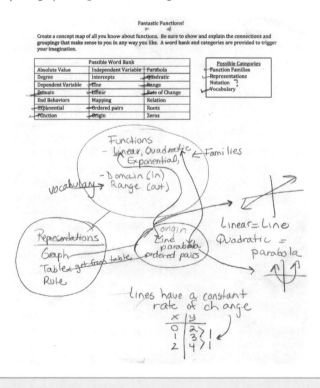

Strategy

Misconception Check

A misconception check is a list of statements about which students will agree or disagree (or mark True or False) and explain why they believe as they do. This is especially useful to surface common errors and misconceptions. Once students have responded, you can group students according to their answers—either answers that are alike to have specific further tasks ready or different answers to discuss and defend their positions.

Simplifying Expressions

Mark each statement as True or False. Explain your thinking.

1. Like terms are defined by the combination of variables in the term.
2. Any terms that have a common variable can be added or subtracted.
3. The same integer operation rules apply when simplifying expressions as when solving an integer problem.
4. The order of operations does not apply to algebraic terms.

Strategy

Quick Write

This is a free write for students to recall, model, draw, or calculate anything relating to the topic. This can be posed as a question, such as "What do you know about ratios?" A word bank or skill list can be provided to stimulate students' thinking.

What Do You Know About Ratios?

What Do You Know About Ratios?

Please write, draw, or anything else you know to do to show me what you know about ratios. Be sure to include what is a ratio, and for what they are used. The word bank is there to help you if you want.

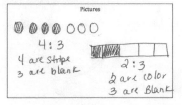

Word Bank
Comparison
Constant of Proportionality
Denominator
Numerator
Part
Proportion
Ratio
Scale
Unit rate
Whole

Pictures

4 : 3
4 are stripe
3 are blank

2 : 3
2 are color
3 are Blank

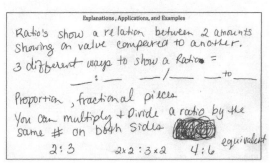

Explanations, Applications, and Examples

Ratio's show a relation between 2 amounts showing on value compared to another.
3 different ways to show a Ratio =
___ : ___   ___ / ___   ___ to ___
Proportion, fractional pieces
You can multiply + Divide a ratio by the same # on both sides
2 : 3   2x2 : 3x2   4 : 6 equivalent

FIGURE 2.1 (Continued)

Strategy

Technology

There are many ways to use technology as a preassessment that do not have to be expensive. Certainly, clickers or calculator-based technology that allows you to survey and graph class data is effective. However, not everyone has these kinds of technology available. Consider giving a multiple-choice assessment and use Plickers for student responses. For this, assign students a specific card number and their answers will be logged and graphed through your smartphone. For free cards and information on using Plickers, see https://www.plickers.com/library. Survey Monkey, Socrative, and Poll Everywhere are also free sites that can be used, but you may not be able to get individual information, so use them carefully.

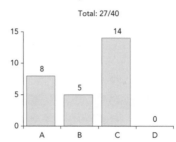

Choose a response that describes you today for "How are you doing?"

A. Blessed Beyond Belief

B. Happy To Be Here

C. Hanging In There

D. Really?

Answer	Card#	first name	last name
C	8	Eight	
–	18	Eighteen	
–	11	Eleven	
B	15	Fifteen	
–	5	Five	
C	40	Forty	
–	4	Four	
–	14	Fourteen	

Another preassessment strategy that becomes formative and summative as well is a strategy I call Frayer Times Four (Smith, 2017). This is an adaptation of a Frayer model. The idea is to design a Frayer-type model for the preassessment. It does not have to be the traditional Frayer model that has sections for Definition, Information, Examples, and Nonexamples. I determine what sections I want to have and design my model that way. I then put the same model on a piece of paper four times: two on the front and two on the back. The first model is for the preassessment. About halfway through the unit, I give the paper back to students. I ask them to look at what they wrote on the first model and cross out anything they now know is incorrect. On the second model, they can correct the errors from the first model and add anything else they have learned. About three fourths of the way through the unit, I repeat this process, with students crossing out anything in the first two models that they now know is incorrect and correcting and adding more information in the third model. Finally, the entire process is repeated after the summative assessment, with all corrections and additional information being added to the final model. This provides a one-page portfolio of growth through the unit and has students continue to reflect on their own learning as well. Figure 2.2 gives an example of the front/back of a Frayer Times Four for solving equations.

TRY IT! FINDING OUT

Purpose: To practice designing a preassessment other than a pretest

Design a preassessment for your next unit. Choose one of the preassessment strategies given in this section.

Sometimes a warm-up problem can serve as a preassessment in unexpected ways. Always be on the watch for unexpected solutions and methods. For example, Ms. Anthony proposed the following problem for her seventh-grade students to solve:

> On a road trip across the country, I drove 145 miles in my first 2½ hours. (I forgot to check mileage earlier.) I planned to drive 8 hours a day. How many miles would I drive in a day?

Ms. Anthony expected all of her students to set up a proportion and cross-multiply to solve. She was looking to see which students did not set up proportions correctly and if any students had difficulty multiplying or dividing with decimals. Ms. Anthony did have students who confused the setup of the proportions and others who did not accurately work with the decimals. However, Ms. Anthony was surprised when she saw that her students used five additional methods. Figure 2.3 shows the methods used in solving the proportional reasoning problem and what can be learned from each.

FIGURE 2.2

SOLVING EQUATIONS FRAYER TIMES FOUR

Frayer Times Four Solving Equations

Name _____

Date _____

Define	Solve
Coefficient	
Constant	$1/3 \, x = 17 \quad 21 = 3(4x + 1)$
Equation	
Expression	
Inverse Operation	$-2x - 4 = 5.31 \qquad \frac{1}{2}(6x - 2) = 2(x + 1)$
Isolate	
Like terms	
Simplify	
Solution/Solve	
Variable	

Solving Linear Equation

In equations, the equal sign shows an equivalence of two quantities that must be maintained.

Operations come in inverse pairs that allow you to undo them.

__Apply__

Write a real world situation that could be solved with an equation, then solve it. Interpret your answer in context.

__Explain__

Choose one of the two understandings listed, and explain its meaning.

Date _____

Define	Solve
Coefficient	
Constant	$1/3 \, x = 17 \quad 21 = 3(4x + 1)$
Equation	
Expression	
Inverse Operation	$-2x - 4 = 5.31 \qquad \frac{1}{2}(6x - 2) = 2(x + 1)$
Isolate	
Like terms	
Simplify	
Solution/Solve	
Variable	

Solving Linear Equation

In equations, the equal sign shows an equivalence of two quantities that must be maintained.

Operations come in inverse pairs that allow you to undo them.

__Apply__

Write a real world situation that could be solved with an equation, then solve it. Interpret your answer in context.

__Explain__

Choose one of the two understandings listed, and explain its meaning.

 Templates can be downloaded at resources.corwin.com/ everymathlearner6-12.

FIGURE 2.3

PROPORTIONAL REASONING PROBLEM SOLVING

Student A	Observations: This is the most common method for solving a proportion. Student misconceptions would primarily be in setting up the ratios correctly or arithmetic mistakes—both of which Ms. Anthony saw in this example. The student began to see that the answer was not making sense but did not have a method for recovery. In addition, if this is the only method with which students are familiar, they may encounter difficulty if there are more than two ratios for which to solve in a problem.
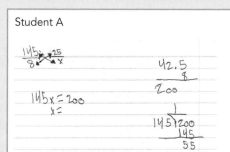	
Student B	Observations: This approach uses a table to find a missing value. The student is approaching the table similarly to a bar model (see Student C) showing groups of 2½ hours and groups of 145 miles. This strategy will be useful in developing the concept of a constant rate of change when learning linear functions. The student ran into some difficulty trying to reach exactly 8 hours but was able to figure out how to find the number of miles in half an hour by dividing 2.5 hours by .5 (half an hour) and determine "how many half-hours were in 2.5 hours." The reasoning of the student was correct, but an addition error resulted in an incorrect final answer.
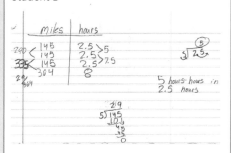	
Student C	Observations: This student has set up a bar model to solve the proportion. This model connects reasoning to solving the proportion that cross-multiplication usually does not. The picture helps students reason about the context and see the meaning of proportionality within the context: As time continues, the number of miles accumulates at the same rate as the original given ratio. This understanding will also develop the concept of a constant rate of change when studying linear functions.
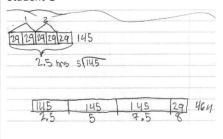	

(Continued)

FIGURE 2.3 (Continued)

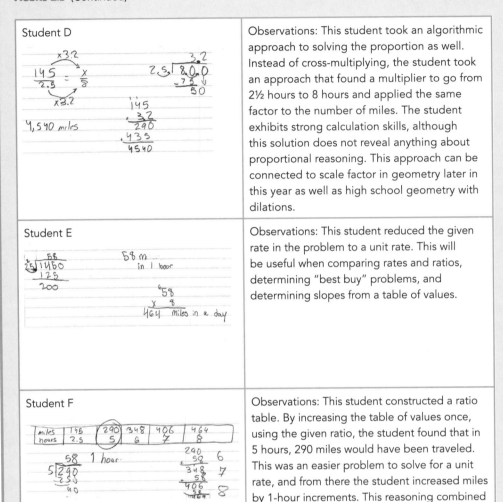

Student D	Observations: This student took an algorithmic approach to solving the proportion as well. Instead of cross-multiplying, the student took an approach that found a multiplier to go from 2½ hours to 8 hours and applied the same factor to the number of miles. The student exhibits strong calculation skills, although this solution does not reveal anything about proportional reasoning. This approach can be connected to scale factor in geometry later in this year as well as high school geometry with dilations.
Student E	Observations: This student reduced the given rate in the problem to a unit rate. This will be useful when comparing rates and ratios, determining "best buy" problems, and determining slopes from a table of values.
Student F	Observations: This student constructed a ratio table. By increasing the table of values once, using the given ratio, the student found that in 5 hours, 290 miles would have been traveled. This was an easier problem to solve for a unit rate, and from there the student increased miles by 1-hour increments. This reasoning combined several of the previous strategies creatively and correctly.

These examples demonstrate how powerful a task can be to provide information about our students' readiness and reasoning. Ms. Anthony posed a problem and allowed her students to work however they wanted. She did not review or suggest a specific method. Had she done so, she would not have gotten the information she did. Instead, she would have found out only who knew how to do the suggested procedure and nothing about the reasoning involved.

In this section, we have looked at different ways to preassess our students for readiness. Because a preassessment is really about how to begin a unit in light of so many different students, it is usually most effective to preassess about a week before the start of the unit. This will give you time to reflect on what you learn about your students and decide how to begin. It is also important to realize that readiness fluctuates greatly and as a result must be assessed continuously. This is the role of formative assessment, which will be developed in Chapter 7.

STRATEGIES TO DETERMINE INTEREST

As described in Chapter 1, interest differentiation can be about designing inquiry and tasks that relate to your students' passions and hobbies. That is incredibly powerful, and research suggests that changing the context of a problem to relate to our students' lives can result in greater investment by students on the task (Walkinton et al., 2014). The study found that when working on a unit on linear equations, students who worked with problems differentiated by interest outscored control students who worked with nondifferentiated problems. The greatest achievement advantage occurred for students who typically struggled with mathematics.

How we find out about our students' interests is really quite easy—you probably do this at the beginning of the year already. Most teachers use interest surveys or inventories or just sharing before, after, and during class about what we like. Finding out about interests should be natural because students want to tell you what they like, and they want you to care about what they like, even teenagers. Sometimes we can get so busy or so focused on what we need to accomplish in class that we forget to simply talk to our students and ask for their feedback. Let them know you are trying something different, and then ask how it worked for them. You might be surprised at the honest and usually sensitive feedback you gain.

Figure 2.4 lists other more formal strategies for finding out your students' interests.

Consider It!

- How do you currently assess your students' interests? Make a list.

- Do you assess for interests in learning as well as their families and hobbies?

- How do you use interest information in the design of learning activities?

FIGURE 2.4

ASSESSING STUDENT INTERESTS

Strategy

All About Me Times

Have fun creating a template for students to create a front page for a newspaper or a magazine cover that is all about them. You can suggest specific items for students to complete and leave it to students' creativity, or provide them with a template. Possible categories include the following:

- Your headline—eight words or less that tell what you consider to be most important about yourself

- You can find me—what do you like to do on the weekends? After school? Hobbies?

- In the future—what are your hopes and dreams for the future?

- Fantastic Favorites—list your favorite food, music, sports, art, hobbies, TV show, movie, book, color, animals. . . . Any favorite at all.

- Mathematics Goals—my mathematics goal for this year is. . . . I am good at. . . . I need help with. . . . Three things I can do to reach my goal. . . .

Strategy

Surveys

Many surveys can be found online, but it may be just as easy to design your own questions based on what you truly want to know. Don't forget to add pictures as cues for English language lerners as necessary.

All About Me and How I Learn!

Read each of the statements below. If it is usually true about you, circle Yes. If it is usually NOT true about you, circle No. Remember, no one is a certain way all of the time!

1.	It has to be quiet for me to learn well.	Yes	No
2.	I don't really hear noise around me when I am concentrating.	Yes	No
3.	I do mathematics work best by myself, but then I will share with others.	Yes	No
4.	I do mathematics work best with others so I can talk and work things out with others' help.	Yes	No
5.	When I get frustrated in mathematics, I usually quit working.	Yes	No
6.	When I get frustrated in mathematics, I keep trying until I get it.	Yes	No
7.	I work best at a table or desk.	Yes	No
8.	I work best on the floor.	Yes	No
9.	I like to play games to learn and practice mathematics.	Yes	No
10.	I like to use a computer or video to learn and practice mathematics.	Yes	No
11.	I like to follow along with my teacher to learn and practice mathematics.	Yes	No
12.	I like to complete worksheets to learn and practice mathematics.	Yes	No
13.	I like to follow exact instructions when doing a mathematics project.	Yes	No
14.	I like to be able to put my own ideas into a mathematics project.	Yes	No

Journals and Interviews

Personal journal prompts to get to know your students work well as some students may be too shy to tell you the truth about how they feel. Writing also will help students self-assess their learning, think about their process of learning, and set goals for learning. Prompts can include the following:

- Today in mathematics, I liked how we _____ but I didn't really like _____.
- My best strategy for graphing a function is _____. I like this strategy because _____. An example of using this strategy is _____.
- This week in mathematics, I learned _____ very well because I learn best when _____.
- One way I learn mathematics best is _____.
- I really struggle to learn mathematics when _____.
- Mathematics is most fun when _____.
- Mathematics is most frustrating when _____.
- My favorite thing I've ever done in mathematics class would have to be when _____.
- It helps me learn when you _____.
- It helps me learn when my friends in class _____.

People BINGO

People BINGO is a fun way to help students get to know each other at the beginning of the year, but if you collect the cards and notice which students signed which squares, you will also learn about your students' interests. Create a BINGO card (with no free space) with statements about students. You can tailor this to mathematics only, but I like to find out about all of my students' interests in order to incorporate them as much as possible in class. Ideas include the following:

- I have brothers and/or sisters (older/younger).
- I have a pet (or pets).
- I play a musical instrument (which one?).
- I sing in the school choir.
- I play a sport.
- I like mathematics.
- I love mathematics.
- Color helps me see things better.
- I am good with numbers.

There is no limit as to what can be put in the squares of the card.

You can have students use the cards in various ways—have them meet each other and sign one square on each other's cards that is true about them. The goal can be a row, corners, full card, or any other pattern you choose.

Students' Interests Tables

Have students form groups of three or four. Make a table with students' names across the top as column labels and down the sides as row labels. Cross out the diagonal cells where the same names meet. Students fill in the cells, finding similarities between the two people whose names form the cell.

(Continued)

FIGURE 2.4 (Continued)

Directions: Write each of your names across the top of the table, and also down the right side of the table in the same order. Two names come together to form each cell. The two students tell each other about themselves and find out a minimum of two things they have in common. Fill in the cell with the commonalities your have found. Fill in the entire table, and be ready to share with the class what you have learned about your group.

Name				

Strategy

Human Likert Scale

Create a 1–10 (or 1–5) scale on a wall in your room. Give students a prompt, such as "How did you like playing a game to practice simplifying expressions today?" and have students put themselves along the wall in response.

 Surveys and Observation tools with answer keys can be downloaded at resources.corwin.com/everymathlearner6-12.

TRY IT! MY PICTURE/MY SONG

Purpose: A creative way to find your students' mathematics interests

1. Provide students with pictures, magazines, and/or word phrases.

2. Have students make a collage to best represent themselves as mathematics learners. Students should include specific areas, such as family, pets, hobbies, interests, mathematical strategies, words that describe how they feel about math, and so on.

As an alternative, students could create and perform a rap song about themselves following the same areas as listed above.

STRATEGIES TO DETERMINE LEARNING PROFILE

There most likely is not a survey or test item that will reveal the complete picture of how a student learns, and even if we could figure it out, the picture is likely to change! There are, however, structures that help us define effective tasks for different learners. When working with learning profile, it is often most effective to create purposefully designed tasks and let students choose the task that is most appealing or with which they think they can best learn or demonstrate learning. When building your classroom community and celebrating the differences in your class, it is important to fully develop the idea that not only do we enter learning at different places, but we all learn in different ways. It is great that we have different ways to make sense of, explain, and demonstrate mathematics.

In Chapter 1, broad categories of learning profile were described. Figure 2.5 provides descriptions of two learning profile structures that are based on ways of thinking or intelligences. Gardner's multiple intelligences is a familiar structure and Sternberg's triarchic theory is another structure not quite as familiar. Both are commonly used to differentiate instruction.

How do we find out which intelligences are represented in our classroom? Carefully observing your students' choices and more natural ways of reasoning can give you insight into your students' learning profiles. In addition, there are survey tools on the Internet that you can use. Figure 2.6 gives survey examples for students to discuss and discover likely aspects of their own learning profiles.

It's important to pause here and note that there are some dangers in how you evaluate and establish learning profiles. Even though these surveys appear to give a diagnostic of student learning, there has been little research evidence to support that these particular styles are assessable. Also, there is worry that teachers may consciously or unconsciously label students as a particular type of learner, which will then limit options and opportunities. Of even greater danger is that students will label and limit themselves. It is often best to have discussions with students about the various types of learning and have students reflect on how they relate to the various descriptions. So please use the inventories accordingly and with caution.

Consider It!

- Think about the students who you believe fit various categories based on the descriptions given in Figure 2.5. Jot their names into the chart.

- Are the tasks and activities you are using in balance to represent diverse thinkers in your class? Are there possible areas that you should consider how to address?

FIGURE 2.5

LEARNING PROFILE INTELLIGENCE DESCRIPTIONS AND LEARNING STRUCTURES

Name	Description	Will Learn By
Multiple Intelligences		
Verbal/ Linguistic *Word Smart*	Likes to read and write to learn and make sense of learning. Usually likes to talk. Uses words to explain concepts, relationships, and ideas.	Saying, hearing, and seeing words; creative wordplay; analogies; similes and metaphors
Logical Mathematical *Number/ Reasoning Smart*	Quick to recognize and apply patterns and relationships. Sequences naturally. Tends to be linear in thinking. Reasons using concepts, relationships, and ideas.	Categorizing, working with patterns and relationships, using organizers and other structures, breaking processes into smaller steps, providing detail and explanation
Visual-Spatial *Art Smart*	Appreciates and interprets pictures, charts, graphs, diagrams, and art. Uses visuals, either pictures or imagery, to depict concepts, relationships, and ideas.	Visualizing, dreaming, using multiple colors, creating pictures, slideshows, or storyboards
Musical *Music Smart*	Can use various forms of music to show concepts, relationships, and ideas. Can use music or rhythm to aid memorization or practice of skills.	Singing or humming, setting facts to rhythms or familiar tunes and jingles, tapping or clapping, playing music in the background while working
Body Kinesthetic *Body Smart*	Models concepts, relationships, and ideas through movement and objects. Often jumps into a task without reading directions. Taps, shakes a foot, paces, etc.	Engaging in hands-on tasks, physical movement, manipulatives
Interpersonal *People Smart*	Sensitive and aware of others in the expression and learning of concepts, relationships, and ideas. Demonstrates understanding through empathy. Usually has deep friendships and may have a lot of friends.	Cooperative groups. Thrives in a healthy learning community. Natural leaders and communicators
Intrapersonal *Self Smart*	Interprets concepts, relationships, and ideas in terms of experiences or impact on self. Aware of personal thoughts, feelings, likes, and dislikes.	Opportunity to self-reflect, independent work, pursuing own interest, or relating learning to prior experiences and interests
Naturalist *Nature Smart*	Recognizes concepts, relationships, and ideas in nature or the impact on nature. Enjoys relating things to their environment and making connections to nature.	Observations, exploring natural phenomenon, patterning

Sternberg's Triarchic Theory		
Analytical *School Smart*	Detail oriented about concepts, relationships, and ideas. Appreciates outlines, graphic organizers.	Comparing, analyzing, critiquing, evaluating, seeing the parts and the whole, using criteria, judging, thinking logically, sequencing, ranking, defending (Doubet & Hockett, 2015)
Practical *Street Smart*	Relates concepts, relationships, and ideas to experiences and the real world. Is concerned about when and how the learning will be used in life.	Relating learning to the real world and/or prior personal experiences, putting principles into practice and action planning, demonstrations, teaching, convincing
Creative *Imagination Smart*	Thinks "outside the box" about concepts, relationships, and ideas. Has unique and original thoughts, connects, examples, and explanations. Imagines what could be, ways to improve ideas, and what would happen if. . . .	Open-ended prompts that allow for creative solutions, making new or unusual connections, predicting, transforming, analogies, representing creatively, noticing differences and changes, humor

 Surveys and Observation tools with answer keys can be downloaded at resources.corwin.com/everymathlearner6-12.

There is power in teaching students some of the various ways people can think and learn, and they will probably find ways they like to learn or mathematics strategies they like to use better than others, as long as you reinforce that this should never define or limit them. As students mature through the grades, they will be able to recognize learning situations in which they can apply some of their strengths, such as a visual or creative learner designing icons to accentuate notes in a lecture or a logical learner creating tables or flowcharts for a multistep process. The goal is to understand that we learn together and from each other in many different ways.

In the end, no matter what we do, there is no absolute determination on learning profile. We can gain insights into our students and design lessons and tasks according to profile structures (multiple intelligences, Sternberg triarchic theory, or modality)

Consider It:

- What are the pros and cons of using surveys in helping students identify their own learning profile strengths?

- How can you invoke the various aspects of learning profile in your teaching and activity designs without boxing students into a certain label?

FIGURE 2.6

LEARNING PROFILE SURVEY TOOLS

Tool

Multiple Intelligence Survey

Students use a highlighter to mark the statements most true about them and total each box. There is not a title in the boxes so that students do not choose a title they like best and then color all the options. It is hoped that students will honestly reflect on what is *most* true of them, not just what they like or could possibly do. The full survey and answer key are available at resources.corwin.com/everymathlearner6-12.

Multiple Intelligences Inventory

For each statement rate yourself from 0 – 4 as to how strongly you agree with the statement. Transfer the scores to the answer key at the end of the survey, and total the columns to see your strengths.

Statement	Score
1. I like telling stories and jokes.	—
2. I really enjoy mathematics.	—
3. My favorite problem-solving strategy is to draw a diagram.	—
4. My favorite problem-solving strategy is to use tools or manipulatives.	—
5. My favorite problem-solving strategy is to think about numbers in beats or rhythm.	—
6. My favorite special is gym since my favorite problem-solving strategy would be to apply numbers to the outdoors.	
7. I get along well with others.	—
8. I like my alone time.	—
9. I like word games like Scrabble.	—
10. I like logic puzzles and brainteasers.	—
11. I daydream a lot.	—
12. When I look at things, I like to touch them.	—
13. I like to listen to music and to sing.	—
14. I love to go walking in the woods and looking at trees and flowers.	—
15. I like working with others in groups to learn mathematics.	—
16. I like to work alone without anyone bothering me.	—
17. I can explain my mathematics in writing.	—
18. I like to find out how things work.	—
19. I like to imagine word problems in my head.	—
20. I move my body a lot when I'm explaining a problem.	—
21. I like to have music playing when I'm doing my mathematics homework.	—
22. I like to do my mathematics homework outside.	—
23. I like helping teach mathematics to other students.	—
24. I am willing to share my answers but prefer not to teach others.	—

25. I like learning mathematical vocabulary and use it correctly.	—
26. I love playing checkers or chess.	—
27. In a mathematics book, I like to look at the pictures or graphs rather than read the words.	—
28. I like to tap my fingers or play with my pencil during a mathematics lesson.	—
29. I play a musical instrument well.	—
30. If I have to memorize something, it might help me to relate it to something outside.	—
31. Friends come to me to ask my advice in learning mathematics.	—
32. I like to think independently in mathematics and often come up with my own solutions.	—
33. If I have to memorize something, I make up a rhyme or saying to help me.	—
34. I like to put things in order.	—
35. If I have to remember something, I draw a picture to help me.	—
36. I prefer to build and use solid figures when solving problems.	—
37. If I have to memorize something, I make up a song or rhyme to remember it.	—
38. If something breaks, I look around me to see what I can find to fix the problem.	—
39. I have many friends.	—
40. I have one or two good friends.	—
41. If something breaks, I read the directions.	—
42. If something breaks, I look at the pieces and try to figure out how they work.	—
43. If something breaks, I study a picture of it to help me.	—
44. If something breaks, I play with the pieces to try to fit them together.	—
45. If something breaks, I tap my fingers to a beat while I figure it out.	—
46. I would like to apply the mathematics I'm learning to the environment.	—
47. If something breaks, I try to find someone who can help me.	—
48. If something breaks, I like to fix it by myself.	—

Tool

Sternberg Triarchic Theory

Students mark T or F on each of the statements, then transfer their answers onto the answer key. Students count and total the number of True in each column to see whether their predominant learning intelligence is Analytical, Practical, Creative, or an equal combination.

Mark each sentence T if you like to do the activity or F if you do not like to do the activity.

1. Think about the characters when I'm reading or listening to a story. ___
2. Design new things. ___
3. Taking things apart and fixing them. ___
4. Comparing and contrasting strategies or representations ___
5. Coming up with ideas. ___
6. Learning through hands–on activities. ___
7. Evaluating my own and other kids' work. ___
8. Using my imagination to solve problems or apply math. ___
9. Putting into practice things I learned. ___
10. Thinking clearly, in a step-by-step order, and figuring things out. ___
11. Thinking of other solutions. ___
12. Working with people in teams or groups. ___
13. Solving logic problems and puzzles. ___
14. Noticing things others often ignore. ___
15. Solving problems between people. ___
16. Thinking about my own and others' mathematical strategies. ___
17. Thinking about mathematics in pictures and images. ___
18. Advising friends on their mathematics problems. ___
19. Explaining difficult ideas or problems to others. ___
20. Supposing things were different. ___
21. Convincing someone to do something. ___
22. Using hints to draw conclusions. ___
23. Drawing in mathematics ___
24. Learning by interacting with others. ___
25. Sorting and classifying. ___
26. Inventing new games or approaches in mathematics. ___
27. Applying my knowledge. ___
28. Using graphic organizers or images to organize my mathematical thoughts. ___
29. Creating something new. ___
30. Adapting to new situations. ___

Tool

Modality

This is a screening instrument to determine whether students are most likely to learn mathematics visually, auditorally, or kinesthetically. Students give themselves a score from 1 to 3 on the strength of each statement. They transfer their scores to the score sheet and total the columns.

Math Modality Preference Inventory

Read each statement and give yourself a score (3, 2, or 1) as to how strongly each statement applies to you. Try not to use 2 very often!

Often - 3   Sometimes- 2   Seldom/Never- 1

_____ 1) I need to write math down when learning in order to remember it.

_____ 2) I learn best from a lecture and not from a textbook.

_____ 3) I learn best in math when I can do something with my hands, like using counters or other models.

_____ 4) I need it to be quiet when I study math.

_____ 5) I hate taking notes. I want to just listen to lectures and I will remember and learn that way.

_____ 6) I learn and study math better when I can move—pace the floor, shift positions, tap, etc.

_____ 7) It's hard for me to understand math when someone just tells about it without writing it down.

_____ 8) I have difficulty following written solutions on the board unless someone also explains the steps.

_____ 9) I learn math best when I can manipulate or use hands-on examples.

_____ 10) I like to work a problem out in my mind. I usually get the right answer that way.

_____ 11) I can remember more of what is said to me than what I see.

_____ 12) I usually can't verbally explain how I solved a math problem, but can show it to someone.

_____ 13) I enjoy writing in math and show my steps to stay organized.

_____ 14) The more people explain math to me, the faster I learn it.

_____ 15) I've always liked using my fingers to figure out math.

_____ 16) When taking a math test, I can often see in my mind the page in my notes or in the text where the explanations or answers are located.

_____ 17) I don't like reading explanations in my math book; I'd rather have someone explain the new material to me.

_____ 18) It helps when I take a break and move around when I study math.

_____ 19) I get easily distracted or have difficulty understanding in math class when there is talking or noise.

_____ 20) I wish my math teachers would lecture more and write less on the board.

_____ 21) If I look at my math teacher when he or she is teaching it helps me to stay focused.

_____ 22) I get easily distracted or have difficulty understanding in math class when there is talking or noise.

_____ 23) It helps me when I repeat the numbers or talk to myself when working out math problems.

_____ 24) I enjoy figuring out math games and math puzzles when I learn math.

Learning Styles Inventory Scoring Guide

Write your score for each statement beside the appropriate number below, then add all the scores in each column.

1)___	2)___	3)___
4)___	5)___	6)___
7)___	8)___	9)___
10)___	11)___	12)___
13)___	14)___	15)___
16)___	17)___	18)___
19)___	20)___	21)___
22)___	23)___	24)___

Total

Visual   Auditory   Kinesthetic

The largest number in the total of the three columns above indicates your dominant learning style.

Visual learners learn best by seeing. Visual learners benefit from taking notes, charts, graphs, diagrams and color.

Auditory learners learn best by listening. Auditory learners benefit from listening to lectures with minimum notes and from discussions and talking to themselves when working alone.

Kinesthetic (or tactile) learners learn best by moving, touching or doing. Kinesthetic learners benefit from hands-on activities, writing and rewriting notes, and games.

Surveys with scoring keys can be downloaded at resources.corwin.com/everymathlearner6-12.

and then watch to see what works with individual students. Details on designing differentiated tasks and activities according to learning profile as well as readiness and interest are given in detail in Chapter 4.

CONCLUSION

Understanding our students in depth—who they are, what they are interested in, and how they will best learn—is something we as teachers must study if we want to most fully reach our students. Teaching is much more complex than delivering information, and our students' learning is dependent on how well we understand and address what each student needs to learn. In the end, the time we spend getting to know our students as learners not only helps them learn to the best of their abilities but also communicates care and concern for them as individuals. The relationships and lessons we build for our students through differentiation will not only best help our students reach their greatest potential but also develop in them a lifelong love of learning.

FREQUENTLY ASKED QUESTIONS

Q: Isn't readiness differentiation just tracking in the classroom?

A: There are times when addressing readiness is necessary. Students who do not have essential perquisite understanding for a new topic need to have the missing content and skill addressed in order to be successful, but not all students need that. In the same way, students who are more advanced should have the opportunity to continue to grow and stretch. This is not to say that this differentiation is all that will happen in the classroom for students. A differentiated classroom is flexible in how tasks are designed and students are grouped, with approximately one third of the time being based on readiness. With tracking, on the other hand, students are grouped together based on determined achievement criteria, and that is the course of study on which they stay. Most tracked systems say that students can move into a different level as they gain knowledge, close gaps, or accelerate, but the likelihood of that happening is very slight given that a slower and lower curriculum is usually designed for more struggling students and an enriched and accelerated curriculum is designed for more advanced learners. Over 50 years of research show that the gaps rarely close and often widen.

Q: Is there a difference between learning profile and learning style?

A: Yes there is. Learning profile includes everything that encompasses ways that students take in information, make sense of the information, and get information to long-term memory. It includes gender, culture, intelligences (ways of thinking), and cognitive style. Learning style has meant many different things over the years—from the physical setup of the room to visual, auditory, and kinesthetic learning models. There are currently about 71 "learning style" models! I am not sure anyone knows what the term means any longer.

Q: How do I know whether to differentiate by readiness, interest, or learning profile?

A: The choice to differentiate by readiness, interest, or learning profile is largely dependent on a teacher's decision-making process. What is the apparent need to address in the learning? Is it about what challenges students will be able to handle? Then readiness is the vehicle. If it is about motivation, then interest. If you want a way for students to most proficiently make sense of learning and move the learning into memory, then you want to choose learning profile. Often it does not have to be one clear avenue. Often these are combined in task design. For example, I can design a task based on a few of the multiple intelligences that best fit the learning goal and then provide extensions and supports to aid the readiness of the student. Finally, I can ask students to choose the task they are most interested in completing. I have now combined all three aspects of differentiation. How to design tasks is addressed in Chapter 4.

Keepsakes and Plans

What are the keepsake ideas from this chapter, those thoughts or ideas that resonated with you that you do not want to forget?

Who Our Learners Are:

1.

2.

3.

Readiness:

1.

2.

3.

Interest:

1.

2.

3.

Learning Profile:

1.

2.

3.

Based on my keepsake ideas, I plan to:

1.

2.

CHAPTER THREE

TEACH UP

MAKING SENSE OF
RIGOROUS MATHEMATICAL CONTENT

The second foundational key to effective differentiation is to know the mathematics content in depth. Differentiation will be purposeful and effective only when the mathematics standards are analyzed and form the basis of instruction and activities. In this chapter, you will find the following:

If I were to ask you how to complete this sentence, what would you say: "The most basic idea in the learning of mathematics is . . . "? What did you say? Patterns? Number sense? Calculations? Perhaps you went a different way and said applications. Or modeling. As many times as I ask teachers this question, I receive a wide variety of answers. I have never heard anyone complete the statement in accordance with the original quote, however. According to John Van de Walle (2007), "The most basic idea in the learning of mathematics is . . . mathematics makes sense." Truthfully, I didn't think of that answer the first time I saw this quote either! The more I ponder it and the more I work with teachers in constructing powerful mathematics lessons, the more I realize that it should be everyone's (not just teachers but administrators, parents, coaches, etc.) mantra. I am just wondering—are there some of you right now thinking that mathematics *doesn't* make sense? Do you have students who would not believe the statement that mathematics makes sense?

This is a chapter on mathematical content and trying to make sense of it, which is foundational to differentiation. If we design differentiated tasks before we have clear conceptual understanding, knowledge, and skills of the content we are teaching, we are probably dooming ourselves to a lot of extra planning and sometimes frustrating classroom experiences, with little growth or achievement to show as a result. To paraphrase something Carol Ann Tomlinson once said (personal communication), "If we are somewhat foggy in what we are teaching, and then differentiate, we end up with differentiated fog." This is not our goal.

MATHEMATICS MAKES SENSE

Our brains are sense-making machines. In fact, our brains naturally seek patterns and meaning making in order to store to long-term memory (Sousa, 2015). We now know that in order for an idea or concept to be stored in long-term memory, it needs to make sense and be relevant to the learner. Unfortunately, we often do not teach math as if it is a sense-making subject. We tend to teach skills, or problem types, and then practice, practice, practice . . . until we reach the next skill to be taught. I would not be surprised if mathematics was the instigator of the phrase "drill and kill." However, if we can begin to view mathematics as sense-making, we can break this pattern, both for ourselves as teachers and for our students. Most teachers I meet have never been taught to understand mathematics, only how to do it—even as mathematics majors in college. It makes sense, then, that many teachers struggle to make mathematics understandable for their students, especially if mathematics just naturally made sense to us throughout our schooling.

We have learned from cognitive science that the human brain is not well designed for memorizing data. It is most efficient and effective when it works with patterns, connections, meaning, and significance—with personal meaning being the most important (Sousa, 2015). Without the necessary time to make sense of learning, students naturally resort to memorization. Thus, the most effective way for students to learn mathematics is to prioritize understanding rather than memorization. It is our job to provide lessons that can make that happen.

How do we begin to make sense of mathematics? The first step is to clarify the big ideas that are the foundation for the topic(s) being taught in the unit. Sometimes these essential understandings are embedded in the standard we are addressing, and sometimes they can be seen in some of the exploration tasks in a resource, but it is almost always up to the teacher (or a collaborative team if you are working in one) to determine.

THEMES AND BIG IDEAS IN MATHEMATICS

There are some big ideas in mathematics that are true throughout mathematics, for every grade level and every course. Figure 3.1 provides a few of these concepts and understandings.

This figure is just the beginning of thinking in terms of broad conceptual understanding in mathematics. These understandings span units and grade levels as you can see. They are as true in kindergarten as they are in calculus. Let's take another step. For any mathematical unit based on a group of standards to be taught, the content can be divided into what students will come to know, understand, and be able to do. In the differentiation literature, this is referred to as KUDs (Tomlinson & Imbeau, 2014; Tomlinson & Moon, 2013).

The **K**now in KUD are about facts that can be memorized. Our mathematics content is filled with Knows; math facts, vocabulary, formulas, and steps to a procedure (such as how to plot points) all fall under the Know category. If you can look it up, it is probably a Know. On the other hand, **U**nderstandings are conceptual. They are big ideas and have many layers. Understandings connect the content across units, as well as connect mathematical content to other subjects. Understandings remain important and true over years,

Consider It!

- What is the difference between knowing, understanding, and doing mathematics?

- What does it look like when students exhibit understanding of mathematics? How is it different from students who know *how to* do mathematics but don't *understand* mathematics?

FIGURE 3.1

GENERAL CONCEPTS AND UNDERSTANDINGS IN MATHEMATICS

Concept	Understandings
Mathematical Operations and Properties	• Each operation in mathematics has meanings that make sense of situations, and the essential meaning of each operation remains true in every context and number system. • Every mathematical operation has specific properties that apply to it, and these properties are the basis for how these operations can and cannot be used. • The properties of operations provide the reasoning for mathematical explanations.
Number Sense and Estimation	• Developing mental mathematics strategies that reason about numbers, quantities, and the operations with numbers provide flexibility and confidence in working with numbers. • Estimation allows for establishing the reasonableness of an answer.
Units and "Unitizing"	• Determining the "base entity" in a given context or problem (e.g., apples, balloons, rate or ratio, variable, term, and possibly a function) allows you to make sense of the problem, plan a solution path, and make comparisons. • Units in measurement describe what is being measured, and what is being measured has a specific type of unit.
Equality	• An equal sign is a statement that two quantities are equivalent. That equivalency must be maintained throughout any mathematical manipulations or operations.
Shape and Geometry	• Shapes and their properties describe our physical world. • Shapes are categorized and grouped according to their properties. • Relationships among shapes can be described in many ways, including algebraically.
Modeling and Representation	• There are many different representations for a given problem or situation, and each representation can highlight or reveal different aspects of the problem. • Mathematical models represent real-world contexts and provide for connections, comparisons, and predictions.

Some of these understandings were developed alongside the teachers of West Irondequoit School District, NY.

as seen in Figure 3.1, and in fact, it is powerful if the same understandings are used over time to clearly show students that all mathematics topics are connected. Finally, the **D**o is what you expect students to be able to do if they truly Know and Understand. Be careful not to list specific task activities (e.g., "make a poster to show steps for Questions 3 through 8") in the Do category. You are looking for the mathematics within any task that indicate knowledge and understanding. The Do will always start with a verb. To push students to demonstrate understanding and not only knowledge or skills, be sure to include high-level verbs from Bloom's Taxonomy and Webb's Depth of Knowledge, which will be discussed later in this chapter. Let's look at an example of how a KUD can be developed for both a middle school and an advanced algebra unit.

SEVENTH-GRADE UNIT ON RATIONAL NUMBERS

Sample Common Core standards:

Solve real-world and mathematical problems involving the four operations with rational numbers.

Apply and extend previous understandings of multiplication and division of fractions to multiply and divide rational numbers.

    a. *Understand that multiplication is extended from fractions to rational numbers by requiring that operations continue to satisfy the properties of operations, particularly the distributive property, leading to products such as (–1)(–1) = 1 and the rules for multiplying signed numbers. Interpret products of rational numbers by describing real-world contexts.*

    b. *Understand that integers can be divided, provided that the divisor is not zero, and every quotient of integers (with nonzero divisor) is a rational number. If p and q are integers, then –(p/q) = (–p)/q = p/(–q). Interpret quotients of rational numbers by describing real-world contexts.*

    c. *Apply properties of operations as strategies to multiply and divide rational numbers.*

    d. *Convert a rational number to a decimal using long division; know that the decimal form of a rational number terminates in 0s or eventually repeats.*

The next example develops a KUD in Figure 3.3 for an Algebra 2 class studying trigonometry.

FIGURE 3.2

SEVENTH-GRADE RATIONAL NUMBERS KUD BASED ON STANDARDS

Students will **K**now . . .	Students will **U**nderstand that . . .	Students will demonstrate knowledge and understanding through the ability to **D**o . . .
K1: New Vocabulary: Rational Number, Convert	**U1:** Our numbers follow a pattern that stays the same in all types of numbers.	**D1:** Give several examples of how "negative" mean "opposite" in mathematics.
K2: How to add, subtract, multiply, and divide rational numbers.	**U2:** A negative in mathematics means "opposite."	**D2:** Convert a rational number to a decimal using long division.
	U3: A number can be represented different ways, and there can be many different forms of numbers that are equivalent.	**D3:** Explain the different processes for operations with rational numbers.
K3: The decimal form of a rational number terminates in 0s or eventually repeats.	**U4:** Only things that are alike can be added or subtracted.	**D4:** Represent real-world contexts with rational numbers.
	U5: Rational numbers can be used to represent situations in the real world, which include both positive and negative values.	**D5:** Model/demonstrate/illustrate how rational numbers follow the same patterns as integers. (Compare/contrast integers and rational numbers.)
K4: How to use division to convert between rational numbers and decimals.	**U6:** Operations with rational numbers follow the same patterns as operations with fractions and integers.	**D6:** Explain how the pattern of multiplying negatives results in a positive or negative product and how it relates to "opposite."
		D7: Add, subtract, multiply, and divide rational numbers.
		D8: Convert rational numbers to a decimal equivalent.

ADVANCED ALGEBRA UNIT ON TRIGONOMETRY

Sample Common Core standards:

Understand radian measure of an angle as the length of the arc on the unit circle subtended by the angle.

Explain how the unit circle in the coordinate plane enables the extension of trigonometric functions to all real numbers, interpreted as radian measures of angles traversed counterclockwise around the unit circle.

Prove the Pythagorean identity $sin2(\theta) + cos2(\theta) = 1$ and use it to find $sin(\theta)$, $cos(\theta)$, or $tan(\theta)$ given $sin(\theta)$, $cos(\theta)$, or $tan(\theta)$ and the quadrant of the angle.

Graph trigonometric functions, showing period, midline, and amplitude.

Choose trigonometric functions to model periodic phenomena with specified amplitude, frequency, and midline.

Relate the domain of a function to its graph and, where applicable, to the quantitative relationship it describes.

FIGURE 3.3

ADVANCED ALGEBRA TRIGONOMETRY KUD BASED ON STANDARDS

Students will Know . . .	Students will Understand that . . .	Students will demonstrate knowledge and understanding through the ability to Do . . .
K1: Vocabulary: Unit circle, arc, subtend, radian, period, midline, amplitude, sine, cosine, tangent, maximums, minimums, subtended, periodicity.	**U1:** There are different measurement systems that can be equated, but most have more common uses in specific contexts and areas of study.	**D1:** Prove Pythagorean identities and use them to find sine, cosine, and tangent values and the quadrant of the angle.
K2: Values of trig functions are interpreted counterclockwise around the unit circle.	**U2:** The unit circle in the coordinate plane enables the extension of trigonometric functions to all real numbers.	**D2:** Graph trigonometric functions showing period, midline, and amplitude. Interpret the key features within a context.

D3: Choose trigonometric functions to model periodic phenomena with specified amplitude, frequency, and midline. |
K3: How to find trig values in radical form (similar triangle method) and using technology.		**D4:** Relate the domain of a function to its graph and to the quantitative relationship it describes.
K4: Shapes and characteristics of the graphs of trig functions.	**U3:** Trigonometric functions are transformed in the same way as all other functions.	**D5:** Explain how the trigonometric functions in the unit circle relate to all real numbers.
K5: Graph functions by hand and with technology for angle from 0 to 2π.		**D6:** Explain the impact of transformations on trigonometric functions. Relate the changes to a real-world context or vice versa.
K6: Radian measure of an angle is the length of the arc on the unit circle subtended by the angle.	**U4:** Trigonometry can be used to model cyclical situations in the real world.	**D7:** Explain what a radian is, and convert back and forth between radians and degrees.

For a function that models a relationship between two quantities, interpret key features of graphs and tables in terms of the quantities, and sketch graphs showing key features given a verbal description of the relationship. Key features include: intercepts; intervals where the function is increasing, decreasing, positive, or negative; relative maximums and minimums; symmetries; end behavior; and periodicity.

As you looked through the understandings in the above units, I hope you thought of other units or topics for which the understandings would also work. For example, in the seventh-grade unit, "**U1:** Our numbers follow a pattern that stays the same in all types of numbers" is true for every unit that explores number's and operations, so it could also be used in integer units in sixth and seventh grades, number systems units in algebra, and even in the advanced algebra unit on trigonometry to connect the unit circle and trigonometric ratios to the real numbers (instead of "**U2:** The unit circle in the coordinate plane enables the extension of trigonometric functions to all real numbers"). The given understanding (**U2**) in the advanced algebra unit is a more topical understanding than the **U1** in the seventh-grade unit, which is an overarching understanding. Both types of understandings (topical and overarching) are appropriate and useful for building conceptual understanding and connecting mathematical topics across units and years.

When the same understandings are referred to over and over again, students make the connection with prior knowledge instead of learning the current skill or topic as a *new* thing that they now need to master. This is the power of understanding mathematics. As we learn more and more, the concepts and connections become the building blocks upon which we grow our knowledge and skills. Instead of learning rational numbers as a completely new topic with new procedures to be memorized, students can logically see that this is the same idea as fractions that they have been learning since third grade and integers that they began in sixth grade! Now the connections are made, the same principles and patterns apply, and we just learn new details with a new number group. Math makes sense!

You might have noticed that the KUDs provided were all numbered (K1, K2, etc.). This is not necessary, but it helps significantly when

FIGURE 3.4

WRITING A UNIT KUD

Area	Tips
Know	• The Know category is based on FACTS. These can include vocabulary and definitions, math facts such as trigonometric values, patterns such as integer operation "rules," and so on. • Know statements are straightforward—if you know it, you know it. • Knows are usually written as a list: Bullets are fine. • "How to" do something would be considered a Know. You either know the steps, or you don't.
Understand	• The Understanding category is based on CONCEPTS. They are big connecting ideas. They can be general principles and generalizations. Most often, Understandings provide a "why" to what you are learning. • Understandings have several things you would need to "know" in order to fully be able to understand and explain. Thus, the Know statements should be directly related to one or more Understandings. • Understandings are written in complete sentences and can be preceded by the phrase "Students will understand THAT." For example, "Students will understand quadratic functions" is not an understanding. Quadratic functions are a topic. Instead, "Students will understand *that* quadratic functions follow the patterns and similarities of all families of functions" would be an understanding. • Understandings are revisitable. That is, if a student can come to understand in depth in a single lesson, it is probably not an understanding. • Most units have two to five understandings.

(Continued)

FIGURE 3.4 (Continued)

Do	• The Do category states the mathematical evidence that students should be able to exhibit if they both Know and Understand the content in the unit. It is not where lesson activities are listed—that would be in a specific lesson plan.
	• Do statements usually begin with verbs, because they describe the actions students should be able to do.
	• Be sure to include actions that will have students think like the professional—for example, "explain the impact of changing a sample population" is the work of a statistician.
	• Include higher order verbs to ensure that students are demonstrating understanding (explain, justify, generalize) as well as factual knowledge and skill (define, graph).
	• Do statements will include the skills of the unit.

referring back to the KUD for planning and for communicating with others. Figure 3.4 suggests some design tips when writing KUDs for your unit.

For most teachers, writing the Understandings for a unit is the most challenging aspect of unpacking standards.

For additional examples of understandings correlated by grade or course, topic, and skill, refer to Figure 3.1 and/or download Additional Understandings in Secondary Mathematics from resources.corwin.com/everymathlearner6-12.

TRY IT! KUD LIST

Purpose: To practice explicitly expressing what students should Know, Understand, and be able to Do as a result of learning based on the standards for the unit.

What are the big ideas or understandings undergirding one of your units? As you look at a unit, what are the K, U, and D? For help and additional ideas for writing understandings, review Figure 3.1. You can also download a unit template to help guide your work.

Most mathematics instructional resources provide the standards being addressed, and many give "essential questions" for each lesson. Some of these are more helpful than others, but in and of themselves, they are often insufficient. For most teachers, developing KUDs for their unit is the most challenging part of differentiation. However, it is worth the effort. The depth at which we come to know our content through this process has many benefits:

- We see connections among mathematics more readily.

- We are ready to answer unexpected questions (see Chapter 4).

- We plan purposeful and targeted lessons (see Chapter 4).

- We recognize conceptual gaps and misconceptions in our students more readily (see Chapter 7).

- We build cohesive units that ensure instruction, tasks, and all forms of assessment reach the desired learning outcomes (see Chapters 4 and 7).

- Differentiation based on anything less may not target essential learning for all learners and thus not have the intended results.

TEACHING UP

One of the misconceptions about differentiation that I have often heard is that differentiation "dummies down" curriculum. Nothing could be further from the truth. Research clearly shows that everyone can learn mathematics at high levels (Boaler, 2015). This is the essence of teaching up. We believe that all students can learn, we can hold all students to high expectations, and we must provide the necessary support for students to accomplish the goal. This is fully developed through clarity of curriculum and expectations, instructional decisions (see Chapter 4), and our classroom culture (see Chapter 5).

The discussion of how mathematics should be taught has been going on for a long time. The National Council of Teachers of Mathematics (NCTM) in 1989 first formally proposed what teaching and learning mathematics might look like through the publication of *Curriculum and Evaluation Standards for School Mathematics*. The Professional Standards for Teaching Mathematics in 1991 and the Assessment Standards for School Mathematics in 1995 followed this. In 2000, NCTM updated these publications with *Principles and Standards for School Mathematics*. These publications and others, including *Adding It Up* (Kilpatrick, Swafford, & Findell, 2001) from the National Research Council in 2001, began a serious conversation about what it means to learn mathematics. The learning of mathematics in the mathematics community has never been about memorization and speed. In 2001, the National Research Council in *Adding It Up* (Kilpatrick et al., 2001) suggested five strands for mathematical proficiency: conceptual understanding, procedural fluency, strategic competence, adaptive reasoning, and productive disposition. All of these publications and resulting conversations and research have laid the foundation for what teaching and learning in mathematics should be ideally—balancing conceptual understandings and reasoning with procedural skills and strategies, embedded within real-world contexts.

Most recently, we have NCTM's (2014) publication of *Principles to Actions* describing today's mathematics classroom. The first three principles for school mathematics in NCTM's (2014) *Principles to Actions: Ensuring Mathematical Success for All* are as follows:

- Teaching and Learning—Effective teaching should engage students in meaningful learning that stimulates making sense of mathematical ideas and reasoning mathematically.

- Access and Equity—All students have access to a high-quality mathematics curriculum with high expectations and the support and resources to maximize learning potential.

- Curriculum—A curriculum that develops important mathematics along coherent progressions and develops connections among areas of mathematical study and between mathematics and the real world.

So how do we do it? How do we teach and design units and lessons to accomplish all of this? How do we "teach up" to ensure a high-quality mathematics education for all students? The beginning is certainly clarifying the understandings and basing units and instruction around conceptual understandings with embedded skills. While digging into our standards, we need to make sure that we are teaching at or above our grade level or course expectations. Chapter 4 will provide more specific design strategies for helping students to reach appropriate course-level content as well as enrichment and engagement ideas.

Teaching up also involves designing lessons, asking questions, and choosing tasks at a high level of cognitive demand. There are two structures commonly used to determine if we are conducting class at a high level: depth of knowledge (DOK) and cognitive demand.

Both structures have four levels, two levels defined as lower and two defined as upper. DOK, a structure designed by Norman Webb in the late 1990s, was originally designed for mathematics and science standards but has been expanded for all content areas. Cognitive Demand (Smith & Stein, 1998) is a structure specifically for mathematics. Figure 3.5 gives the level names for each framework and their characteristics.

FIGURE 3.5

STRUCTURES FOR COGNITIVE COMPLEXITY

Level	Depth of Knowledge	Cognitive Demand	Description
Lower Level 1	Recall	Memorization	• Reproducing facts, rules, formulas, procedures, or definitions from memory • No connection to concepts
Lower Level 2	Skill/Concept	Procedures Without Connections	• Use information in a familiar situation • Involves two or more steps • Algorithmic. Use a procedure rotely • Very little ambiguity or reasoning involved • No student explanations required
Upper Level 3	Strategic Thinking	Procedures With Connections	• Requires reasoning, developing a plan or a sequence of steps • Some complexity in the task or question • Procedures are to develop connections and conceptual understanding • Multiple representations • Takes cognitive effort
Upper Level 4	Extended Thinking	Doing Mathematics	• Requires an investigation, time to think and process multiple conditions • Requires complex and nonalgorithmic thinking • Explore and understand the nature of mathematical concepts, processes, and relationships • Mathematics of the real world

TRY IT! HOW RIGOROUS IS IT?

Purpose: To practice determining the level of rigor in a given task or problem.

For each of the following tasks, determine the DOK or cognitive demand level. Answers are at the end of the chapter—but don't cheat!

1. Some shoes that I have wanted were just placed on sale! Their original price was $74.99 but now they are on sale for $63.75. I'm wondering if this is a good deal.

   a. What is the percent of decrease from the original price?

      I still didn't have enough money saved up to buy the shoes, so I had to wait. Now the store has an ad that all sale items have been reduced by one third of the sale price.

   b. What is the new sale price?

   c. What is the overall percent of decrease from the original price?

   d. Explain why your answers are correct. Can I just add the original percent decrease and the additional sale decrease to find the overall decrease? Why or why not?

2. Find the next two terms in the arithmetic sequence:

   $\frac{2}{5}, \frac{3}{5}, \frac{4}{5}, \ldots$

3. I drove from Phoenix to New York for a total of 2,408 miles. I am hoping to average 55 miles per hour on the trip. I want to drive about 8 hours a day to allow time to stop for lunch and get a good night's sleep. About how many miles per day should I plan to drive and how many days will this take me?

4. Conduct a survey of the freshman class to generate any bivariate data that interest you (for example, number of hours on social media and grade point average). Determine an appropriate sample and how you will randomly sample to gather data. Determine the best display for your raw data (minimum of two) and interpret your data. Consider:

- Do you believe there is a correlation? Causation? How could you know?

- What questions can you ask for further exploration of your data?

- What distributions or statistics might be helpful for interpretation?

5. Use algebra tiles to model simplifying expressions and solving equations. Explain how the tiles model each symbolic step in the process.

   a. $3(x - 1) = 15$ b. $2x + 4 = x - 4$

Most mathematics instruction in the United States occurs at Levels 1 and 2. Level 1 should be a supporting level to enable students to function at Levels 2 and 3. Please understand that these levels are not necessarily hierarchical—that is, you do not move through the levels in order. In fact, starting with a Level 4 task is often a great starting point to create the need to learn the facts, formulas, procedures, and other skills in Levels 1 and 2. Our aim should be for the majority of students' work to be at Levels 2 and 3. In Chapter 4, we will further discuss the selection and design of higher level tasks.

TRY IT! HIGHER AND HIGHER

Purpose: To recognize the complexity with which you most often challenge your students and to push for higher levels.

Make a list of the tasks and questions you have used in class over the past week or two. Write the complexity level (DOK or cognitive demand) next to each one. At what level are most of the tasks and questions with which your students engage? Do you need to make any adjustments? See if you can bump up some of the tasks and questions you have identified as lower level.

There is yet another consideration to teaching up: helping students understand what it means and looks like to be an active learner of mathematics.

WHAT LEARNING MATHEMATICS WITH UNDERSTANDING LOOKS LIKE

How students engage with learning mathematics is equally as important as the content they are learning. In fact, if they are not invested in the process of learning, they may not learn the content to the depth we desire and certainly don't remember it beyond the immediate unit (or sometimes even the next day). As mentioned before, this is not a new way of thinking but has rarely been made an integral part of a standards document or mathematics learning.

----------●

Consider It!

What does it look like when students are involved with learning mathematics? What verbs come to mind?

The realization of how important it is that students develop "mathematical habits of mind" has prompted our current focus on describing and expecting that the way students learn mathematics shifts along with the content of what students are learning. Today's standards documents describe student actions for learning in various ways. The Common Core State Standards have described them through the Standards for Mathematical Practice. Other states that have not adopted the Common Core also have process standards that are very similar, and some states that are not using the Common Core State Standards are using the Standards for Mathematical Practice as part of their state's standards document. These behaviors are written as standards to raise the importance of students' actions and thinking in learning mathematics effectively and are not only expected in the classroom but also expected to be assessed as a part of end-of-year testing. Although there are slight differences in the descriptions of each process, the intent and descriptions are consistent from state to state. Figure 3.6 shows alignment among the Standards for Mathematical Practice with other states' process standards. At the time of this writing, other states were looking at amending their standards that may not be reflected in this figure.

The full descriptions of each of these mathematical behaviors can be accessed at the following websites:

- Common Core Standards for Mathematical Practice: http://www.corestandards.org/Math/Practice/
- Nebraska Mathematical Processes: https://www.education.ne.gov/math/Math_Standards/Adopted_2015_Math_Standards/2015_Nebraska_College_and_Career_Standards_for_Mathematics_Vertical.pdf

- Oklahoma Mathematical Actions and Processes: http://sde
  .ok.gov/sde/sites/ok.gov.sde/files/documents/files/OAS-Math-
  Final%20Version_2.pdf

- South Carolina Process Standards: https://ed.sc.gov/scdoe/
  assets/file/agency/scde-grant-opportunities/documents/
  SCCCRStandardsForMathematicsFinal-PrintOneSide.pdf

- Texas Process Standards: http://www.abileneisd.org/cms/
  lib2/TX01001461/Centricity/Domain/1943/Texas%20
  Mathematical%20Process%20Standards%20Aug%202014.pdf

- Virginia Standards of Learning Mathematics Goals: http://
  www.pen.k12.va.us/testing/sol/standards_docs/mathematics/
  index.shtml

WATCH IT!

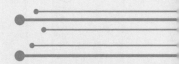

In this video, two teachers discuss the importance of teaching and modeling the eight standards for mathematical practice. The students in the video have been explicitly taught these standards from the beginning of the school year and discuss the role of perseverance (SMP 1) and reasoning (SMP 3) after a group task. As you watch Video 3.2, *Putting the Standards for Mathematical Practice at the Heart of Differentiation*, consider the following questions:

1. How might the teacher have established how students participate in and engage with mathematics content in deep and meaningful ways?

2. What are the pros and cons in the students' actions in learning mathematics with the Standards for Mathematical Practice in mind?

3. How effectively do you explicitly teach and address the practices in your mathematics classroom?

4. Why do you believe there is such an emphasis on mathematical practices (or processes or habits of mind) in the learning of mathematics today?

Video 3.2 Putting the Standards for Mathematical Practice at the Heart of Differentiation

Although the various documents may give different names, there is agreement on what learning mathematics should look like. Combined into a simplified list, here are six aspects of active mathematics learning. Remember that these are describing student actions—not teacher actions! I believe we all do these things as teachers of mathematics. In fact, if we want our students to exhibit

FIGURE 3.6

STANDARDS FOR MATHEMATICAL PRACTICE (SMP) AND OTHER PROCESS STANDARDS

SMP	NE	OK	SC	TX	VA
Make sense of problems and persevere in solving them	Solve mathematical problems	Develop a deep and flexible conceptual understanding	Make sense of problems and persevere in solving them	Use a problem-solving model that incorporates analyzing given information, formulating a plan or strategy, determining a solution, justifying the solution, and evaluating the problem-solving process and the reasonableness of the solution	Mathematical problem solving
Reason abstractly and quantitatively		Develop mathematical reasoning	Reason both contextually and abstractly		Mathematical reasoning
Construct viable arguments and critique the reasoning of others	Communicate mathematical ideas effectively	Develop the ability to communicate mathematically	Use critical thinking skills to justify mathematical reasoning and critique the reasoning of others	Communicate mathematical ideas, reasoning, and their implications using multiple representations, including symbols, diagrams, graphs, and language as appropriate	Mathematical communication
Model with mathematics	Model and represent mathematical problems	Develop the ability to conjecture, model, and generalize	Connect mathematical ideas and real-world situations through modeling	Create and use representations to organize, record, and communicate mathematical ideas	Mathematical representations

SMP	NE	OK	SC	TX	VA
Use appropriate tools strategically		Develop strategies for problem solving	Use a variety of mathematical tools effectively and strategically	Select tools, including real objects, manipulatives, paper and pencil, and technology as appropriate, and techniques, including mental math, estimation, and number sense as appropriate, to solve problems	Mathematical problem solving
Attend to precision		Develop accurate and appropriate procedural fluency	Communicate mathematically and approach mathematical situations with precision	Display, explain, and justify mathematical ideas and arguments using precise mathematical language in written or oral communication	Mathematical problem solving
Look for and make use of structure		Develop the ability to conjecture, model, and generalize	Identify and utilize structure and patterns	Analyze mathematical relationships to connect and communicate mathematical ideas	
Look for and express regularity in repeated reasoning		Develop the ability to conjecture, model, and generalize	Identify and utilize structure and patterns		
	Make mathematical connections	Develop a productive mathematical disposition		Apply mathematics to problems arising in everyday life, society, and the workplace	Mathematical connections

these behaviors, we need to model them as well as explicitly teach them to and expect them from our students.

Let's take a closer look at how to implement some of these actions.

Make sense of problems—reason and interpret mathematical situations. This is the obvious beginning, right? But how often do your students barely look at a problem before saying "I don't get it." We often read the problem to the students, interpret the problem for them, and give the first step. It is no wonder that so many students do not know how to make sense of problems for themselves. When students engage in learning mathematics, they wrestle with the context of a problem, what they are looking for, possible ways to start the problem, and multiple solution paths or representations. In addition, when students make sense of problems, they begin to discuss the mathematics they see in a real-world situation and describe a real-world situation that would require the mathematics being learned.

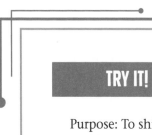

TRY IT! HOW STUDENTS MAKE SENSE OF PROBLEMS

Purpose: To shift "sense-making" to students when facing a new problem

Give the students a rich problem to solve.

1. In partners, have Partner A (student whose birthday is coming next) read the problem and Partner B interpret the problem in his or her own words. This should also include what the solution will look like (for example, ___ feet). Discuss as a class or check in on students' interpretations.

2. Have Partner B suggest a way to start the problem to Partner A. Partner A then suggests another way to start, or agrees to the idea of Partner B, and explains why it will work.

3. Have partners generate strategies to represent and solve the problem.

4. Either together or alone, students go on to solve the problem.

Communicate mathematically—Students explain their thinking mathematically and ask questions of, or build on, other students' explanations. Students who communicate mathematically use correct mathematical vocabulary and multiple representations to communicate their thinking. Beware of accepting only an answer or a retelling of steps as an explanation. Explanations need to include reasoning and the meanings and properties of operations to be considered robust.

TRY IT! STUDENT DISCOURSE

Purpose: To teach healthy mathematical discourse skills

1. Direct mathematical conversations so that they are among the students as much as possible. Do not interpret and redirect questions and answers. Teach students to restate what other students have said. To provide structures for discourse, give students sentence starters such as the following:

   - I agree with _____ because _____

   - Another way to think about this is _____

   - I did it a different way. I _____

   - I disagree with _____ because _____

   - I would like to add on to what _____ said about _____

   - Can you explain what you mean by _____

   - Can you show _____ in another way

   - I think that _____ because _____

2. As the teacher, stay with a student who might be struggling or unsure in his or her communication. Ask questions to help the student clarify his or her thinking rather than move on to another student.

3. Gently correct and provide correct mathematical vocabulary.

Model with mathematics—There are two aspects to modeling mathematics: models of mathematics and how mathematics models the real world. Models of mathematics include using manipulatives such as algebra tiles or models and two-color counters, drawings, tables, graphs, and symbols. Whenever new material is presented in a way that students see relationships, they generate greater brain cell activity and achieve more successful long-term memory storage and retrieval (Willis, 2006, p. 15). We also use mathematics to model the real world. When we solve quantitative problems from the world around us, we are modeling the world with mathematics.

TRY IT! MATHEMATICAL MODELING

Purpose: To make mathematical processes and problems concrete and visual whenever possible

1. It is very important that the concrete or visual model comes *before* the paper-and-pencil process. If the algorithm is taught first, students will not value or want to complete the concrete or visual activity. Also, the concrete or visual task is to develop the conceptual understanding and make sense of the process or algorithm to follow.

2. Connect the concrete or visual explicitly to the skill or process. If it cannot be explicitly connected, it is not a valid model. For example, each step in solving an equation with algebra tiles correlates to the written symbolic step. Once students can correctly solve equations with the manipulative, the process of solving on paper is just recording the process they have already learned with the tiles in mathematical symbols. The role of inverse operations and "unwinding" the order of operations now makes sense instead of being steps to memorize.

3. Challenge students to represent problems in as many different ways as they can through manipulatives and various representations.

Choose and use tools appropriately—Tools can be anything! We usually think of physical tools such as two-color counters, rulers, protractors, and calculators or computers. However, tools can also be mental strategies such as estimation strategies or the distributive property for multiplying a monomial and a trinomial. Knowing which tool or strategy will be appropriate and useful in a given situation is a necessary skill for solving problems and a practical life skill. Often we distribute the tools we will be using in a lesson; for example, today we need compasses. Instead, build a toolbox with all of the mathematical tools in the classroom for table groups or an area where all tools are stored, and challenge students to select the tools they think they will need based on a lesson's description.

TRY IT! THE TOOLBOX

Purpose: Have students select and defend a variety of mathematical tools

1. For a lesson, explain to the students what the task will be and ask them to choose the tools they think they will need.

2. After the task, ask students to reflect on the tools they chose. Did they get what they needed? Why or why not? Did they choose extra tools that were not needed? Why did they select that tool? What have they learned for future selections?

Recognize and use patterns and structures—The more students work with mathematics, the more they can recognize mathematical structures. For example, integers alternate between evens and odds. An even root can only be taken of a positive number to have a real answer, and the root will be positive. An odd root, on the other hand, can be taken of either a positive or negative value, and the root will have the same sign as the radicand. Structure includes understanding why a process works, such as solving a proportion or factoring a trinomial, instead of simply memorizing the steps needed to complete the process. Using a pattern as a mathematical practice at the secondary level is most often related to repeated reasoning rather than finding and using a specific element in a pattern. For example, practicing multiplying exponential factors with the same base repeatedly should lead students to recognize that the product will have the same base and an exponent that is the sum of the exponents in the factors ($x^3 \cdot x^5 = x^8$). Instead of giving students an algorithm, such as the "rules" for adding integers, try modeling thinking about the structures and patterns that are inherent in the operations and use multiple problem examples to find the patterns that lead to the generalized steps.

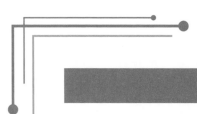

TRY IT! PATTERN HUNT

Purpose: To make sense of mathematical rules or procedures and recognize mathematical structures that give hints to solutions

1. Give students several problems to solve that use manipulatives, drawings, models, and so on, but not rules or steps. For example, use two-color counters or number lines to model integer addition and subtraction.

2. Generate a list of the problems and their answers from using the models.

3. Have the students find the "shortcuts" or patterns they recognize. For example, after several repetitions and generating a class list of problems and answers, students will see that multiplying two factors with the same sign will have a positive product, but multiplying two factors with opposite signs will have a negative product.

4. This will undoubtedly be the algorithm or rule you wanted to teach, and instead it will be a student discovery.

Attend to precision—Perhaps undergirding all other of these mathematical practices is the ability to attend to precision. Precision includes using correct vocabulary. It includes noticing whether an equation has a plus or minus sign and attending to all other notation. It includes knowing facts and formulas and efficiently using various strategies for operations and problem types. It includes knowing when and how to apply the properties of operations in multiple contexts.

TRY IT! CATCH ME

Purpose: Have students catch you any time you are not mathematically precise

1. Prepare a problem presentation with which you will make several precision errors.

2. Use incorrect or slang vocabulary. Make arithmetic and algebraic mistakes.

3. Tell students in advance that you will be making several errors or imprecise vocabulary, and their job is to find your imprecisions.

4. You can also divide the class into two teams and award points as students collaborate to find errors and imprecisions.

Clarifying content and teaching students how to actively learn mathematics is essential for all mathematics instruction. It is certainly necessary for effective differentiation, which is based on solid curriculum. Just how do rigorous and explicit content, mathematical learning practices, and differentiation fit together?

CONCLUSION

We have developed a complete picture of clarifying content for designing differentiated instruction. We have also discussed the actions students need to employ to learn mathematics with understanding. Effective teaching is not about delivering information or creating meaning. It's melding the two to help students see the meaning in the information they are learning (Sousa & Tomlinson, 2011).

As we prepare to dig into explicitly designing differentiated mathematics instruction, consider the changes in how we teach mathematics as a whole. Figure 3.7 compares the "before and after" of teaching mathematics today, adapted from David Sousa (2015).

FIGURE 3.7

BEFORE AND AFTER OF MATHEMATICAL REASONING

We used to teach mathematics as . . .	But now we teach mathematics as . . .
Problems to be calculated	Situations about which we reason
Procedures to be memorized	Operations that are based on properties with multiple representations and strategies
Isolated topics	Connected concepts
A speed activity for prowess	Problem solving and reasoning for prowess
Teacher led and valued	Student discovered and valued
Something forgettable	Understood, so remembered

There are two keys to differentiation: know your content and know your students. In the previous chapter, we learned how to get to know our students as learners. In this chapter, we looked at knowing our content in depth. In the next chapter, we will look at how knowing our content and our students comes together in powerful differentiation.

FREQUENTLY ASKED QUESTIONS

Q: With the Common Core standards and other state standards so closely aligned, do we really need to go through the work of writing a KUD? Aren't they written somewhere?

A: There are many posts about big ideas online. Some are good and can be a resource. However, some are labeled "conceptual understanding" but are actually fact or skill based. These are not understandings. In addition, there is nothing like the struggle to make sense of the standards to help your own learning and clarify what you want students to come away with. Remember that we want our students to take a challenge and struggle with things that are challenging . . . we need to do the same.

Q: What if my students can't explain their thinking?

A: Chances are pretty good that your students have been asked to tell how they got an answer in mathematics, and this has always been what an "explanation" was. They need to be taught how to construct a mathematical explanation. This can be done by modeling first and foremost, but also ask questions such as "How did you know to do that?" or "What allows you to do that in mathematics (e.g., you can do this by using the distributive property, etc.)?"

Q: What about students who can't reach the standard?

A: First, be very careful of drawing these types of conclusions. Research is showing that almost all students, given time and support, can reach standards. With that said, some students are significantly behind in their mathematics learning. It is very important to teach the grade- or course-level standards in class. When we draw conclusions that certain students are not able to reach the standard and lower the expectations, or worse, lower the instruction level, we widen gaps, not close them. Truthfully, most students can reach the standards given support and, if appropriate, more direct intervention. The Response to Intervention (RTI) structure is designed to help students significantly behind in learning to close gaps and reach as close to grade level as possible, if not actually reach the standard. However, even given the RTI structure, remember that Tier 1 instruction is on grade level through differentiated techniques. Chapter 4 will more specifically address how to design instruction for readiness, as well as interest and learning profile.

Keepsakes and Plans

What are the keepsake ideas from this chapter, those thoughts or ideas that resonated with you that you do not want to forget?

Mathematics Makes Sense:

1.

2.

3.

Themes and Big Ideas in Mathematics:

1.

2.

3.

Teaching Up:

1.

2.

3.

What Learning Mathematics With Understanding Looks Like:

1.

2.

3.

Based on my keepsake ideas, I plan to:

1.

2.

TRY IT ANSWERS

1. DOK 3/procedures with connections. This is a multistep application of computational algorithms. It would be a high DOK 2 if it were not for the explanation requirement.

2. DOK 1/memorization. This is a straightforward algorithm to find a common difference, and the algorithm is probably not needed because the pattern is so simple.

3. DOK 2/procedures without connections. This item is a basic application of computational algorithms. Other than recognizing the need for division, the context does not add depth to understanding the process for solving the problem.

4. DOK 4/doing mathematics. This is an example of what mathematicians do in the real world.

5. DOK 3/procedures with connections. This task uses models to make sense of the algorithms that will be used in simplifying expressions and solving equations prior to formal symbolic instruction.

CHAPTER FOUR

STEP UP

HOW TO MAKE PROACTIVE PLANNING
DECISIONS THAT DEEPEN THINKING

For many educators, when they think of differentiation, it is the
task or activity they are usually picturing, rather than the intentional
design behind the task. This chapter will provide you with a variety of
strategies for differentiation in order to match your learners' needs
with deep content. In this chapter, you will find the following:

Decisions, Decisions	Classroom Structures
Differentiation and KUDs	Frequently Asked Questions
Strategies for Differentiation	Keepsakes and Plans

"I have this great activity. . . ." That is how most teachers begin thinking about instruction in general and especially differentiation. It is very hard not to think that way. Yet, effective and purposeful differentiation is dependent on the integration of knowing both your students' learning needs and the depth of content as described in the preceding chapters. And so the foundations are in place and it is time to design. Purposeful differentiation is all about decisions.

DECISIONS, DECISIONS

At its simplest, differentiation is a series of decisions about the most impactful learning opportunities for each student. However, there are a lot of decisions to be made: What classroom structures will work best and for which segments? What should be differentiated? How should it be differentiated? What strategies will be effective?

Before you start feeling overwhelmed, remember that in a differentiated classroom, not everything is differentiated. That statement often causes a great sigh of relief among teachers. It is not even desirable to differentiate everything if you could. In a differentiated classroom, very purposeful decisions are made as to what should and should not be differentiated.

There is an ebb and flow in a differentiated classroom—times when the whole class is together to establish common language and ground work for the topic or exploration; times for group or partner work, sense-making, exploration, and various tasks; times for individual work to practice; and times for the teacher and students to check for their understanding and assess their progress. Within any lesson, students move in and out of these various structures depending on the components and design of the lesson.

DIFFERENTIATION AND KUDs

The starting point of effective differentiation is clear and explicit content (see Chapter 3). So what do we do with the content once it is unpacked into a KUD? In any classroom there are three areas that can be differentiated: Content, process, and product. Content describes what we teach, which was discussed in Chapter 3. Process describes what students will do in order to learn the content (this chapter), and product describes how students will show what they have learned (Chapter 7). From Chapter 1 you remember that we can differentiate any of these areas by readiness, interest, or learning profile. As you look at planning differentiated tasks, the "Know, Understand, and Do" should be the driving force. However, not everything should be differentiated. As you think about your content, consider the following:

- *Know*—Can be differentiated. To make the determination of which "Knows" can be differentiated, determine what is essential information and what is not. Essential knowledge (such as key grade-level vocabulary, formulas, number systems, and other specifics in the standards) is nonnegotiable and the content is not differentiated, although the methods by which students learn the facts may be differentiated or students who already have mastery may also have a differentiated task. If the "Know" is good to know, it may be differentiated. For example, a specific application of a skill may be differentiated. Not every application of exponential functions needs to be taught to every student, nor could they possibly be. Different specific contexts may be given to different groups of students based on readiness or interest.

- *Understand*—The Understandings for a unit are not differentiated. All students need to develop the same connections, concepts, and big ideas that give purpose to the mathematics being learned, although they may be reached at different depths and by different means. So the tasks to reach the understandings may be differentiated, but the understandings themselves are not.

- *Do*—The Do in the KUD is written in a way to show what students should be able to do as a result of the mathematical learning in the unit but does not include the specific tasks by which the learning is exhibited. The Do is entirely differentiable based on the types of tasks and demonstrations designed. How students show what they know and understand is wide open. The number of aspects and complexity at which they demonstrate skills may be negotiable based on readiness.

Figures 4.1 and 4.2 give examples of how the KUD can guide differentiation. The figures use specific Ks, Us, and Ds from the seventh-grade unit on rational numbers and the advanced algebra unit on trigonometry KUDs found in Chapter 3. Notice that not all of the KUDs for a unit could possibly be used in a single lesson. Specific Ks, Us, and Ds were chosen from the unit plan for use in different lessons. These KUDs are used to design the differentiated tasks for the lesson. The examples provide tasks for readiness, interest, and learning profile differentiation as examples, but for an actual lesson, the teacher would make the decision as to the manner of differentiation and not try to do all three. Likewise, not all of the tasks would be used in a single lesson but could be used over the course of the unit if desired or needed for repetition or review, or the teacher could decide to choose the method for differentiation that is most appropriate for the lesson given specific students' needs.

FIGURE 4.1

SEVENTH-GRADE DIFFERENTIATION IDEAS BASED ON KUD

KUD From Unit Plan Being Addressed in This Lesson:

K1: Vocabulary:

Rational Number

K2: How to add, subtract, multiply, and divide rational numbers.

U2: A negative in math means "opposite."

U4: Only things that are alike can be added or subtracted.

U6: Operations with rational numbers follow the same patterns as operations with fractions and integers.

D1: Give several examples of a negative meaning "opposite."

D3: Explain the different processes for operations with rational numbers.

D5: Model/demonstrate/illustrate how rational numbers follow the same patterns as integers. (Compare/contrast integers and rational numbers.)

D6: Explain how the pattern of multiplying negatives results in a positive or negative product and how it relates to "opposite."

D7: Add, subtract, multiply, and divide rational numbers.

Example for Readiness Differentiation	We have learned how to work with integers, and you have been working with fractions since at least third grade and decimals since fourth grade. In this unit, we have somewhat combined these areas into one: rational numbers. Rational numbers are numbers that can be written as a ratio of integers. This means that rational numbers can be expressed as positive or negative fractions, decimals, or whole numbers. Today, we will formalize how we work with rational numbers and how they are really the same thing as what you have been doing.

Tiered Worksheets:

Group 1: Independently complete table of operations with fractions, decimals, integers, and rational numbers. Explain the connections among the three number systems.

Group 2: Independently complete specific problem types (add, subtract, multiply, and divide with fractions, decimals, integers, and rational numbers) and explain how to do each type. Finally, draw conclusions as to why operations with rational numbers are not really new. Two-color counters and fraction strips are available for students if needed.

Group 3: Complete the same task as Group 2 with teacher guidance or supervision. Two-color counters and fraction strips are used to reinforce the meaning of negatives and common denominators.

Tier 1

Working with Rational Numbers (Tier 1)

Fill in the table with steps, rules and/or patterns for each type of number system.

	Fractions	Integers	Rational Numbers
Add			
Subtract			
Multiply			
Divide			

Explain how operations with rational numbers combine what you already know about integers and fractions. Give examples to support your explanations.

Tier 2-3   Working with Rational Numbers (Tier 2)

1) Working With Fractions	
Add: $\frac{2}{5} + \frac{3}{4} =$	Explain: How do you add fractions?
Subtract: $\frac{6}{7} - \frac{2}{3} =$	Explain: How do you subtract fractions?
Multiply: $\frac{4}{9} \cdot \frac{3}{4} =$	Explain: How do you multiply fractions?
Divide: $\frac{1}{3} \div \frac{5}{6} =$	Explain: How do you divide fractions?

(Continued)

FIGURE 4.1 (Continued)

2) Working With Integers	
Add: −7 + 4 =	Explain: How do you add integers?
Subtract: −3 − 8 =	Explain: How do you subtract integers?
Multiply: 8 · −4 =	Explain: How do you multiply integers?
Divide: $-132 \div -4 =$	Explain: How do you divide integers?

3) Working With Rational Numbers	
Add: $\frac{-2}{5} + \frac{3}{4} =$	Explain: How do you add rational numbers?
Subtract: $\frac{6}{7} - \frac{-2}{3} =$	Explain: How do you subtract rational numbers?
Multiply: $\frac{4}{9} \cdot \frac{-3}{4} =$	Explain: How do you multiply rational numbers?
Divide: $\frac{-1}{3} \div \frac{-5}{6} =$	Explain: How do you divide rational numbers?

Explain how operations with rational numbers combine what you already know about integers and fractions. Use the examples above to support your explanations.

The worksheets for this example can be downloaded at resources.corwin.com/everymathlearner6-12.

Example for Interest Differentiation	We have learned how to work with integers, and you have been working with fractions since at least third grade and decimals since fourth grade. In this unit, we have somewhat combined these areas into one: rational numbers. Rational numbers are numbers that can be written as a ratio of integers. This means that rational numbers can be expressed as positive or negative fractions, decimals, or whole numbers. Today, we will formalize how we work with rational numbers and how they are really the same thing as what you have been doing. Choose *one* of the following tasks. You may work alone or with a partner. 1: Complete a worksheet of problems with fraction/decimal, integer, and rational number operations. Complete a compare and contrast Venn diagram (three circles) on the operations with fractions, integers, and rational numbers. 2: Complete an "Always, Sometimes, Never" fact sheet on operations with fractions/decimals, integers, and rational numbers. Use examples

	to support your answers (for an answer of sometimes show when it is true and when it is false). Draw conclusions about how operations with rational numbers combine the rules of working with fractions, decimals, and integers.
	3: Design a four-pane window foldable for operations with fractions, decimals, integers, and rational numbers. Give steps for each operation (or pair of operations) with examples. In the center of the foldable, explain how operations with rational numbers are built from operations with fractions, decimals, and integers.
Example for Learning Profile Differentiation (Differentiated by Sternberg's Triarchic Theory)	We have learned how to work with integers, and you have been working with fractions since at least third grade and decimals since fourth grade. In this unit, we have somewhat combined these areas into one: rational numbers. Rational numbers are numbers that can be written as a ratio of integers. This means that rational numbers can be expressed as positive or negative fractions, decimals, or whole numbers. Today, we will formalize how we work with rational numbers and how they are really the same thing as what you have been doing. *Analytical Task: It's in the Cards.* Students create problems by drawing cards designated as fractions, integers, or rational numbers. They will also draw an operation card to determine the operation of the problem. Students complete several problems with a minimum of one of each operation with fractions and integers and a minimum of two each with rational numbers. Conclude by explaining the steps to add, subtract, multiply, or divide rational numbers and how these steps relate to the steps of integer and fraction operations. *Practical Task: Dear Sixth Grade.* Write a letter to sixth graders explaining how important it is to learn fraction and decimal operations and the meaning of integers really well by the time they leave sixth grade so that they can have a very easy time with rational number operations. Tell them what a rational number is, and show them how to add, subtract, multiply, and divide rational numbers (use at least one negative rational number in each problem example) with problem examples. Finally, explain why operations with rational numbers are really just a combination of the rules of fractions and integers. *Creative Task: A Picture Is Worth a Thousand Words.* Create a visual representation showing operations with all forms of rational numbers. Your visual should include at least one example of every operation with each type of number and, most important, how (and why) operations with rational numbers are a combination of operations with integers and with fractions. Your visual could be a mind map, a cartoon, a graphic organizer, a poster, or any other idea you have. Please run your idea by me before starting on your rough draft.

FIGURE 4.2

ADVANCED ALGEBRA DIFFERENTIATION IDEAS BASED ON KUD

KUD From Unit Plan Being Addressed in This Lesson: **K1:** Vocabulary: Unit circle, radian, arc, subtend **K6:** Radian measure of an angle is the length of the arc on the unit circle subtended by the angle. **U1:** Different measurement systems can be equated, but most have more common uses in specific contexts and areas of study. **D7:** Explain what a radian is, and convert back and forth between radians and degrees.	
Example for Readiness Differentiation	All students will explore a hands-on activity determining the number or radii that will fit in the circumference of any given circle. This will be accomplished by bringing in several different circular plastic tops or plates and having students use yarn to estimate the radius of each circle and then determine how many radii fit around the circumference. Regardless of the size of the circle, a little more than 6 radii will fit—this should connect to their prior knowledge, and students should be able to estimate the number to be 2π and connect this to the formula for circumference (Note: sometimes it is easier to ask how many are in a semicircle so that the number, a little more than 3, triggers the thought of π). Define an arc of one radius length as a radian. 1 (Craftsman): You have now found why the formula for the circumference of a circle is $C = 2\pi r$. Use the fact that there are 2π radian around any circle's circumference and your expertise with converting units or with ratios and proportional reasoning to find two different ways to convert between degrees and radians. Take a copy of the unit circle with degrees labeled and write in the corresponding radian measures. Hint: Radian measure stays in terms of π. Do not give any decimal approximations! Extra challenge: If I memorize the radian and degree equivalencies for 0, 30, 45, 60, and 90 degrees, how can I find other quadrant angle equivalencies without converting? (e.g., 150 degrees? $3\pi/4$ radians?) 2 (Apprentice): You have now found why the formula for the circumference of a circle is $C = 2\pi r$. There are 2π radians in a full circle. How many degrees are in a full circle? Use this equivalence to determine how many radians are in a half-circle. In 90 degrees? 60 degrees? 45 degrees? Choose a ratio of radians to degrees (hint: use either 2π or π) to use as a conversion factor to convert any radians to degrees and degrees to radians. Test your reasoning on the conversions you have previously found first, then try to find the number of radians in 150 degrees and 80 degrees. How many degrees in $\pi/12$ radians? $\pi/5$ radians? (Note: You can also convert between radians and degrees using a proportion. If time, see if you can set up a proportion to solve the same problems you just converted.)

3 (Novice): You have now found why the formula for the circumference of a circle is C = 2πr. This means that in a semicircle, there are π radians. You have also converted between units in the past, using a conversion factor (think mph to feet per second conversion). Use the fact that π = 180° to set up a conversion factor to convert either degrees to radians or radians to degrees. Some questions to review before trying the mathematics:

- What form of 1 do we use for a conversion factor?

- To what do you need to pay attention when dividing units for conversion? (Hint: How do you "cancel" the units from which you are changing?)

Use your conversion factor to convert various degrees to radians and radians to degrees problems.

Closure for all: Explain what a radian is and how it relates to the circumference formula. Convert 145 degrees to radians and 3π/4 to degrees.

Example for Interest Differentiation	Choose one of the following ways to discover radian measure.

1: Use computer software to draw a circle with a radius about 2 inches so that the circle is big enough to see other constructions. Use the arc tool to segment the circumference into arcs exactly the length of the radius. Draw radii from the center of the circle to the endpoints of each arc. How many complete arcs can you get in the circumference? What approximate fraction of the radius is left? Does this number sound familiar? How does it relate to the formulae of the circumference of a circle? Each interior angle that subtends a complete arc has the measurement of 1 radian. How many radian are in a full circle?

2: Construct a circle with a radius about 2 inches using a compass. (This is just to ensure the circle is large enough to work with . . . the exact radius is not important.) Take a Wikki Stix (or piece of string or chenille) and measure the radius from your compass marks. Cut your measuring tool off, and use it to measure the number of arcs it will form around the circumference of the circle. Mark the endpoints of each arc. Use multiple pieces of your Wikki Stix (or yarn or chenille) to connect the center of your circle to the endpoints of each arc. How many complete arcs can you get in the circumference? What approximate fraction of the radius is left? Does this number sound familiar? How does it relate to the formulae of the circumference of a circle? Each interior angle that subtends a complete arc has the measurement of 1 radian. How many radians are in a full circle?

3: Take one of the cans that have been brought in. Notice that there is a mark at a spot on the rim of the can to mark the beginning and end of the circumference of the can.

(Continued)

FIGURE 4.2 (Continued)

	• Carefully roll the can, beginning and ending with the mark for one complete rotation, and measure the distance it has rolled.
	• Measure the diameter of your can.
	• Divide the distance rolled by the diameter.
	• Repeat with different-sized cans.
	• What do you find out? How many diameter are in the circumference? How many radii? How do these relate to the formulae of the circumference of a circle?
	• Each interior angle that subtends a complete arc has the measurement of 1 radian. How many radian are in a full circle?
	Now that you have discovered what a radian is, you can use your knowledge to convert between radians and degrees. We will look at two methods: conversion factors and proportions. You may use either method that you think is easier. (Continue with guided instruction to show two methods.)
	Practice converting several different problems, working alone or with up to two partners.
	Closure for all: Explain what a radian is and how it relates to the circumference formula. Convert 145 degrees to radians and $3\pi/4$ to degrees.
Example for Learning Profile Differentiation (Differentiated by Modality— Visual, Auditory, or Kinesthetic)	All students will explore a hands-on activity determining the number or radii that will fit in the circumference of any given circle. This will be accomplished by bringing in several different circular plastic tops or plates and having students use yarn to estimate the radius of each circle and then determine how many radii fit around the circumference. Regardless of the size of the circle, a little more than 6 radii will fit—this should connect to their prior knowledge, and students should be able to estimate the number to be 2π and connect this to the formula for circumference (Note: sometimes it is easier to ask how many are in a semicircle so that the number, a little more than 3, triggers the thought of π). Define an arc of one radius length as a radian.
	(Visual) Draw a unit circle showing 0°, 30°, 45°, 60°, 90°, 120°, 135°,150°, 180°, 210°, 225°, 240°, 270°, 300°, 315°, 330°, and 360°. Write in the corresponding radians you have already discovered (this should be for 0°, 180°, and 360°). How can you determine the radian measure of a 90° angle? A 270° angle? The other angles in the circle? Complete your unit circle with radian measures.
	Use the fact that 180° = π to set up either a conversion factor or proportion to solve for the angles in the unit circle. You should be able to convert from radian to degrees or degrees to radians.
	Make a mini-poster or postcard with a unit circle, explaining what a radian is and giving directions for converting between radians and degrees and degrees to radians.
	(Kinesthetic) Group will go back to the unit circle taped to the floor at the back of the room. Start with one student standing on 0° / 360°. Find the

card that says 0 and 2π, and the student places that card where he or she is standing on the unit circle. Another student stands at 180° and finds the π card to place on the circle. Next, two more students try to determine the radian measure for 90° and 270° using logical arguments and find corresponding radian cards to place. Once the quadrantal angle measures are placed, students should discuss a conversion strategy that could work to find the remaining angles in the circle. Students now take turns drawing a card with a degree measurement, stand at that spot on the unit circle, convert to radians, and place the appropriate radian card on the circle until the circle is completed with both degrees and radians. If time allows, repeat this process by drawing radian cards, going to that spot on the unit circle, converting to degrees, and placing both cards on the circle.

Create a "tag team" presentation on how to convert from degrees to radians and radians to degrees. Present at least one of each example.

(Auditory) Use a diagram of a unit circle showing 0°, 30°, 45°, 60°, 90°, 150°, 180°, 210°, 225°, 240°, 270°, 300°, 315°, 330°, and 360°. Write in the corresponding radians you have already discovered (this should be 0°, 180°, and 360°).

Discuss with your group:

How can you determine the radian measure of a 90° angle? A 270° angle? The other angles in the circle?

How could you set up a conversion factor or a proportion to solve for any angle measure in degrees given radians or radians given degrees? Test your theory on several known angle measures.

Formalize your process for converting between radians and degrees, and fill in the remaining angle measures on your circle.

Create a short skit or write a dialogue explaining what a radian is and how to convert between radians and degrees. Be sure to explain why the conversion factor works.

The examples in Figures 4.1 and 4.2 clearly show different types of tasks based on readiness, interest, and learning profile. However, it is possible that these can be combined in different ways, such as giving choices within a specific readiness level or designing tasks by learning profile and allowing students to choose the task that is most interesting to them.

It is also important to keep in mind the depth of knowledge/cognitive demand level (see Chapter 3) of the tasks. Low-level differentiated tasks may not have the desired learning outcomes for which we are hoping, because the tasks are low level. Differentiated tasks should be high level and implement the mathematical practices, conceptual understanding, and problem-solving skills to have the greatest impact on the learning of mathematics.

Consider It!

As you look over the differentiation suggestions in Figures 4.1 and 4.2, what conditions would prompt a teacher to choose readiness or interest or learning profile for the specific lesson?

STRATEGIES FOR DIFFERENTIATION

Choosing whether to differentiate by readiness, interest, or learning profile should be based on recognizing student need coupled with decisions about keeping learning fresh and engaging. Each area of differentiation has its specific strengths. Figure 4.3 provides the rationale for choosing a specific mode of differentiation.

FIGURE 4.3

DIFFERENTIATION FOCUS

Differentiation Aspect	Purpose
Readiness	Provides appropriate and realistic challenge and has the best potential for growth and understanding because students feel up to the appropriate challenge
Interest	Addresses intrinsic motivation and creates connections and a sense of fun in learning
Learning profile	Eases the learning process so that our brains can get learning into and out of memory. It is "more likely to evoke positive emotional responses, engaging affective filters to open access to the brain's processing centers" (Willis, 2006).

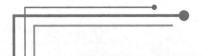

TRY IT! WRITE A KUD FOR ONE LESSON

Choose an upcoming lesson and write a brief KUD for the specific lesson (not the entire unit if the unit's KUD is not already developed). If you have used the unit template (see Chapter 3) to write your KUD, select the specific K, U, and D for one lesson. Determine how you will differentiate to best meet your students' learning needs for the lesson (readiness, interest, or learning profile) and why.

Once you have decided on the particular manner of differentiation, consider the following recommendations and strategy ideas.

READINESS DIFFERENTIATION

Readiness differences are probably the most visible of all student learning differences and usually the area of most concern given our high-stakes testing environment. It can also seem the most daunting to address for a teacher.

Readiness differentiation begins with determining where each student is at this moment in his or her understanding and knowledge of the content. This is based on current pre- or formative assessment (for details, see Chapters 2 and 7). A teacher once told me that she did not preassess her students or use much formative assessment because she knew that her students didn't know anything. Be careful with assuming what your students know or don't know without supporting evidence. It is this clarifying evidence that allows us to appropriately address readiness concerns and discover the specific misconception or skill gap that needs to be addressed. According to Judy Willis (2006), "Challenging students at reasonable, appropriate levels is one of the most powerful strategies for success, but teachers must carefully monitor the level of challenge. If goals do not provide sufficient challenge to engage students, or if the challenge exceeds students' levels of capability, frustration replaces motivation" (p. 25).

With differentiation, our goal is not to create 30 lesson plans or tasks to address each student in the moment but rather to look for common patterns in errors or misconceptions to address. In this way, when addressing readiness, groups of students can receive the same task at the appropriate level of challenge without constructing an abundance of variations.

TIP FOR ELL/SPECIAL EDUCATION STUDENTS

It is important to truly assess what students know and understand about the mathematical content and not to be hampered by language constraints. Use multiple methods for assessing your students, including drawings, gestures, and practicing repeating key vocabulary with diagrams and steps to assess the mathematical readiness apart from language readiness.

We often think of "high-middle-low" tasks when addressing readiness. This doesn't necessarily have to be the case. There might be only two different tasks that are needed or perhaps more levels of tasks needed depending on the makeup of the class. Sometimes readiness differentiation is not based as much on the content mastery as on other aspects of readiness such as independence. For example, some students may be able to self-start on a task, while others need more modeling and help getting started. One structure for differentiation could be to have one group of students with the teacher to get started, while the other students are starting independently on the same task. At a certain point, flip the groups so the original group with the teacher is now working independently, and the students who had begun independently now have a time to check in and extend their thinking with the teacher.

Another way to differentiate by readiness is to have different points within whole-class direct instruction when students who are ready to begin independent (or paired) work move out of the whole-class instruction. Students not quite ready will continue with the teacher to see more examples and hear further explanation. At another stopping point, students are given another opportunity to work independently. Continue in this way until all students are working without guidance. Sometimes students who have moved to work independently may find they were not quite ready after all. They are then able to check back in with the groups still working with the teacher as needed. It may be that some reluctant learners will not choose to work apart from the teacher if given the option—do not give that option.

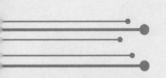

WATCH IT!

As you watch Video 4.1, *Planning and Implementing Readiness Differentiation*, consider the following questions:

1. How can readiness groups be determined?

2. How were differences in readiness addressed through the specific tasks and/or stations?

3. How did the teacher plan the tiered (readiness) tasks for the various levels?

4. How did the teacher manage the tasks, making sure that students had the correct level?

5. How were students engaging with, or reacting to, their specific tasks?

Video 4.1 Planning and Implementing Readiness Differentiation

STRATEGIES

Tiered Activities

The primary strategy used for differentiating by readiness is called a tiered activity. One reason a tiered activity is the building block for readiness differentiation is that just about anything can be tiered. Designing tiers is based on whatever the instructional approach is in the mathematics class—questioning, practice problems, a specific task—all can be tiered by adjusting for various readiness levels. The essential key is to not weaken or change the learning objective when designing different tiers, although the same essential understandings and skills may be addressed at different levels of complexity, abstractness, and open-endedness (Tomlinson, 2014, p. 133).

To create a tiered activity:

1. Explicitly establish the essential understanding and skills to be addressed.

2. Brainstorm possible structures or activities that will elicit the essential learning—this is wide open. The activity should be interesting, be high level, and cause students to use and reflect on the essential understandings and skills. Consider the activities you have already used first and check for the complexity level of the task and for whom the task as written is most appropriate.

3. If you are designing from scratch, write your first task for the highest group of students in the class. If you are using a preexisting activity that is not for the highest group of students, hold on to it for the appropriate tier and jump to designing the top tier. Once you have designed your top task, go through your class roster and record the students who will be able to engage with this task.

4. Design your next task. It could be the same task as the original task with additional supports, models, or smaller steps embedded. It could also be a different task. Once this task is designed, review your roster and make a list of the students for whom this task is most appropriate.

5. Continue this process until you have the number of tasks designed to appropriately challenge all of the students in your class.

The readiness example in Figure 4.4 showed a form of a tiered activity by creating tiers for a worksheet.

Figure 4.4 shows a template for creating a tiered activity.

FIGURE 4.4

TIERED ACTIVITY ORGANIZER

Tiered Activity Organizer

Standard(s):

From Unit's KUDs, choose the specific K, U, and/or D for the Tiered Activity

Know:

-
-
-

Understand:

-
-

Do:

-
-
-

Tier	Task	Students who will do this task
1		
2		
3		
4		

This template can be downloaded at resources.corwin.com/everymathlearner6-12.

Figures 4.5 and 4.6 give examples of how specific KUDs from the unit's standards lead to developing activity.

FIGURE 4.5

SEVENTH-GRADE SOLVING EQUATIONS

Standard:

- Apply properties of operations as strategies to add, subtract, factor, and expand linear expressions with rational coefficients.

- Use variables to represent quantities in a real-world or mathematical problem, and construct simple equations and inequalities to solve problems by reasoning about the quantities.

Know:

- Vocabulary: coefficient, constant, inverse operations, isolate, simplify, solution, term, variable

- Distributive property with algebraic expressions

- A solution to an equation is the value or values of a variable that will make the equation true. Substituting the found value will provide a check for correctness.

- The steps to solving an equation are based on reversing the order of operations and using inverse operations to isolate the variable.

Understand:

- Algebra is grown-up arithmetic.

- Only things that are alike can be added (like terms, simplifying expressions).

- Different forms and representations of an expression can show how quantities are related and lead to problem solutions.

- An equal sign shows that two quantities are equivalent, and this equivalence must be maintained throughout the process of solving the equation.

Do:

- Model and solve multistep algebraic equations.

- Model and solve real-world situations with algebraic expressions and equations.

- Explain how solving an algebraic equation relates to arithmetic with rational numbers.

Whole Class:

We have been solving equations in this unit. We began by looking at how algebra can model real-world situations. We learned the process of solving an equation by using algebra tiles to solve for an unknown before we ever wrote an equation on paper. We have continued to use the models to make sense of the process as we grew from one step to two steps to multisteps with the distributive property before we learned the symbolic notation to record the solution process. Today we want to combine all of the segments of our work by looking at multistep real-world problems that can be solved using algebra. You may work alone or with a partner in your color group.

(Continued)

FIGURE 4.5 (Continued)

Tier	Task
Orange	(a) Students complete several real-world multistep problems that involve rational coefficients and constants.
	(b) Students are asked to write and solve their own context problems based on a given equation. For example, *write a real-world problem that could be solved by the equation* $\frac{3}{4}(x+1)=10$. *Solve your problem in context.*
	(c) Explain how solving a multistep equation involves all of the arithmetic you have learned in mathematics. Include the following vocabulary (at least) in your explanation: variable, coefficient, constant, equivalent (equivalence), equal sign, addition, subtraction, multiplication, division, integers, fractions, rational numbers, inverse operations, isolate.
Purple	(a) Students complete several multistep equations to review the process. Equations advance from integer coefficients and constants to fractional coefficients to rational numbers. Algebra tiles are available as needed, and there is a section for sketching the models on the task sheet.
	(b) Students apply their equation-solving knowledge to real-world application problems. Most of the problems involve integer coefficients and constants, but the final challenge problem involves rational numbers.
	(c) Explain how solving a multistep equation involves all of the arithmetic you have learned in mathematics. Be sure to include the four operations and how they are used as inverses to solve, the integer rules, working with rational numbers, and so on, in your explanation.
Blue	(a) Students complete several multistep equations to review the process. Equations advance from integer coefficients and constants to a few challenge problems with rational numbers. Algebra tiles are used for the integer equations, and there is a section for sketching the models on the task sheet for all equations.
	(b) Students apply their equation-solving knowledge to real-world application problems. Most of the problems involve integer coefficients and constants, but the final challenge problem involves rational numbers. There are hints along the way to remind students of how to set up the equations and expressions correctly, such as "*What operation is involved in the equation? How many of the unknown are there in the context?*" Algebra tiles and sketches are also used to make sense of the problem context.

	(c) Explain how to solve a multistep equation and how it involves all of the mathematics you have learned over the years. Make a two-column table for your explanation. On the right, choose one of the multistep equations you solved in Part 1 on your sheet. Show every step on a separate line. On the left, explain what you did at each step, why it was correct to do mathematically, and how it is like other arithmetic you have learned.
Green	Students complete the Blue task with the teacher helping the group review and get started. There are also specific checkpoints for the teacher to initial throughout the task.

 A template to create a tiered activity can be downloaded at resources.corwin.com/everymathlearner6-12.

ADVANCED ALGEBRA POLYNOMIAL FUNCTION END BEHAVIORS

Standard:
Graph polynomial functions, identifying zeros when suitable factorizations are available and showing end behavior.

Know:
• Vocabulary: Polynomial function, zero, roots, maximum, minimum, end behavior • The basic shape, number of zeros, and end behaviors of a polynomial function relate to the degree of the function. • The lead coefficient and constant of a polynomial function determine the transformations of the function. • Factorization or other solution methods to find zeros of the function equation solves for the roots of the function. • Not all roots of a function are Real ($\mathbb{R}$), and some roots are repeated more than once.

Understand:
• Families of functions share the same characteristics and properties in all representations. • The function equation of a polynomial function can give enough information for an accurate sketch of the graph of the function.

(Continued)

Chapter 4 | Step Up   97

FIGURE 4.6 (Continued)

Do:

- Sketch graphs of polynomial functions from their equations.
- Analyze and graph polynomial functions.
- Describe the transformations of any polynomial function on the parent function based on the lead coefficient and constant.

Whole-Class Introductory Discussion:

- Can you predict how people will act or what they will do?
- What characteristics would you look for in doing so?
- Can you predict a family member better than a stranger?
- How well can you predict what your friends will think?
- What factors will affect people's behaviors?
- What else can be predicted in the world by behavior (e.g., stocks, economy, weather, etc.)?
- How are world behaviors predicted (data, graphs, etc.)?
- How can we predict what an extension of a graph might do?

If you don't have a piece of a graph, could you predict what a graph might look like or how it will behave? Based on what? Today you are all going to investigate characteristics of the graphs of polynomials. You will graph specific polynomial functions on your calculator and sketch them. Your goal is to draw conclusions about their general behaviors based on specific attributes of the equation. (Discuss what end behaviors and zeros are if the students do not already know these terms.) Each group will share their findings when finished in order for all to have a complete picture. Tomorrow we will relate the work we have been doing with polynomials to the graphs of polynomial functions and graph by hand.

Note: Although the groups were written from the highest to more basic tiers, they are listed below in presentation order, most basic to most complex, to show the complete scope of the lesson. Students were required to take notes on the presentations to complete the notes for the lesson. No teacher instruction was given.

Tier	Task
M	Students are given four quadratic equations, two with positive lead coefficients and two with negative lead coefficients. They graph the parabolas in their graphing calculators and copy the graphs onto their worksheets. This is repeated with four cubic, four quartic, and four quintic polynomial functions. • Describe the end behaviors of a graph based on the degree of the polynomial. • Describe the change in the graph based on the sign of the lead coefficient. • Test your hypotheses with equations and graphs of your own.

A	Students are given several even degree polynomials to graph, followed by several odd degree polynomials to graph in their calculators and copy on their worksheets. • What conclusions can you draw from your graphs about the end behaviors and the degree of the polynomial? • How do the roots of the function seem to relate to the degree? • Students are given other polynomial functions and asked to predict the basic shape of the graph and then to sketch a graph. • Students are given graphs of polynomial functions and asked to estimate what the function might be.
T	Students are given the following polynomials to graph in their calculators and copy on their worksheets: • $Y_1 = (x + 1)(x - 2)$ • $Y_2 = -(x - 3)^2$ • $Y_3 = 2x^2 + 5x + 6$ Describe the behavior of the graph, including its relationship to the x-axis and its end behaviors. Do you see any patterns? Repeat the process and answer the same questions with the following polynomials: • $Y_1 = (x + 3)(x + 2)(x - 1)$ • $Y_2 = (x - 2)(x + 1)^2$ • $Y_3 = -x^3 + 2x - 5$ What conclusions can you draw? How can you predict the number of times a graph will touch or cross the x-axis? Based on your observations, describe how a graph behaves from its equation. Include end behaviors and x-intercepts.
H	Students are given multiple polynomials to graph. Some should be in factored form. Include both even and odd degrees and both positive and negative lead coefficients. • Draw conclusions about how the equation of a polynomial can predict the behavior of a graph. Include end behaviors and roots. • Test your conclusions by writing polynomial equations and predicting and sketching their corresponding graphs. Check your prediction with a graphing calculator.

 A template to create a tiered activity can be downloaded at resources.corwin.com/everymathlearner6-12.

As mentioned earlier, most strategies and tasks can be "tiered" simply by creating additional versions to most appropriately challenge students. Some examples of the adjustments that can be made to adjust appropriate challenge and complexity (Tomlinson, 2014) from a more basic readiness level to a higher readiness level are as follows:

- From *foundational* (close to current experience) to *transformational* (removed from text or experience) information and ideas

- From *concrete* (manipulatives, hold in hand, event based, etc.) to *abstract* (intangible, symbolic, etc.) representation, ideas, applications, and materials

- From *simple* (use idea or skill being taught) to *complex* (combination of ideas or multiple abstractions) resources, research, issues, problems, skills, and goals

- From a *single facet* to *multiple facets* in a task

- From a *small leap* (few unknowns or gaps, relative familiarity with task) to *great leap* (relative unfamiliarity with a process or elements)

- From *more structure* (specific directions, modeling) to *more open* (few directions and less modeling)

- From *clearly defined problems* (more algorithmic, specific applications) to *fuzzy problems* (less defined, open ended, multiple answers)

- From *less independence* (guidance and check-in points with teacher) to *greater independence*

- From *slower pace* to *quicker pace* of learning concepts and repetition

The next example shows how a specific strategy can be tiered to address students' readiness.

Think Dots Think Dots is a strategy conceived by Kay Brimijoin that places six different questions or tasks onto separate cards with pips (die spots) on the opposite side. Figure 4.7 shows a picture of Think Dots. Think Dots can be used in a variety of ways. Students can individually roll a die and complete the task they roll, or a group of students can work together with one student rolling a die and facilitating the work on the task. The lead and the roll then is passed to the next student.

FIGURE 4.7

THINK DOTS

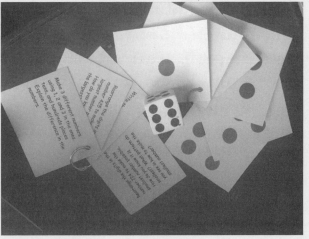

© Nanci Smith

To create a set of Think Dots:

1. Design six questions or tasks that ask for information or are an application of the lesson content. Design this first set at a high level for the highest students in your class. There are a variety of methods by which you can design the six cards:

    a. You could use the six levels of Blooms, one for each card.

    b. Choose six of the eight Standards for Mathematical Practice to design specific questions or tasks for the lesson content.

    c. Consider multiple representations for a task or process.

    d. Use the following prompts to design targeted tasks:

        i. Describe

        ii. Analyze

        iii. Compare and contrast

        iv. Demonstrate or model

        v. Change an element of the problem and describe how it will affect the results

        vi. Diagram or illustrate

2. Design additional sets to address the various readiness levels in your class. Consider the following ways to design multiple levels:

   a. Provide manipulatives or models for more concrete examples.

   b. Shorten directions or provide step-by-step directions.

   c. Have fewer facets per problem.

   d. Provide more basic applications.

   e. Have greater check-in points with the teacher.

Figure 4.8 gives a sixth-grade example on least common multiple (LCM) and greatest common factor (GCF), and Figure 4.9 gives an algebra equations example.

FIGURE 4.8

LCM AND GCF THINK DOTS

	Tier 1
○	Describe three different methods for finding a common factor.
○ ○	Charmy eats spaghetti every third day. She watches TV every second day. Explain how to find the number of times in a month that she eats spaghetti and watches TV on the same day.
○ ○ ○	Compare and contrast finding LCMs and GCFs. Explain when each is used.
○ ○ ○ ○	Give examples of how people use GCFs and LCMs in life—sometimes without even knowing it!
○ ○ ○ ○ ○	Create a word problem that involves both a GCF and an LCM to solve.
○ ○ ○ ○ ○ ○	Compare and contrast the use of factor trees and Venn diagrams in finding GCFs and LCMs.

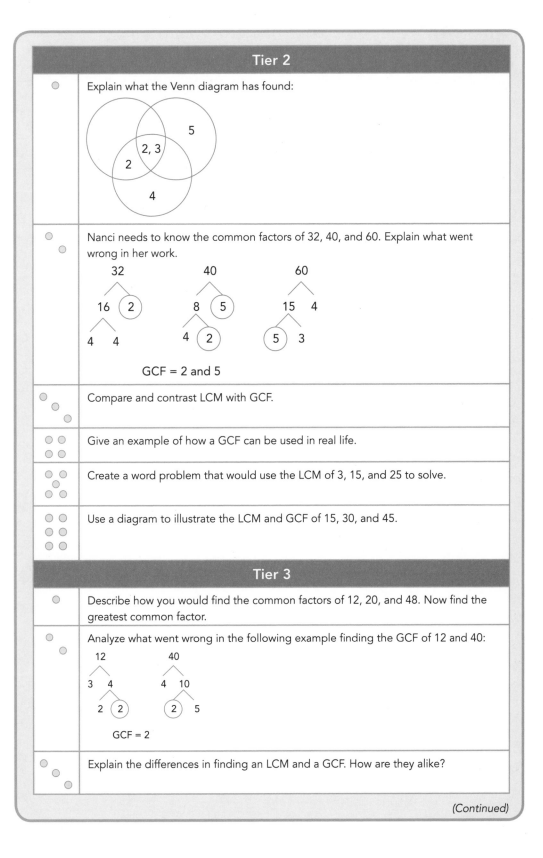

Tier 2

○ Explain what the Venn diagram has found:

5

2, 3

2

4

○
 ○ Nanci needs to know the common factors of 32, 40, and 60. Explain what went wrong in her work.

32   40   60

16 (2) 8 (5) 15 4

4 4 4 (2) (5) 3

GCF = 2 and 5

○
 ○
 ○ Compare and contrast LCM with GCF.

○ ○
○ ○ Give an example of how a GCF can be used in real life.

○ ○
 ○
○ ○ Create a word problem that would use the LCM of 3, 15, and 25 to solve.

○ ○
○ ○
○ ○ Use a diagram to illustrate the LCM and GCF of 15, 30, and 45.

Tier 3

○ Describe how you would find the common factors of 12, 20, and 48. Now find the greatest common factor.

○
 ○ Analyze what went wrong in the following example finding the GCF of 12 and 40:

12   40

3 4 4 10

2 (2) (2) 5

GCF = 2

○
 ○
 ○ Explain the differences in finding an LCM and a GCF. How are they alike?

(Continued)

FIGURE 4.8 (Continued)

○ ○ ○ ○	Give an example of how someone might use a least common multiple in his or her life. When do you use an LCM versus using a GCF?
○ ○ ○ ○	Find the LCM of 15 and 21. How do you know your answer is correct (and don't say because we did the math!)?
○ ○ ○ ○ ○ ○	Use a diagram to illustrate the LCM and the GCF of 9 and 12.

FIGURE 4.9

EQUATIONS THINK DOTS

Tier 1	
○	a, b, c, and d each represent a different value. If $a = 4$, find b, c, and d. $a + c = b$ $b - a = c$ $cd = -d$ $d + d = a$
○ ○	Explain the mathematical reasoning involved in solving card 1.
○ ○ ○	Explain the many roles a variable can have in mathematics. Give examples.
○ ○ ○ ○	Create an interesting word problem that is modeled by $3x - 1 \leq 5x + 7$. Solve the problem.
○ ○ ○ ○	Diagram how to solve $3x + 4 = x + 12$.
○ ○ ○ ○ ○ ○	Given $ax = 15$, explain how x is changed if a is greater or a is lesser in value.

Tier 2	
○	a, b, c, and d each represent a different value. If $a = -1$, find b, c, and d. $$a + b = c$$ $$b + b = d$$ $$c - a = -a$$
○ ○	Explain the mathematical reasoning involved in solving card 1.
○ ○ ○	Explain how a variable is used to solve word problems.
○ ○ ○ ○	Create an interesting word problem that is modeled by $2x + 4 = 4x - 10$. Solve the problem.
○ ○ ○ ○ ○	Diagram how to solve $3x + 1 = 10$.
○ ○ ○ ○ ○ ○	Explain why $x = 4$ in $2x = 8$, but $x = 16$ in $\frac{1}{2} x = 8$. Why does this make sense? Why wouldn't the x-value just double or divide in two?
Tier 3	
○	a, b, c, and d each represent a different value. If $a = 2$, find b, c, and d. $$a + b = c$$ $$a - c = d$$ $$a + b = 5$$
○ ○	Explain the mathematical reasoning involved in solving card 1.
○ ○ ○	Explain in words what the equation $2x + 4 = 10$ means. Solve the problem.
○ ○ ○ ○	Create an interesting word problem that is modeled by $8x - 2 = 7x$. Solve the problem.
○ ○ ○ ○ ○	Diagram how to solve $2x = 8$.
○ ○ ○ ○ ○ ○	Explain what changing the "3" in $3x = 9$ to a "2" does to the value of x. Why is this true?

Take an activity you currently use in class. Think about the appropriate readiness level of the task as it is currently written. For which students in class is the task most appropriate? How can you create other tiers of the same task for the remaining students in class? Design the various tiers and try them out.

A final way by which you can think of differentiating by readiness is through scaffolding and compacting. Compacting addresses advanced students while scaffolding provides additional supports for those students who will need it.

Compacting has the following basic steps:

1. Identify and document the skills and understandings that the students have mastered based on assessments and the unit's KUD.

2. Identify and document the skills and understandings that the students have *not* mastered based on assessments and the unit's KUD.

3. When the class is working with and learning content that the students have already mastered, they will work on a related study or area of application. Students will rejoin the class to learn content that has not previously been mastered.

4. All students will remain accountable for the learning of all content within the unit on the summative assessment.

Too often we expect students to complete work they already know how to do, no matter the repetition or boredom, while the rest of the class catches up to "what they already know." For example, we tell students to do the same work as everyone else, and when they are finished, they can do something more. This in essence punishes students for being advanced or learning quickly! We also expect them to not be a discipline problem while this is happening. Compacting allows bright students to work independently on related studies, dig deeper into content and application, and continue to learn and grow instead of holding stagnant. It provides the opportunity to use some of the wonderful tasks we could do "if only there was time," because now there is time for certain students. In addition, compacting provides the time for these bright and gifted students to dig deeply into the concepts and understandings in the unit through tasks and explorations that replace other class assignments. Notice that compacting *replaces* certain assignments within the unit—it does not *add on to* the existing assignments for "students who finish early."

Scaffolding, on the other hand, is a general term for providing the support that will enable students to be successful with any given task. Possible supports include the following:

- Hint Envelopes—provide a list of hints for specific sections or steps to a problem. Think of what you would ask students if they were struggling at any given point in the task, and record these in order. Put the hints (either as a list or separately on slips of paper) into an envelope for students to access as needed.

- Models—provide models or partial models of what is expected in the task. This is especially effective with procedures for solving numerical operations. When providing a model, be careful not to give away too much of the information with which you want students to wrestle and make sense.

- Reciprocal Teaching—use mixed readiness pairings to have the first student "teach" the process to the second student as the second student writes and solves the problem as the "teacher" teaches. Roles then reverse. Begin with the student who has the stronger readiness level as the first teacher. Be ready for pairs of students who may need help from the beginning.

TIPS FOR ELL/SPECIAL EDUCATION

When considering ELL students, scaffolding may need to be more about language than mathematics. Provide a word box with illustrated definitions to help students master language and concepts in the units. In addition, illustrated steps to a particular process will help students struggling with language to connect steps and the process to prior knowledge and reasoning.

- Mini-teach—pull a small group of students who need an additional example or coaching through a problem.

A final reflection on addressing student readiness. Whatever structure or task you are designing for students, remember the following:

Students with less developed readiness will benefit from

- Someone to help them find and make up missing information and skills in order to close gaps and move ahead
- More direct instruction and practice
- A higher degree of structure and concrete materials to make sense of activities
- Fewer steps, less reading, a slower pace, and tasks closer to personal experiences

Students with greater developed readiness will benefit from

- Skipping practice of previously documented mastered skills and understanding
- Complex, open-ended, abstract, and multifaceted problem-solving tasks
- A quick pace for mathematical skill mastery and a slower pace for building depth of conceptual understanding and problem solving (Tomlinson, 2014, pp. 18–19)

INTEREST DIFFERENTIATION

When I began differentiating, I thought that in order to differentiate by interest, I needed to figure out my students' hobbies and then directly relate them to the mathematical topic at hand. That became very difficult. It is possible to get stumped trying to relate the specific content to students' specific interests. This is usually because we approach the connection through a skill or fact rather than a concept. For example, we can hook students' interests when studying proportional reasoning, percent increase and decrease, or systems of equations by looking at getting the best bargain when shopping. We can study geometry through the lens of art, architecture, or even ancient Egypt. We can even introduce algebraic reasoning and skills through the lens of mystery unknowns such as "I'm thinking of two numbers when multiplied together have a product of –12 but when added together have a sum of 1." Finding concepts that intrigue our students, and relating our studies to them, is one way to differentiate by interest.

Research also suggests that changing the context of a problem can result in greater investment by students on the task. One study that was conducted with high school students changed the context of word problems from a typical textbook problem to something the students were interested in—such as shopping, computers, music, and use of cell phones—without changing any of the numbers or mathematics required. Half of the 141 students in the study were given the original problems in the unit, and the remaining students were given problems with the context tailored to their interests. The group that received problems with their interests represented performed better and learned faster during the unit and were still performing better on more complex problems that were not adjusted four units later (Walkington et al., 2014).

We know from cognitive science that we can also intrigue and hook our students through connections (as described above), appropriate challenge or a puzzle-like quality, and novelty (Sousa, 2015). These qualities can be integrated at the beginning of a lesson as a hook or through the tasks we choose. Perhaps the most important way to create interest in our students is through modeling our own enthusiasm and choosing intriguing tasks.

The most common way that we differentiate by interest is by offering choice. This can be done in a wide variety of ways from using choice boards to designing activities into which choices are built.

WATCH IT!

As you watch Video 4.2, *Planning and Implementing Interest Differentiation*, consider the following questions:

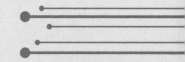

1. What tips can you take from how the teacher plans for interest differentiation? What would you say was the most important tip about the design of multiple activities?

2. How does the teacher use interest to assign groups? How does, and how should, a teacher react to students' individual choices?

3. How do the students respond to the choices they made?

4. What are the advantages of allowing students to choose their tasks? What would be the disadvantages?

5. What can you take from the video clip to apply to your classroom when providing choices?

Video 4.2 Planning and Implementing Interest Differentiation

STRATEGIES

Contracts

Contracts is a general term for any strategy that provides students with an opportunity for students to work somewhat independently on material that is balanced between teacher-assigned and student-choice tasks. Contracts can be used as formative or summative assessments or as a learning progression through the unit. No matter what the structure, a quality design will include the following:

- Specific content goals from the KUD, including knowledge and skills that need to be practiced and mastered

- Application of skills and knowledge into context and problem-solving situations

- Specific working conditions for students follow to assume responsibility for learning

- Student choice

- Criteria for success

There are many structures by which a contract can be designed. The first example is based on a strategy by Carol Cummings (2000) called a menu. The menu provides three sections: main dish (imperatives), side dish (negotiables), and desserts (optionals). Figure 4.10 gives an example of a geometry menu on similar figures.

FIGURE 4.10

SIMILAR FIGURES MENU

· ·

Menu: Similar Figures

Final Due Date: April 17

Check-In Dates: Meet with Teacher to determine

<u>Imperatives (Must Complete All)</u>

1. Write a mathematical definition of "Similar Figures." It must include all pertinent vocabulary, address all concepts, and be written so that a fifth-grade student would be able to understand it. Diagrams can be used to illustrate your definition.

---

2. Generate a list of applications for similar figures, and similarity in general. Be sure to think beyond "find a missing side . . . "

3. Develop a similar figures lesson to teach younger students who are just beginning to think about similarity.

Negotiables (Choose 2)

1. Create a book of similar figure applications and problems. This must include at least eight problems. They can be problems you have made up or found in book, but at least three must be application problems. Solve each of the problems and include an explanation as to why your solution is correct.

2. Show at least five different applications of similar figures in the real world, and make them into math problems. Solve each of the problems and explain the role of similarity. Justify why the solutions are correct.

3. Create an art piece using similar figures. On the back, explain the mathematics of your work including which shapes are similar, the transformations used to create the images from the original, and any other interesting mathematics you ran into during your creation.

4. Write a FAQ sheet on similar figures. Please write a minimum of five questions and answers. They need to incorporate correct vocabulary, steps needed and the possible issues in solving problems correctly, and why we need to learn about similarity.

Optional (To go above and beyond)

1. Make a photo album showing the use of similar figures in the world around us. Use captions to explain the similarity in each picture.

2. Write a story about similar figures in a world without similarity.

3. Write a song about the beauty and mathematics of similar figures.

4. Create a "how to" or book about finding and creating similar figures.

 The menu can be downloaded at resources.corwin.com/ everymathlearner6-12.

Another example of a type of contract is called a think-tac-toe. This is a 3 × 3 table (or other size of your design) from which students will choose tasks. Most often, students are to choose one task from each row but do not have to make a tic-tac-toe. In designing a think-tac-toe, each row of options should relate to the same concept, skill, or topic. With careful design, it will not matter which tasks the students choose since the tasks in the same row all relate to the same outcome. Figure 4.11 gives an example of a seventh-grade proportional reasoning think-tac-toe task.

FIGURE 4.11

PROPORTIONAL REASONING THINK-TAC-TOE

• Create a word problem that requires proportional reasoning. Solve the problem and explain why it requires proportional reasoning.	• Find a word problem from the text that requires proportional reasoning. Solve the problem and explain why it was proportional.	• Think of a way that you use proportional reasoning in your life. Describe the situation and explain why it is proportional and how you use it.
• Create a story about a proportion in the world. You can write it, act it, videotape it, or present it in another story form.	• How do you recognize a proportional situation? Find a way to think about and explain proportionality.	• Make a list of all the proportional situations in the world today.
• Create a pict-o-gram, poem, or anagram of how to solve proportional problems.	• Write a list of steps for solving any proportional problem.	• Write a list of questions to ask yourself beginning with encountering a problem that may be proportional through solving it.

Directions: Choose one option in each row to complete. Check the box of the choice you make, and turn this page in with your finished selections.

 The think-tac-toe can be downloaded at resources.corwin.com/everymathlearner6-12.

A final way to address interest is to use novel and fun approaches, such as games. There are many commercial and computer-based games that can practice mathematical skills. There are also many games that can be easily made for your students.

Matching Games

Matching games can be made out of any set of problems. Consider bumping up the readiness level by creating three cards to match instead of two. For example, for factoring quadratics, use one card for the problem, one card for the factors, and a third card for the solution set. Another example of adding a third category would be a word problem, the expression to set up the problem, and the answer. To make the game easier to play as a memory-style game, consider running the card types in different colors, such as the problem in blue, factors in green, and solution sets in pink. If you don't want to take the time and trouble to make copies in color, mark the backs of the cards with a P (problem), F (factors), and S (solution set). This allows students to turn over one of each kind of card to see if they match, rather than turning over three problem cards that don't have a chance to match. Note that if you do create a game with three categories to match, a natural readiness differentiation would be to give some students two categories to match and other students three.

Triplets

Triplets is a card game played similar to a rummy game with students taking turns drawing and discarding cards and trying to get three cards to match. The playing instructions are as follows.

Instructions:

1. One student will deal each player three or six cards face down. Three cards should be used to introduce the game, and six cards are used for a more challenging version.

2. Place the remaining cards in a pile in the center and flip up the top card.

3. The player to the right of the dealer has the first move. He or she may either draw a card from the top of the pile or pick up the top card from the discard pile. The player will then discard one card from his or her hand.

4. Play continues until a player has one (three cards) or two (six cards) sets of three cards each with equivalent answers, at which time the player places his or her discard face down and shows the two triplet matching cards to all players.

A deck of cards is made of 30 cards comprising six different sets of five possible matches. To begin, determine six different "targets" for the topic on which cards will match. For example, if you are creating a linear functions game, the targets can be six different functions. Once the targets are established, create four more cards that will match with the target, such as a slope card, a y-intercept card, a point on the line, and a table. You could also include perpendicular lines or graphs depending on with what you want your students to work on. Figure 4.12 shows a triplets linear function example.

FIGURE 4.12

TRIPLETS LINEAR FUNCTION CARDS

Target	$y = 2x + 1$	$y = -2x - 1$	$x + y = 5$	$y = 1/2x + 2$	$y = 5x - 2$	$x = y$
Card	$m = 2$	$m = -2$	$m = -1$	$m = 1/2$	$m = 5$	$m = 1$
Card	$b = 1$	$b = -1$	$b = 5$	$b = 2$	$b = -2$	$b = 0$
Card	(1/2, 2)	(1, −3)	(−4, 9)	(10, 7)	(−1, −7)	(114, 114)
Card	x y −1 −1 0 1 1 3 2 5	x y −1 1 0 −1 1 −3 2 −5	x y −1 6 0 5 1 4 2 3	x y −1 1.5 0 2 1 2.5 2 3	x y −1 −7 0 −2 1 3 2 8	x y −1 −1 0 0 1 1 2 2

Triplets Linear Function Cards can be downloaded at resources.corwin.com/everymathlearner6-12.

For any game, you can adjust readiness simply by adjusting cards. It will still address interest because it is a game, and students recognize that everyone is playing the game and do not tend to notice if different levels of the game are going on. For example, in the linear functions game above, perhaps you would want all equations in slope-intercept form with only integer coefficients and constants for a more basic tier of the game. On the other hand, perhaps you want to raise the readiness level and include some cards with the distributive property, various forms of the equations such as general form, point-slope or intercept forms, graphs, and even tables with the x-values out of order and not increasing by 1. These adjustments to the game do not change the interest factor, and all students continue their study of linear functions.

Build-a-Square

Build-a-Square is a puzzle game originated from puzzles called "Crazy 'Noun'" puzzles, such as the Crazy Plane puzzle, that my children played with when they were in elementary school. There were nine cards with halves of planes, or whatever was on the puzzle, on each edge. For example, there could be the front of the plane with a propeller on one edge and the tail section on the edge of a different tile. Aligning the cards in a 3 × 3 formation where every edge met between cards made a complete and unique plane that completed the puzzle. Build-a-Square was born! Simply put problems and/or answers on the edges of the cards. Cards are then matched based on the answers of the problems. Matching edges could include a problem and the correct answer or two problems that have the same answer. Figure 4.13 shows a completed Build-a-Square puzzle for eighth-grade slopes.

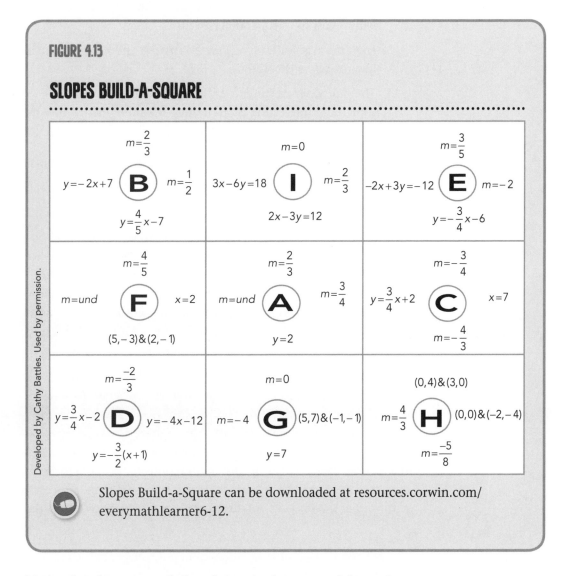

FIGURE 4.13

SLOPES BUILD-A-SQUARE

Developed by Cathy Battles. Used by permission.

Slopes Build-a-Square can be downloaded at resources.corwin.com/everymathlearner6-12.

Notice that there are symbols or letters in the center of the cards. These act as an answer key for the teacher instead of having to check every connecting side. Students can also record the letters to turn in as an answer key. If you do not want to use letters that will orient the cards as to which way they are placed, consider using symbols that will rotate with the square card, such as stars, ovals (ellipses!), squares, parallelograms, and so on. Having square cards rather than rectangular, as well as symbols that do not give away orientation, greatly increases the difficulty of the puzzle!

Neuroscience supports the advantages to students when learning with interest. They include the following:

1. High motivation leads to greater attention, increased willingness to learn, and persistence.

2. High motivation leads to greater interest, and high interest is intrinsically motivating.

3. The motivation a student experiences when learning something interesting is often more rewarding than when he or she is learning for "award" (Sousa & Tomlinson, 2011).

When designing for interest differentiation and allowing students choice of task, be aware of possible snares. Even though we encourage students to choose a task based on their best learning outcomes, sometimes students choose poorly. Students may choose a task based on the task a friend has chosen instead of the task that seems most interesting or accessible to them. One way to avoid this is to explain the options and have students write their choices on a note card or sticky note. Once students record their choices, tasks are given out or groups are formed. This can be done the day before the activity, and then the teacher forms groups or assigns tasks for the next day based on the students' choices.

In addition, when students choose a task, whether designed by interest or learning profile, they may often choose a task because it appears easier to them. When offering choice, be careful to design tasks that remain true to the learning goals, have a reasonably similar complexity level, and require the same amount of effort and time commitment. That way, if students choose a task because it appears easier, it will be because it appeals to how the student best learns rather than because of discrepancies in the design of the task.

LEARNING PROFILE DIFFERENTIATION

Learning profile differentiation is often a comfortable starting place for differentiation. The learning profiles themselves suggest appropriate task design, and students can be offered the choice of task to complete based on their interests. Chapter 2 gives detail about the specific structures of the learning profile intelligences (Sternberg's triarchic theory and Gardner's multiple intelligences).

WATCH IT!

As you watch Video 4.3, *Planning and Implementing Learning Profile Differentiation*, consider the following questions:

1. How are the tasks the teacher chose aligned to Sternberg's learning profile?

2. What is the teacher's goal in designing learning profile differentiation?

3. What was the advantage in offering a choice of two tasks within the same learning profile for students?

4. How do each of the seemingly different tasks all address the same learning objective?

5. How do you think the students reacted to being placed in learning profile groups based on their own survey responses and discussion the previous day?

Video 4.3 Planning and Implementing Learning Profile Differentiation

When designing learning profile tasks, keep in mind that the thinking and reasoning involved in a task is more important than the actual task activity. In Chapter 2, the types of reasoning related to the various learning profiles are outlined.

STRATEGIES

Sternberg's Triarchic Theory

Robert Sternberg (2005) suggests that students organize learning primarily in one of three ways: analytically, practically, and creatively. Most students will be a combination of two, and occasionally a student will be evenly balanced among all three. Tasks can be aligned according to these descriptions. Figure 4.14 provides task examples for each area of Sternberg's theory of intelligence.

FIGURE 4.14

STERNBERG-ALIGNED TASKS

Intelligence	Possible Tasks for Mathematical Concept or Skill
Analytical The ability to analyze and think in linear and logical-sequential ways. Analytical learners tend to be "school smart."	• Bullets • Lists • Steps • Worksheets • Tables, charts • Venn diagrams • Timelines • Sequencing • Flowcharts • Compare and contrast • Puns and subtleties • Identify key parts • Find the error • Evaluating • Sorting and classifying • Appealing to logic • Critique and criticize • Explaining difficult problems to others • Making inferences and deriving conclusions • Graphic organizer • Timeline • Venn diagram • Patterns • Classifying • Definitions • Cause and effect • Codes • Graphs • Database • Blueprints • Newspaper • Fact file • Worksheets

Practical	
The ability to put ideas into action and apply ideas to the real world. Practical learners draw from personal experiences. Practical learners tend to be "street smart."	• Working your way out of a problem • Notes to self (what questions to ask myself, how to make sense of the learning or topic for myself) • Here is a problem; explain what happened • Analogies • Draw real-world examples • Advising and convincing others (advice columns) • Hands-on activities • Taking things apart and fixing them • Understanding and respecting others/friendships/resolving conflicts • Putting things into practice • Adapting to new situations • Explaining how things can be used • Developing a plan to address a problem • Help classmates understand • Scenarios • Role-plays • WebQuest • Job shadowing • Dialogs • Newscasts • Letters to the editor • Flyers • Demonstrations • Experiments • Surveys • Field trips • Petitions • "Cheat sheets" • Lesson plans
Creative	
The ability to imagine possibilities and think outside the box.	• Figure out a way to explain • ABC or other creative "books" or guides on a topic • How to represent • Make your own interpretation • Pictures or news bulletins to describe

(Continued)

FIGURE 4.14 (Continued)

Creative students think of their own ways to explain and demonstrate and often have unique and correct solution paths. Creative learners are "imagination smart."	• Designing new things • Alternative solutions and methods • Thinking in pictures and images • Noticing things other people tend to ignore • Suppose something was changed. . . . What would happen if? • Acting and role-playing • Inventing • Become a . . . and use your new perspectives to help us think about . . . • Use humor to show . . . • Explain or show a new and better way to . . . • Figure out a way to explain . . . • Pictures, picture books, doodles, and icons • Songs • Riddles • Mime or charades (think vocabulary!) • Play • Bumper stickers or headlines to summarize learning

Figure 4.15 provides an example of differentiation by Sternberg's triarchic theory to summarize simplifying radicals.

FIGURE 4.15

STERNBERG SIMPLIFYING RADICALS TASKS

Analytical	Determine the steps for simplifying radicals. Make a flowchart or list of directions that are so clear a sixth-grade student would be able to use it to simplify radicals.
Practical	Generate a list of questions with answers to guide a person's thinking about how to simplify radicals. Include examples. A friend should be able to understand the "whys" of simplifying radicals from thinking in this way.
Creative	Write a story of the life of a radical as it is being simplified. Explain what is happening to it and why. OR Create a visual medium to explain how to simplify radicals.

The following example in Figure 4.16 gives an example of solving absolute value equations differentiated by Sternberg's triarchic theory.

FIGURE 4.16

STERNBERG SOLVING ABSOLUTE VALUE EQUATIONS

∙∙

Please choose one of the following options to show me everything you know about solving absolute value equations and inequalities. No matter which option you choose, **be sure to include the following:**

- The mathematical definition of absolute value (Hint: Don't say *always positive!*)
- Hints and warnings of which to be aware when working with absolute value
- How to represent your solution(s) (set notation, graphing, other?)
- Four sample problems chosen from among the bank of problems given, two from each column

Analytical	Make lists of steps teaching how to solve an absolute value equation and another list of steps teaching how to solve an absolute value inequality. (You will have a total of two lists.) After each list, show a sample problem from the bank that clearly labels each step from your list. Complete an additional two problems for a total of four. Give hints and warning with each step. Don't forget to put the definition of absolute value somewhere and how to represent your answers, too!
Practical	Make a cheat sheet for yourself (no, you can't *really* use it on the test . . .) with reminders and tips of how to solve absolute value equations and inequalities. Your cheat sheet should be complete enough that someone who didn't study and is fairly clueless would be able to follow the tips and examples and do well on the test. Don't forget to include the definition of absolute value, how to show answers, and also the four examples.
Creative	Your textbook publisher has hired you to write supplemental material for the series. They want you to write an "Absolute Value for Dummies" book. Your book will follow the pattern of a "Dummies" book, which has very few words on a page but lots of diagrams, illustrations, and important tips and warnings. Start with "What is an Absolute Value . . ." and go through how to solve equations and inequalities involving absolute value (total of four as described at the top), complete with how to show the solution.

Multiple Intelligences

Gardner's multiple intelligences may be the most familiar of all the learning profile structures. Keep in mind that when you design a lesson based on multiple intelligences, you do not have to design tasks for all of the eight (or nine if you include existentialist) intelligences. Choose the most appropriate tasks for the topic—do not try to force a task to an intelligence just to have it. Figure 4.17 provides possible task ideas for the different multiple intelligences.

FIGURE 4.17

MULTIPLE INTELLIGENCE TASKS

Intelligence	Possible Tasks for Mathematical Concept or Skill
Linguistic "The word player"	• Use storytelling to explain . . . • Write a poem, short story, or news article about . . . • Create a mnemonic to remember a process or math facts • Give a presentation • Lead a class discussion • Create a talk show radio program or PSA announcement
Logical/mathematical "The questioner"	• Interpret or translate the concepts into a mathematical formula or explain a formula in terms of concepts • Demonstrate, model, or justify a mathematical skill or concept • Make an instruction book on the skill or concept • Design a test with answer key • Demonstrate how this topic can be linked to other topics we have learned
Spatial "The visualizer"	• Chart or graph . . . • Design a computer presentation, bulletin board, or mural about . . . • Create a piece of art that demonstrates . . . • Make a video finding the concept or skill in the real world
Musical "The music lover"	• Write a song, jingle, or rap that explains . . . • Explain how the music of a song relates . . . • Create a jingle or rap to memorize . . . • Use sheet music to learn fraction addition
Bodily/kinesthetic "The mover"	• Create (and/or perform) a skit that explains . . . • Choreograph a dance that shows steps to a procedure or concept • Build a model • Use manipulatives to learn, practice, or demonstrate . . . • Make or play a game that includes the concepts and skills

Interpersonal "The socializer"	• Conduct a class meeting that discusses . . . • Organize or participate in a group task • Tutor another student • Peer teach
Intrapersonal "The individual"	• Create a personal analogy for . . . • Write notes to self, journal entries, and reminders about the skill or concept • Work independently
Naturalist "The nature lover"	• Describe any patterns you detect • Explain how the concept or skill can be found in the environment • Show how the concept or skill could be applied in nature

Source: Adapted from Sousa (2015, p. 204).

Figure 4.18 gives an example of a high school geometry lesson on proof with tasks designed by multiple intelligences.

FIGURE 4.18

PROOF MULTIPLE INTELLIGENCES

High School Geometry	
Logical/ mathematical	Generate proofs or rationales for given theorems. Be ready to explain your thinking and help us remember them!
Verbal/ linguistic	Write in paragraph form why the theorems are true. Explain what we need to think about, or what needs to be in place, before using the theorem.
Visual/spatial	Use pictures to explain and/or illustrate the theorem.
Body/ kinesthetic	Use Geogebra, other computer software, or manipulatives and models to discover and explain the theorems.
Musical	Create a jingle or rap to sing the theorems so that we can remember them. Include reasoning about why they are true.
Intrapersonal	Write a journal entry for yourself explaining why the theorems are true, how they make sense, and a tip for remembering them.
Interpersonal	Create a game of Taboo on the theorems we are learning. Find partners to play with.
Naturalist	Find pictures in the environment that show (or could show with a little help) the theorems we are learning.

Modality

Another common way that teachers will differentiate tasks is based on learning modalities: visual, auditory, and kinesthetic. This is a learning preference (often referred to as a learning style) rather than a learning intelligence, and thus the research has not shown that using this structure directly increases student achievement. However, designing tasks according to modalities can increase buy-in and student interest. Figure 4.19 provides different possible tasks for each area.

FIGURE 4.19

MODALITY TASKS

	Possible Tasks
Visual	• Make graphs, charts, illustrations, posters, or other visual aids for learning mathematics. • Write visual notes—add icons, color, and other symbols to highlight and explain notes • Color-coding solutions • Read or write mathematical texts, such as write a paragraph to explain . . . • Draw pictures to model or explain . . . • Design/use graphic organizers
Auditory	• Oral presentations or discussions • Present infomercials or PSAs (or other skits) • Create question lists • Books/instructions on tape/recording answers on tape • Self-talk (Whispies) • Interviews
Kinesthetic	• Use math manipulatives • Games • Skits • Create gestures to fit steps to a process • Model mathematics with concrete materials • Play charades to reinforce mathematical vocabulary or concepts of numbers

Figure 4.20 gives a sample lesson on the angle relationships formed when parallel lines are cut by a transversal differentiated with modality in mind.

FIGURE 4.20

EQUIVALENT FRACTIONS

Parallel Lines Cut by a Transversal	
Visual	Make posters showing all the angle relations formed by a pair of parallel lines cut by a transversal. Be sure to color-code definitions and angles, and state the relationships between all possible angles. (Note: This has been left purposefully open and somewhat vague to encourage students to reason about the best representations.)
Auditory	Play Shout Out (groups of three or four): All players have a diagram of parallel lines cut by a transversal with the angles numbered. One player serves as a reader and draws a clue out of the envelope, such as "name an angle supplementary to angle 1." All other players shout out a correct angle number. Each player scores a point if he or she can prove the angle is correct. The next player becomes the reader, and play continues.
Kinesthetic	Walk It Tape two parallel lines cut by a transversal on the floor with masking tape (or tape a large diagram on butcher block paper to the floor). Two players stand in assigned angles. As a pair, they have to tell what they are called (i.e., vertical angles) and their relationships (i.e., congruent). Use all angle combinations; even if there is not a specific name, there is a relationship.

For many students, specific strategies for studying may be helpful. Figure 4.21 gives study suggestions based on visual, auditory, and kinesthetic strategies.

FIGURE 4.21

STUDY STRATEGIES

	Study Strategies
Visual	• Color-code notes • Create your own study icons and symbols to help you recognize important information, new information, and information about which you are not quite sure yet • Make and use flash cards • Make tables and bulleted notes • Keep study area clean and clutter free • Sit toward the front of the class to make eye contact with the teacher
Auditory	• Read notes out loud • Tape-record notes and replay them • Say the steps to solve a problem out loud as you write them • Discuss explanations and procedures with a friend or family member • Put it to music—create your own jingles and mnemonics
Kinesthetic	• Use flash cards as a match game • Make foldables or other manipulatives to help you study • Use manipulatives to check your answers • Squeeze a stress ball or other squishy object as you study—bring it to a test with you • Take frequent stretch breaks

CLASSROOM STRUCTURES

A final consideration in planning for differentiation is how the classroom should be structured, including movement. In a differentiated classroom, multiple structures for working conditions are used flexibly. A given class might consist of whole class, small groups or pairs, and individual work. There is no specific pattern for how or when different configurations are used, but among these, there is generally an ebb and flow. The most typical pattern in a mathematics class is starting whole, moving into guided practice in pairs or groups, and ending with individual practice. This structure may be appropriate at times but should not be the only sequence used. In fact, this series of arrangements is in contrast to a constructivist approach to learning mathematics where students engage in an activity to explore and make connections before formal whole-class instruction. A constructivist approach begins with a small group or paired activity to engage with sense-making and introduction to a topic, concept, or application, and then we come together to discuss findings, solidify key ideas, and get any further direction before moving into small groups or pairs for further exploration and finally ending with individual practice. These are just two possible classroom progressions. Depending on the day and the lesson, any combinations can be designed.

Most of the differentiated tasks described earlier in the chapter could be done in small groups, pairs, or individually. You need to make the decisions based on the complexity of the task and perhaps students' preferences for work. The working structure for a specific task could also be a matter of choice for the student.

In designing a differentiated lesson, the classroom structure needs to be considered based on the strength of the structure and the desired outcome:

- *Whole class*—for common knowledge, creating common vocabulary, sharing work, rich discourse
- *Small group*—for collaborative tasks that benefit from multiple perspectives, multiple tasks, problem solving, and encouraging mathematical discourse
- *Pairs*—encourages greater participation as students cannot choose to not talk with only one other person but can hide in a small group
- *Individual*—for individual accountability, practice, and reflection

When choosing the structure for each segment of the lesson, remember above all that students need to take ownership of their learning. As much as possible, learning should be active and students need to be doing the work, which is more difficult to oversee and expect in a whole-class structure than with groups, pairs, or individual task assignments.

CONCLUSION

Remember that differentiation, in essence, is up to the teacher making purposeful decisions about the best ways for each of his or her students to learn and demonstrate important content. There are no ironclad "if-thens." It would be easier if there were—but unfortunately there are not. When designing differentiated tasks for a mathematics lesson, consider the following:

1. Determine the specific KUD for the lesson from the unit's KUD.

2. Determine what should be differentiated and what will not be differentiated. Decide how you want to differentiate by readiness, interest, or learning profile. Remember that these can also be combined. Base your differentiation on the students' learning needs and the content.

3. Design or find the differentiated activities or tasks.

   • Most strategies you already use can be differentiated. Look at the strategy or task, and decide which students would best benefit from it as written. Determine what would prevent other students from learning well with the task or strategy as written. Adjust the strategy or task accordingly, or determine a related strategy or task for other learners.

   • Gather a collection of ideas from colleagues, resources, the Internet, and your imagination. Instead of choosing the one task that you think will best work, decide which students may benefit from a particular approach or task and why. Then use all of the ideas for which students could best benefit.

   • No matter how you are choosing to differentiate, remember that all tasks should address the same broad learning outcome. For example, you might differentiate based on a strategy preference (using proportions or a conversion factor between radians and degrees), but all students are still exploring unit circles and systems of angle measurement using strategies and models.

4. Decide which parts of the lesson will be done in which classroom arrangement: whole class, small groups, pairs, or individually.

This chapter provides many different ways to differentiate for your students. Please remember that these are ideas from which you will choose. If you are continuing your journey in differentiation, I hope this provides you with further ideas and examples. If you are at the start of your journey, consider some advice. Do not try to do too many things at once, combine too many aspects of differentiation into single lessons, or become overwhelmed. Start with what makes most sense to you. Start with a single activity that is differentiated. Start small, but start.

FREQUENTLY ASKED QUESTIONS

Q: How do you decide whether to differentiate by readiness, interest, learning profile, or a combination?

A: The decision by what to differentiate is largely a teacher decision. The overwhelming factor is the need you see in your students for differentiation. If there are learning gaps in essential prerequisite learning, readiness needs to be the choice. Readiness can also be accomplished through learning profile or interest differentiated tasks with mixed readiness and either adjusting readiness within the tasks or having students with a higher readiness coaching those with a lower readiness. Learning profile provides specific structures by which to design tasks, and students can be given the choice of tasks, which will make it an interest differentiation. Keep in mind the purposes of interest (motivation) and learning profile (ease of learning) in making your choices. Sometimes, you might want to choose a specific structure or aspect simply because it has not been used in quite a while and you need some variety in class.

Q: How often should lessons or tasks be differentiated?

A: There is no correct number of times to differentiate. When a teacher is first beginning the journey of differentiation, trying to differentiate one task or lesson every week or two is probably enough. It becomes easier and more natural the more often you try, though. In fact, you will find that over time, it becomes as natural to plan a differentiated lesson as it does a whole-class lesson. Often, you will find that the whole-class lesson does not work any longer because you will recognize the students for whom the lesson will not work or fit and wonder what to do about them. That's when you realize that it's happened . . . you are now fully differentiated.

Keepsakes and Plans

What are the keepsake ideas from this chapter, those thoughts or ideas that resonated with you that you do not want to forget?

Differentiation and KUDs:

1.

2.

3.

Strategies: Choosing to Differentiate

1.

2.

3.

Strategies: Readiness

1.

2.

3.

Strategies: Interest

1.

2.

3.

Strategies: Learning Profile

1.

2.

3.

Classroom Structures:

1.

2.

3.

Based on my keepsake ideas, I plan to:

1.

2.

3.

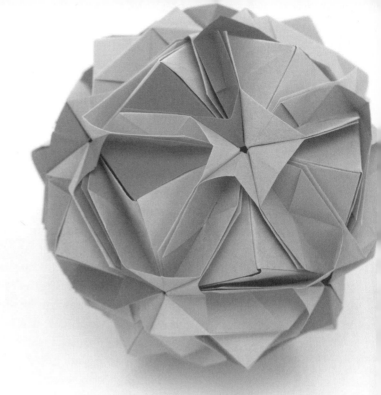

CHAPTER FIVE

SET IT UP

ESTABLISHING THE RIGHT TONE TO MAKE DIFFERENTIATION DOABLE

W here learning takes place is one of the intangible factors affecting students' learning. A safe learning environment where students collaborate and grapple with deep concepts, view mistakes as learning opportunities, and where a growth mindset is taught, promoted, and expected will enable differentiation and learning to flourish. In this chapter, you will find the following:

A Healthy Learning Environment	Everybody Learns
Embracing Fair	Frequently Asked Questions
	Keepsakes and Plans

I once worked in a district where the attitude seemed to be that the students just couldn't . . . whatever. You fill in the blank. Students would look at you and say, "We don't do that here. Don't you know we are from (name of district)?" or "I can't do that. I'm from (district), you know." Sitting around a conference table working on lessons and activities with a group of teachers in this district, I quietly tallied how many times I was told that their kids couldn't do something. In frustration, I finally told the teachers that they were right. Their kids couldn't do these things. However, it was probably more about the teachers' mindset and attitudes about the students rather than the students themselves. They had said "these kids can't . . ." Twelve times in 20 minutes. On digesting this information, one teacher finally said, "Well, maybe they can. But they won't." Most likely you have worked with students also who "won't." Establishing a learning environment where all students are willing to try, are not afraid to fail, and value both as part of the learning process is foundational to all learning, especially to learning in a differentiated mathematics classroom.

We have now looked at most of the essential components of building a differentiated mathematics classroom: understanding the big picture of differentiation; getting to know our students as learners; clarifying mathematical content through determining what students should Know, Understand, and be able to Do; and purposefully choosing and designing tasks and activities based on our students and content. Designing instruction to invite students to learn is essential for differentiation, but building the learning community in which learning takes place is equally important. It is possible to design a beautiful lesson and have it fail because the classroom environment was not established and maintained for successful differentiation or the learning of mathematics. The learning environment is often one of the intangibles that makes or breaks the quality of student learning.

A HEALTHY LEARNING ENVIRONMENT

Students today want to belong. They want to be accepted for who they are, strengths and weaknesses, and they want to know that they are known. They come to us with their own experiences and beliefs about their capabilities in mathematics and learning mathematics and how they fit in a mathematics classroom. Sometimes their background experiences can break our hearts if they have been told explicitly or learned experientially that they do not measure up.

As teachers, we quickly recognize the student with whom no one else wants to partner, the withdrawn student who can't wait for the bell to ring, or . . . you name the child. Establishing a classroom community that expects that we all learn together in various pairings or groupings and that embraces and provides a safe place for mistake making in the mathematical learning process can go a long way to establishing a safe environment where students both know each other and are known. This collaboration and belonging does not "just happen." It is taught and nurtured.

WATCH IT!

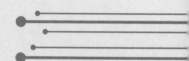

While watching Video 5.1, *Establishing and Maintaining a Healthy Classroom Environment,* consider the following questions:

1. What similarities and differences do you see among the teachers' approaches to developing a healthy mathematics classroom environment?

2. What is the role of student leadership and ownership in a healthy learning environment?

3. What are indicators of a healthy mathematics learning community?

4. How does classroom management affect the learning environment?

5. What tip do you want to remember and try to implement?

Video 5.1 Establishing and Maintaining a Healthy Classroom Environment

Since much of learning mathematics and designing differentiated learning tasks depends on collaboration, expectations for group functioning should be taught and maintained. For example, Figure 5.1 shows a poster from Jayne DeMeuse's classroom in Green Bay, Wisconsin, that promotes positive group work.

During the first weeks of school, I spend as much time—and sometimes more—establishing my environment, norms, and routines as I do with content. I hear the panic in your mind right now as you think, "But we have so much content to get through now!" I understand, but firmly know that a strong and healthy learning environment will increase effective learning and thus stretch your learning time over the long haul. In fact, recent brain research connects the physiology of the brain and the learning environment with the ability to learn (Sousa & Tomlinson, 2011; Willis, 2006).

FIGURE 5.1

GROUPS

© Jayne Demeuse

According to David Sousa and Carol Ann Tomlinson (2011), before a brain is able to pay attention to the learning process, students must feel physically safe and emotionally secure. If a student is feeling strong negative emotions, the limbic system of the brain kicks in and stops cognitive processing and at the same time increases memory of the negativity in order to support survival. By contrast, a positive learning environment increases endorphins in the bloodstream, which creates a positive feeling. This, in turn, stimulates the brain's frontal lobe to support a positive memory of the learning objective as well as the experience. Finally, a negative learning environment leads to increased cortisol in the bloodstream, which raises the learner's anxiety level and shuts down any processing of the lesson content (the brain considers it to be low priority) to prioritize the stressful situation over the content. So you see, a healthy learning environment is much more important to establish and maintain than we might have given it credit. Our own physiology prevents us from learning when we don't feel safe and accepted!

The relationships we build among our students affect the learning of our students. One way to have students make connections yet show their own uniqueness is an activity called "Uniquely Me."

TRY IT! UNIQUELY ME

Give students an index card on which they put their names at the top and number from 1 to 5. Students will write a *true* statement about themselves on each line. Warn students that these will be read out loud, so each statement should be appropriate to be shared in class.

- Line 1—Write something that is true about yourself that is also true of **almost everyone** else in the room (I'm a math student).

- Line 2—Write something that is true about yourself that is also true of **most** people in the room (I like to be challenged in mathematics).

- Line 3—Write something that is true about yourself that is also true of **some** people in the room (I have more than one pet).

- Line 4—Write something that is true about yourself that is also true of a **few** people in the room (I play the drums).

- Line 5—Write something that is **uniquely true about you** (I am a twin).

  - The teacher randomly draws a card from the stack and reads the first statement. If the statement is true about you as a student, stand up. If not, stay seated.

o Read the second statement. If it is also true, the student stays standing. If it is no longer true, the student sits down. Once a student is seated, he or she stays seated throughout the reading of the rest of the card.

o Continue to read through the card with students sitting down as the statements are no longer true about them.

o When the last statement is read, hopefully only the student whose card is being read will be standing.

(Smith, 2016)

In a healthy learning environment, everyone should feel accepted and welcome, and all students make the other students feel welcome and accepted too. So how do you do it?

- Begin by modeling what it looks and sounds like to listen to each other, find out about each other, and appreciate each other.

- Use "get to know each other" activities such as People Bingo and Interest Inventories, especially at the beginning of the year.

- Continue community-building activities throughout the year as quick energizers. For example, keep the "Uniquely Me" cards and use them throughout the year, not just as a one-time activity. Watch for break down of the community, to avoid the typical cliques and outcasts that are often found within a classroom.

- For more specific activities, look at the following Try It! activities.

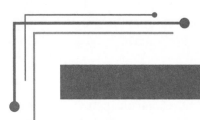

TRY IT! ALL FRIENDS

Purpose: To get to know one another and continue to build relationships

1. Have the class number off by twos, dividing the class into two groups. Have the "ones" form a tight circle, then turn out so that the students' backs are toward the center of the circle and the students are facing out. Have the remaining students (the "twos") face one of the "ones," forming an outer circle. This structure is called "Inside-Outside" circles or a Wagon Wheel.

2. The teacher stands in the very center of the concentric circles so that he or she can lean in any direction and hear the conversations occurring. The teacher in the center poses questions, and each pair of students tells each other their answers.

3. Questions can be anything that will help students get to know each other and make connections. It would be appropriate to share mathematics experiences as well. Examples might include the following:

   • What is your favorite music group or song? Favorite movie?

   • What social media do you prefer to use?

   • Do you like working with others when you learn mathematics or would you rather work alone? Why?

   • What do you look forward to this coming year, in general? In math?

4. After both partners answer the question, the teacher rotates one of the circles. For example, you might have the outside circle rotate three to the left. Now everyone has a new partner and another question is asked.

5. Continue this for the allotted amount of time, alternating which circle rotates, the number of spaces rotated, the direction of the rotation (left or right), and ensuring that after each rotation, students are with a new partner.

Note: This structure is very effective to review content as well. Give each student a review mathematics problem (or a current practice problem, application, etc.). Students work each other's problems in notebooks or whiteboards (for more complex problems, I put the answers on back) and then check their answers with their partner. When all students have finished, they trade cards with their partners, and then the circle rotates. With every rotation, students are "experts" with a new problem and a new partner.

All Friends is a great activity to build class community and, as noted, can be used throughout the year in a wide variety of ways. The next activity emphasizes the importance of working together and listening to each other.

TRY IT! HE SAID, SHE SAID

Purpose: Developing listening and reporting skills

To encourage students to actively listen to one another, have a share-out be only something that was heard from someone else.

1. Following an introductory paired activity (questionnaire or other get-to-know-you game), have students introduce each other to the class.

2. Whenever students work in pairs or groups throughout the year, challenge students to only share something they heard or learned from their partner or group member, rather than something they have said themselves.

It can sometimes be a challenge to listen, for all of us! We often are thinking of what we want to say rather than listening to what the person talking is saying. We can interrupt each other without thinking. The next activity is designed to help a class listen to one another and time responses. It may seem overly simple for a secondary class, but I have found students enjoy this activity and laugh a lot through the process.

TRY IT! COUNT TO 10

Purpose: Develop discourse skills

This activity is very quick and usually pretty funny. I do this to establish strong listening and responding habits.

1. Tell the class that we are going to count to 10 together. Easy, right?

2. Here is the catch: I will begin by saying "one." Only one person can count the next number, so if two people talk at the same time, we have to start over.

3. If there is too long of a gap before someone says the next number, we have to start over. I've had a class take 3 months to make it to 10! Finally, one student stood up and started pointing to other students to get the count to 10. (In my book, that was cheating, although it did show strong leadership and creativity.)

4. As students continue to interrupt, speak at the same time, or have speaking gaps during whole-class discourse, be sure to remind students that we are learning to listen to each other and time our responses. It is important that as we talk together, we truly listen to each other and think about how and when to reply. This exercise practices that skill.

One way to establish that we all learn together and with each other is to be sure to continually mix groupings and pairings of students. We want students to wonder with whom they will be working today. We encourage the idea that we can all learn from everyone else in the classroom. This is especially true in a differentiated classroom, where the design of student groups is very purposeful and based on the design of the task and the type of differentiation. This is the definition of flexible grouping.

Often, as mentioned earlier, when I ask pairs or groups to share out, I only allow the speaker to share something that someone else said. This greatly increases the importance of listening to and understanding each other as we work together. In a learning community, students need to appreciate each other, especially their similarities and differences.

EMBRACING FAIR

I often hear the concern from teachers that if they differentiate, students will ask why different things are happening in the classroom and that students will perceive that it "isn't fair that I have to do this and they get to do that." This is a legitimate concern if you differentiate without establishing an environment to support differentiation. The first step to establishing this environment is to help students understand the basics of differentiation. I explain to students that in our classroom, we are all teachers and we are all learners together, but since we learn differently from each other, sometimes it is necessary for us to do different tasks in order for each of us to learn. Students understand this. Having a frank classroom discussion about what students have liked and disliked in learning mathematics and what has worked or not worked for them will highlight this truth. It is fun to hear a student share what he or she liked in a class and another student immediately respond that he or she doesn't like that very thing. There is a quote often used that says "Fair isn't everybody getting the same thing. Fair is everybody getting what they need." It is important for students to redefine *fair* in this way so that different tasks and assignments become natural and appreciated instead of questionable.

There are several ways to teach students about differentiation, and the amount of detail you explain to students is your preference. Secondary students can certainly understand the structures of differentiation and appreciate a teacher who takes the time to get to know them as learners and explains why certain tasks are going to be designed differently. At a minimum, your students should understand the following:

- We all will have different levels of prior knowledge and mastery, speed at which we learn new concepts and skills, and appropriate levels of challenge to grow. This will change throughout the year, unit to unit, and even skill to skill. Part of my job is to design tasks that ensure that everyone is working equally hard on learning. For this reason, I will differentiate by readiness.

- We all have different types of tasks and applications that will appeal to us as we learn mathematics. Sometimes we will want to try a new type of task and other times we will want to complete a task at which we believe we can be most successful. I will design a variety of tasks from which you may choose how you will best like to learn. For this reason, I will differentiate by interest.

- We all have different ways to make sense of learning, master new skills, and be sure that learning is getting to long-term memory. I need to design tasks to address various ways to learn and make sense of mathematics. For this reason, I will differentiate by learning profile.

As students learn more about differentiation, they naturally learn more about metacognition and what it takes to be an active learner in mathematics. Using the discussion about differentiation and why different groups of students and different tasks will occur over time form the basis of a safe learning environment.

It is interesting that students are usually not concerned if they have a different interest than another or a different learning profile than another. However, readiness can carry a stigma, and that should not be the case. Students with learning disabilities or for whom mathematics is generally a struggle often enter a secondary classroom already discouraged and shut down before anything happens. They carry an invisible "Loser" on their foreheads that affects their effort and interactions. Other students come into class feeling like a "chosen one" for whom math is easy and feeling confident they will continue to receive their excellent grades. Establishing a proper attitude about readiness differences within a mathematics class is crucial for a proper learning environment.

One way to talk to students about readiness differences is to look around the class and point out that there are not as many students wearing glasses as there are students without glasses not as many students are wearing glasses than students without glasses. Since not everyone wears glasses, and if being fair means everyone should have exactly the same things, then no one should be allowed to wear glasses. If you are wearing glasses, please take them off! Have students discuss the silliness of this. Wait for the student who asks about wearing contacts. To this I respond, "It's okay if you are wearing contacts. If we don't know you have extra help, then it's okay." This same principle should apply to learning—if there is support needed, support should be given. At the same time, if you do not need support, you should not have it. The goal is that everyone is able to enter the learning process where they need to enter, be appropriately challenged, and learn!

TRY IT! TARGETING READINESS

Purpose: Develop understanding and acceptance of readiness differentiation

1. Put up a chart with three columns: Too Easy, Just Right, and Too Hard.

2. Ask students to tell how they feel when a task or lesson is too easy. How does it feel when it is too hard? How does it feel when it is just right?

3. List their descriptions in the columns.

4. Tell your students that it is your job as their teacher to hit each student's target and to get it "just right" for each student. The problem is that "just right" is not the same for each student. That is why we might do different tasks or someone may seem to be doing something easier or harder than I am. As your teacher, I want everyone to work equally hard! It is important that we all work hard so that we all learn. Figure 5.2 gives an example of targeting readiness.

TARGETING READINESS

Too Easy	Just Right	Too Hard
• Bored	• Smart	• Bored
• Waste of time	• Proud of myself	• Waste of time
• Mind wanders	• Excited	• Mind wanders
• Slow	• Energized	• Dumb
• Sleepy		• Embarrassed
• Mad		• Mad

Another way to build community, as well as continue to teach our students about differentiation, is to extend some of the "get-to-know-each-other" activities to include talking about our learning profiles as well. Secondary students generally love learning anything about themselves, and discovering their learning profiles either formally or through discussion is usually very impactful and exciting for them. In Chapter 2, "Find Out," there were several methods shared for exploring students' learning profiles. For example, letting students share their favorite mathematical learning activity and asking who else enjoys that will form learning connections. When discussing learning profile with students, have students raise their hands to identify which learning profiles they most naturally align to in mathematics. As students look around the class, they see who learns in similar ways and who does not. This also creates more understanding about differentiation for students and why you will often have different tasks for different students. It creates a learning environment where doing different things is not only acceptable but also appreciated.

EVERYBODY LEARNS

We are all about learning. Sometimes that gets lost. In my classroom, I had a big banner across the back that simply said "Everybody Learns." If students asked why they had to do something, I pointed to the banner. We repeatedly discussed that in our class, everybody learns. In our class, it doesn't matter where you enter learning; it matters that you DO enter learning. It doesn't matter how you want to learn and practice; it matters that you do. And the bottom line of everything we do is that everybody learns. Between understanding that we all learn differently, and that we all can learn, we have the foundation for understanding differentiation.

Unfortunately, mathematics is one of the subjects in which students carry a belief that they are unable to learn. Parents tell their kids that they were not good in math. We often have an uphill battle in mathematics when it comes to learning attitudes. A teacher told me yesterday about a student in her class who constantly says that she isn't any good at math and can't learn math. She then told me that the first time she met the student's mother, the mother introduced her daughter by saying that she isn't very good at math . . . before she ever said her name! These attitudes cannot be allowed in our classrooms.

MINDSETS

Attitudes and belief systems shape everything in our lives, even when we are not aware of them. This is especially true with learning. What we believe, as teachers or students, about what constitutes "smart" or "good at math" affects our effort in learning and even how we talk with one another. We use the term *mindset* (Dweck, 2006) in conversations regularly regarding student attitudes. Dr. Dweck's work describes two types of mindsets: growth and fixed. Figure 5.3 provides examples of each type of mindset and how the different mindsets affect teachers' and students' mathematics beliefs.

FIGURE 5.3

MINDSETS

Teacher Fixed Mindset	Teacher Growth Mindset
I can't do much about the way kids come to me. Some are just too far behind in mathematics.	With support, multiple approaches, and belief in my students, I believe most students can accomplish most tasks in mathematics.
There are some people who just can't learn mathematics.	Everyone is able to learn deep concepts and strategies in mathematics, perhaps at different rates and with different experiences. There is no genetic disposition for or against mathematics learning.
Students can't go far without memorizing math facts.	Knowing math facts certainly eases many mathematical processes, but knowing facts does not precede reasoning. In fact, reasoning can help determine math facts.
I stick to my mathematics textbook because I don't want my students to ask a question to which I don't know the answer.	Learning and reasoning together is the most powerful learning of all—for both the teacher and the students. Most set programs do not give the depth of understanding or problem solving that current standards demand.
Student Fixed Mindset	**Student Growth Mindset**
You are born smart or you aren't, and success comes from genetics. How my parents were in math is how I will be too.	My effort in math has more to do with my success than how I was born.
Challenge is scary.	Challenge is exciting.
Mistakes are wrong and bad.	Mistakes grow my brain.
I am who I am and there isn't much anyone can do about it.	I am constantly changing and growing. New tasks, challenges, and experiences make me who I am.
Math is hard for most people, especially me.	Everyone can be successful at math with effort. Even me.
Math is right and wrong, and you have to be good at memorizing.	Math is about connections, patterns, and problem solving. If you understand the connections and reasoning, most problems can be figured out.
I'm good at math because I know the steps and can do problems faster than most.	I'm good at math because I can problem solve, use multiple strategies and representations, ask good questions, and communicate mathematically.

Dr. Jo Boaler has advanced the study of mindsets, specifically for mathematics. In her book *Mathematical Mindsets,* Boaler (2015) explains that research shows how elastic our brains truly are. In fact, she points out that practicing a task for as little as 10 minutes a day for 15 days has been shown to change the synapses and connections within our brain. This is exciting news. In addition, teaching students about this research has a significant impact on student performance.

> Just telling students that their intelligence is under their own control improves their effort on school work and performance. In two separate studies, students [were taught] how the brain works, explaining that the students possessed the ability, if they worked hard, to make themselves smarter. This erased up to half of the difference between minority and white achievement levels. (Nisbet, 2009)

Even more and more morning announcements at various schools end with the message to "make it a great day . . . or not. The choice is yours." How wonderful to enforce to students that their attitude is in their own control. We also need to empower our students to understand that their effort makes the greatest difference for their success . . . and we probably need to educate our parents as well. No longer shall we allow "But I'm not a math person—and neither is my mom" in our classrooms!

Possible indicators of students' growth mindsets are their willingness to take a risk, make mistakes, combine and invent strategies, and, in general, go for it!

WATCH IT!

As you watch Video 5.2, *Encouraging a Growth Mindset and Productive Struggle*, consider the following questions:

1. How do you think teachers can teach and create a growth mindset with their students?

2. How does the teacher continue to promote and enforce a growth mindset?

3. How do students exhibit a growth mindset?

4. How does the classroom environment and culture add to the mindset disposition of both students and the teacher?

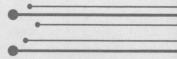

Video 5.2 Encouraging a Growth Mindset and Productive Struggle

One way by which we can establish growth mindsets in students is to simply have phrases and expectations that express growth mindsets. Figure 5.4 shows a bulletin board from Kim Farless's classroom in Queen Creek, Arizona, promoting practical changes in thought processes to promote growth mindset. These changes in thought for our students should also be how we talk to students to promote growth mindsets.

FIGURE 5.4

GROWTH MINDSET BULLETIN BOARD

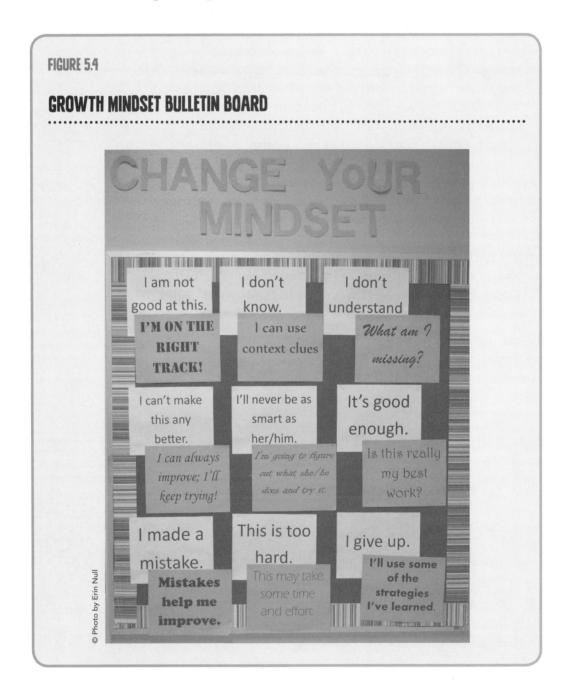

© Photo by Erin Null

Not only is it important to teach our students about having a growth mindset, but we also need them to practice adopting a growth mindset. As mentioned earlier, studies show that understanding how the brain and a growth mindset work can improve students' effort and performance (Nisbet, 2009). The following activities can be done in class to help students develop a growth mindset and a learning environment to support productive struggle.

TRY IT! TRASHING FEARS

Purpose: Establish a safe place to learn mathematics

What fears do your students have about learning mathematics? Have them write their fears on quarter sheets of scratch paper—one fear per sheet. Then wad them up and throw them away! Your fears are trashed because in our classroom, that won't happen. I believe in you, and your classmates will support you until you believe in yourself.

TRY IT! YOUR BRAIN WITH EFFORT

Purpose: To solidify the belief that effort matters most

1. After discussing the plasticity of the brain and the current research on mindset and effort, have students draw a "Before Effort and After Effort" of their brains in mathematics.

2. Have students research or create their own sayings about effort and brain growth in mathematics. Create bumper stickers and posters to hang in your classroom and in the hall. (Adapted from YouCubed.org)

While these Try It! activities will reinforce what a growth mindset is and the importance of effort for your students, it is also important to embed discussion about effort and mindset within a learning task or as part of the closure to a lesson. This will help make growth mindset and the willingness to struggle a more natural part of learning in general and learning mathematics specifically. As part of closure, consider asking students to share what went well and what did not go as well with a given task. You could also ask what was easy and hard about a task for various students. Acknowledging that difficulty and struggle are not only normal but also expected will remove the misconception that struggling with a given mathematical task means that you are not good in mathematics.

PRAISE

Perhaps one of the most powerful, yet easy, adjustments we can make to facilitate a healthy mindset is to be aware of how and for what we praise students. We should continue to praise effort, helpfulness, willingness to make and share a mistake, and great questions. Do not praise results or speed, and NEVER say anything along the lines of "You're so smart. . . ." Try praising students in the following ways:

1. Praise the process, not the person or result. Eliminate words that imply it is about anything other than effort—don't praise good scores or say a student is smart.

   - I am so proud of how long you worked on this.

   - What a great strategy to try!

   - You really caught your mistake there.

   - Thank you for trying so hard and not giving up.

   - I can see that you put a lot of time and thought into this.

2. Give real and specific praise. Keep it real and don't praise something that isn't demonstrating growth or effort. Students will know it is false. Acknowledge growth.

   - It's okay. Everyone makes mistakes and that is how we learn and grow our brains.

   - Look at the progress you made on this problem compared to the last time you tried.

3. Be positive.

   - I know you are struggling right now, but I also know you can do this.

   - I've seen how hard you tried when you ___, so I know you can do it again.

A healthy learning environment is dependent not only on the emotional climate but also on the routines that make differentiation run smoothly.

CONCLUSION

The learning environment is a make-or-break factor in successful differentiation. Creating a culture where students understand and value struggle as the necessary process for success not only promotes the necessary growth mindset in students but also erases the potential stigma of differentiating by readiness. It is clearly understood that everyone in our class works equally hard, works together in various configurations, and is supported and challenged appropriately. In our class, we value and appreciate our differences and recognize that we learn as much, if not more, from others who think and work differently from us. No matter what it takes to learn in our classroom, that is what we are about. For in our class, Everybody Learns!

FREQUENTLY ASKED QUESTIONS

Q: What do we do for a student who will not work until I am standing or sitting with him or her?

A: Students who do not engage with work until a teacher is present have learned that behavior. To break their dependence, do not reinforce it. Help students clearly understand the task at hand and how to take the first step. Have students explain back to you the first step to be sure they understand what they are to do. Once they can tell you what the step is, walk away and have them complete the step on their own while you check in with another student or group of students. Circle back to check on the first students' progress, and then repeat the process with the next step or two. In this way, encourage students' independence while supporting them as needed. This process will allow them to feel successful and develop a growth mindset that focuses on effort.

Q: What do I do with students who refuse to work with other students?

A: There are times when students are not permitted to work together because of a discipline plan, a 504 accommodation, or other legal document. These specifications must be followed. Other than that, do not allow putdowns or refusal to work with other students. It is important that students know and understand how to work with others, whether they are friends outside of class or not. One way to encourage all students working together is to remind students that working groups are flexible, often for a specific task or designated number of minutes. With this said, learning is the most important outcome of our classrooms, and if a specific pairing of students will prevent learning, do not put the students together.

Keepsakes and Plans

What are the keepsake ideas from this chapter, those thoughts or ideas that resonated with you that you do not want to forget?

Healthy Learning Environments:

1.

2.

3.

Embracing Fair:

1.

2.

3.

Everybody Learns:

1.

2.

3.

Mindset and Praise:

1.

2.

3.

Based on my keepsake ideas, I plan to:

1.

2.

3.

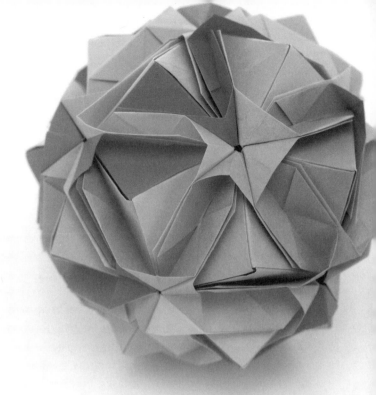

CHAPTER SIX

POWER ON

MASTERING AND MODELING DAILY ROUTINES FOR ACHIEVEMENT ALL YEAR

We continue our look at the learning environment. A safe learning environment for students is based not only on the students' affect but also on the day-to-day running of the classroom. There is a sense of confidence in both the teacher and the students in a class where expectations and routines are understood and well organized. In this chapter, you will find the following:

Classroom Routines	Planning Flexible Time
Assigning Groups	Frequently Asked Questions
Giving Directions	Keepsakes and Plans
Monitoring the Work	

Have you ever noticed how crazy classrooms can look on a teen sitcom? Kids are all over the place, throwing things, talking to each other about anything and everything as long as it has nothing to do with learning . . . you've got the picture. Thankfully that is not how classrooms generally look, although I have seen some that come close. No matter how beautifully a lesson can be designed on paper, learning cannot occur if the learning environment is not set up for success, if routines are not established and used consistently, and if differentiated tasks are not monitored correctly.

CLASSROOM ROUTINES

One of the concerns that many teachers have as they consider differentiating instruction is how to manage different tasks and groups simultaneously. Truthfully, there is not too much difference between managing groups doing the same task and groups doing different tasks. You need to be able to

- Effectively assign groups or partners if that is the classroom structure being used
- Give directions for the various tasks
- Monitor the learning
- Have a plan for students who finish early or need more time

ASSIGNING GROUPS OR PARTNERS

The most important aspect about assigning groups or a partner is determining who should work with whom and why. One hallmark of a differentiated classroom is flexible grouping (Tomlinson, 2001). Flexible groups means that groups can be put together for 10 to 15 minutes for only a specific task, as well as longer-standing groups that will change periodically throughout the year such as assigned seating groups. The specific group you will assign for a given task should be dependent on the task.

Task Groups

If you have designed a differentiated task and want to assign students to groups for the specific task, the first step is to determine by what aspect of differentiation the task is designed: readiness, interest, learning profile, or a combination. For assigned groups, the task will most likely be based on readiness or a previously determined interest or learning profile preference.

When grouping for readiness

- Determine whether the group should be mixed readiness or a homogeneous readiness grouping to address specific needs. There will be time for both. If addressing specific readiness needs, the groups will need to be more homogeneous (but please remember not to use this grouping predominantly).

  o For a more homogeneous grouping, design a tiered activity (see Chapter 4). With your roster, make a list of every student who can do the highest-tier task. Next, list all of the students who can do the next-level task and so on. Continue until all of the students are assigned a specific task. Make random groups from the lists by tasks.

  o For more heterogeneous readiness groups, blend bands of readiness such as high to mid-high, mid-high to mid-low, and mid-low to low. These will be more beneficial working groups than the traditional high-low-middle-middle that usually do not function as well.

When grouping for interest

- Determine if you want to allow students to choose their own groups based on the task or with whom they would want to work. One possible flaw with having students choose their groups on the fly is that they will likely choose a task based on who else chose that task, rather than the task that will most likely work best for them.

- If you want to assign interest groups, survey students for their choices prior to assigning groups. One way is to explain the optional tasks and have students list their top two choices on a sticky note or index card. From the list of their preferences, form the groups. A similar option is to have students write their choice of task prior to forming groups. They can write their choice on a sticky note and then find a partner or small group based on their sticky notes.

When grouping for learning profile

- One option for learning profile groups is to design the tasks according to learning profile and allow students to choose the task they would like to do. If you would like to have groups, follow the strategies for interest grouping above.

- To assign learning profile groups, determine from the task what aspect of learning profile is being accessed. Align this to your knowledge of how your students best learn. Form groups from there.

Standing Groups

Standing groups are groups or pairings that are arranged in advance and maintained for a period of time. Standing groups can be changed on marking periods or four to five times during the year to add variety. There are several ways to form and manage standing groups.

Clock Partners

Clock Partners is a structure to predetermine partners. To make a clock partner, a student asks another student to be his or her partner at a specific time, for example, 12:00. Each student writes the other student's name on the 12:00 line and they now have an appointment at 12:00. A sample clock is shown in Figure 6.1.

FIGURE 6.1

CLOCK PARTNER CLOCK
· ·

Name _____

Clock Partners

The full-size clock can be downloaded at resources.corwin.com/everymathlearner6-12.

On one clock, a variety of partners can be established:

- Allow students to choose their partners for 12:00, 4:00, and 8:00.

- At 2:00, assign a partner who has a similar aspect of mathematical learning profile (see Chapter 2).

- At 6:00, assign a partner with a similar mathematical readiness level—this will need to be in general as readiness can change unit to unit.

- At 10:00, assign a partner who will approach problems in a different manner. This can be through a different preference for representation or how to practice, or a different approach to problem solving.

On one clock, you now have six different partners, three who are student chosen and three who are teacher chosen for differentiation. To use the clock, tell students which appointment time they will be meeting at for the task. If all students are working on the same task, use one of their choices at 12:00, 4:00, or 8:00. If the task is differentiated, use the appropriate time of 2:00 for learning profile (if the same profile aspect is used for the task as was chosen for the clock assignments), 6:00 for readiness, or 10:00 for an open-ended problem-solving task designs the task.

If you are concerned that your students will be insulted or feel disrespected by using a clock that may be similar to an elementary school experience, any structure can work. For example, you could have pairings based on key vocabulary such as "linear, quadratic, exponential, absolute value, and logarithmic," and to assign the specific pairing for a task, the teacher would tell students to meet with their "absolute value function" partners. In general, I have found that high school students enjoy using the clock because if they have seen it in elementary school, it is fun again. However, if middle school students have seen clock partners in elementary school and you are using it again, they may feel that you are disrespecting them as "mature middle school students."

Quadrilateral Groups

Similar to the Clock Partners, quadrilateral groups form groups of four instead of pairs. I have students form their own groups of four with the parallelogram and square shapes, and I assign trapezoid, rhombus, and rectangle groups. You can assign students with similar learning profile characteristics to the trapezoid group, similar readiness to the rhombus group, and a mixed readiness or learning profile group to the rectangle group. Figure 6.2 gives an example of quadrilateral groups.

The names of the group members are written inside the quadrilateral.

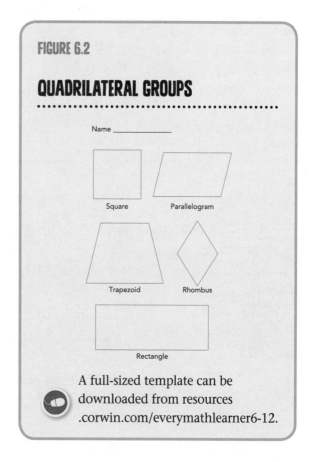

FIGURE 6.2

QUADRILATERAL GROUPS

A full-sized template can be downloaded from resources .corwin.com/everymathlearner6-12.

Moving in and out of groups should not take a long time, although in most classes it does. I have witnessed some classes taking as long as 8 minutes to move to their newly assigned groups and be ready to work. Having groups preassigned saves times. Having students practice moving in and out of groups, including moving any desks if needed, should be practiced so that moving in and out of groups becomes routine.

TRY IT! STOPWATCH DRILLS

Purpose: To move in and out of groups quickly and fluidly

Challenge your students to see how quickly they can form their groups, sit together, and be ready to learn. I conduct stopwatch drills by telling students they will work with their 6:00 partners. . . . Go! Time how long it takes for the class to be seated and ready, and record the time on your whiteboard. Continue practicing at various times to see if you can beat your previous best time. I had all of my classes compete for the quickest time and kept the quickest class period and time in the corner of my whiteboard. This is a fun race but serves to get students moving effectively and quickly. Most classes should be able to move and be ready to learn within 75 seconds.

WATCH IT!

As you watch Video 6.1, *"Clock Partners" Grouping Strategy*, consider the following questions:

1. How does the teacher move students into pairs?

2. How efficiently do students move to be with their partners and begin work?

3. How do the students know the task they are to do with their partners?

Video 6.1 "Clock Partners" Grouping Strategy

GIVING DIRECTIONS

Many students have difficulty following multistep directions—imagine hearing all at once several sets of directions for various tasks, of which you will only be doing one. This only serves to create confusion or cause students to want to do something that another group is doing. Giving directions for differentiated activities can be confusing and so needs to be done carefully. The key to giving directions with differentiated tasks is to give only the directions that are needed to the students who need them.

Directions can be given in different ways. Students can be directed to a specific area of the room and specific instructions given once they are in place. When the students get to the designated area, the activities are set up and students know how to begin.

Stations are one way to implement differentiated tasks. Bear in mind that stations in and of themselves are not differentiated if all students will rotate through all stations, completing exactly the same tasks. However, one option to differentiate stations is to have either choices at each station or readiness differentiation at each station. Figure 6.3 shows Lori Everson's MATH rotations that she uses often for mathematics differentiation: M for Mathematical Games, A for Alone Time, T for Time with Teach (or sometimes Time with Tech), and H for Hmmmm, which is usually something new and challenging. Students often have choices at each station or may do only one or two of the stations based on their current need. Students are told at which station they are to begin, then follow the rotation.

Secondary students are able to follow a task card for directions, and this is my primary way to give directions for multiple tasks. Task cards can be placed in a folder with the supplies needed for the specific task or placed at the location where the task will occur. Often task cards can be put on a group of desks or table where the group will be working on that specific task.

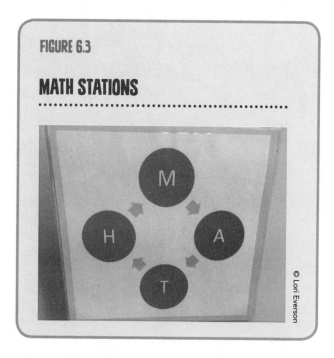

FIGURE 6.3

MATH STATIONS

© Lori Everson

One way you can set up readiness stations is to put tasks in color groups. For example, for a geometry station rotation, two tiers of similar tasks were created. The higher tiered tasks were put in blue folders at each station, and the more basic tiered tasks were put in yellow folders. When students came into class, they were given a blue, yellow, or green sticker. They were then told that they could work alone or with one or two partners of their same sticker color. Students followed their color—blue did blue tasks, yellow did yellow tasks, and the green stickers had to do some blue and some yellow of their own choice. Figure 6.4 shows the readiness folders.

Of course, as students are working, the first step for monitoring the different pairs, groups, or individuals will be to circulate and make sure that everyone understands their task and is working correctly.

FIGURE 6.4

READINESS FOLDERS FOR STATIONS

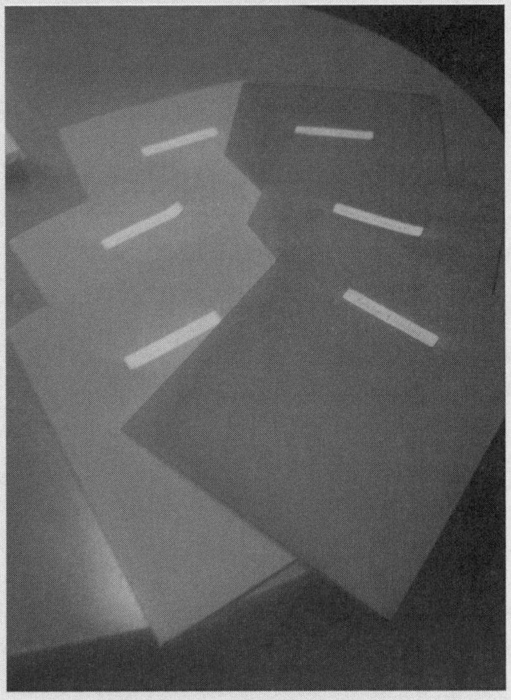

TIPS FOR ELL/SPECIAL EDUCATION STUDENTS

1. Underline key words in the directions on a task card, and provide a picture of what the word means.

2. Whenever possible, reduce the number of words in the directions.

3. Provide a completed step-by-step model for students who are learning the language.

4. Have students practice saying the directions to another student, then showing what the directions mean by modeling or drawing.

MONITORING THE WORK

As mentioned before, monitoring the work in a differentiated mathematics classroom has little difference from monitoring the work when all students are doing the same task. If students are working in pairs or groups, be sure to make your way to each grouping, beginning with the pair or group about whom you have the greatest concern. A word of caution, though: It is possible to get "sucked in" to one specific group, and the rest of the class could grow restless or veer off task while you work with only a small number of students.

It is more effective to talk with struggling groups only about the step they are about to take, whether it is the first step or another step in a process, and then go check other groups while the first group is taking that step and then bounce back to see if they have completed that step. After that, discuss the next step and go check other groups, bounce back to see if Step 2 is completed, and so on. In this way, you do not get caught helping a few students all the way through a task or process and also begin to train independence in those students who tend to be dependent on a teacher's presence in order to begin or to try. It has been suggested that the appropriate time a teacher should spend in any group is 19 seconds—now that is a challenge!

Another tip for monitoring groups is to set some group rules and/or roles. It is important to teach students explicitly the expectations of working together, how to be productive, and how to deal with conflict should there be a problem. Since different groups will most likely be involved in different tasks in a differentiated mathematics class, it is even more important that groups can function independently since they might be the only group on a specific task. The particular roles you choose for your groups are probably not as important as everyone having a role and feeling that they are an important member and need to contribute for the success of the group. Some group roles include the following:

- Director—Reads directions out loud and makes sure that the directions are being followed as the group works.

- Facilitator—Helps the director to keep the group on task and moving. May assign specific jobs to the members to complete the task. Checks to see that everyone is contributing and trying.

- Technician—Helps check accuracy of calculations, may give suggestions for the plan to solve a problem, and makes sure that everyone is recording the group's work if required. May also be in charge of technology if part of the task.

- Material manager—Gathers materials, makes sure all are using the materials appropriately, and, after the group cleans up their area, returns the materials.

- Timekeeper—Budgets the time for each part of the task and makes sure the group continues to make progress and does not waste time.

- Scribe or recorder—If only one finished product is required, the recorder would write the group's conclusions and fill in any graphic organizers or other documents to turn in.

- Encourager—Monitors the group members to be sure everyone is contributing and working hard to do their own jobs and prevents putdowns as much as possible.

As you set up your groups, consider which jobs will be most needed for the group's success and assign specific students to jobs. One word of warning about assigning roles is that a role should not be viewed as an "opt out" of the actual work. For example, the director cannot choose to not work on the task because he or she is monitoring the group's work. I usually require all students in a group to be involved with writing—either all complete a copy of a task, or everyone has to write a part of a group project, and so on. Whatever structure is needed, be sure that there is accountability for all students to work hard, contribute, and learn.

I do not recommend assigning a "spokesperson" as a group role. I want all students to be ready to share the group's work so that they will pay attention to the group's process. I recommend randomly calling students from each group to present, rather than letting students know in advance who will be speaking. It is also important that one of the group rules is that the group is not truly finished until everyone in the group can answer any question about their group work. I often check on this by asking different students in the group a question about their task. If a student is not able to answer me without help, the group is not finished.

TRY IT! TRACKING TRI-FOLDS

Purpose: To monitor or track the progress of all pairs or groups at a single glance

Figure 6.5 shows a picture of Tracking Tri-folds.

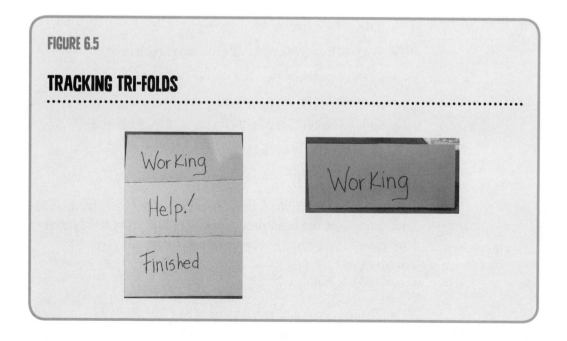

FIGURE 6.5

TRACKING TRI-FOLDS

Working
Help!
Finished

Working

Tri-fold a piece of construction paper or card stock horizontally. In the top section, write "Working." In the middle section, write "Help," and in the bottom section, write "Finished." Fold the paper into a triangular prism. Tell the students to face the side that shows how they are doing (working, need help, or finished) toward the front of the room. At a single glance, the teacher can go to the front of the room and see how the pairs or groups are doing—who is still working, who needs help, or who is finished.

PLANNING FLEXIBLE TIME

One thing on which you can count whenever your students work in groups is that they will not finish at the same time. Planning for "ragged time" will ensure that learning continues and that the classroom environment does not deteriorate. From the beginning of the year, students should have a list of accepted activities to do if they finish early. These activities are called "anchor activities."

Anchor Activities

To continue the learning, anchor activities for mathematics class should be mathematics specific. Possible anchor activities can include the following:

- Finish missing or incomplete assignments
- Play a mathematical game (alone or with a friend)
- Solve a logic puzzle
- Practice mathematical skills through problem cards
- Practice mathematics ACT or SAT problems
- Problem of the day (or week)
- Sudoku or KenKen puzzles
- Help a Friend (with permission)
- Create a mathematical puzzle

The list of anchor activities should start at a more basic level, with fewer options at the beginning of the year, and grow throughout the year. As you compile your anchor activities, consider the following characteristics that would be considered high quality (Tomlinson & Imbeau, 2010):

- Engaging, contain an element of fun
- Focused on essential learning

- Address a broad range of student interests
- Open-ended to allow for multiple solution paths and representations
- Clear directions so that students can work independently
- A check sheet, rubric, or form of monitoring system included for students to gauge quality work

Anchor activities give students who finish early something to extend and stretch their learning. However, some students will require additional time to do their best work to complete their task.

Extra Time

Some students work and process more slowly than others. Time should not be a determining factor as to the amount of effort or the quality of work a student puts into a task. Unfortunately, with firmly set due dates, this can become an issue for students who work and think at a slower pace than others. I am not suggesting that every student who does not finish a task on time has worked hard and just needs more time—we all know students who waste time and do not focus until the last few minutes before something is due. However, for students who honestly could complete a task with maximum effort if given more time, a plan should be in place.

Students who need additional time can request it using a form to explain what they have already completed, why they need more time, when they will continue their work, and their requested due date.

When allowing students to request extra time, it is important that students understand that the request is not a guarantee of extra time. Students should not think that they can put off working on a task and then request extra time.

Appropriate flexible time when students can continue to work on tasks should be brainstormed among the students and the teacher. Possible time slots can include the following:

- Station work
- Warm-up or transition times
- Lunch bunch
- Planned intervention times
- After-school tutoring times
- At home

Figure 6.6 shows a sample of a request for extra time.

FIGURE 6.6

REQUEST FOR EXTRA TIME

Request for Extra Time

Name
_____

Project
_____

Explain what you have done so far:

For what will you use your extra time?

When will you continue your work?

Proposed due date
_____

Teacher Decision:

The full template can be downloaded from resources.corwin.com/everymathlearner6-12.

Using flexible time for students who finish early or need additional time is one of the adjustments that is needed to make differentiation successful. The use of flexible time is actually needed whether or not students are engaged with different tasks because the pace at which students work is one of the learning differences inherent in a class of different students.

CONCLUSION

There is a saying that I understand and appreciate now more than any other time in my life: The devil is in the details. This is true in so many different areas, but especially the classroom. We have all witnessed the demise of order, concentration, and often learning in one way or another due to misplaced papers, interruptions, and various other lack of routines. Sometimes the mundane procedures are just what are needed to allow students to focus on learning and free a teacher's mind to give attention to what is most important.

Consider It!

Brainstorm a list of flexible times throughout the day that can be used for extra time for students who might need it.

WATCH IT!

As you watch Video 6.2, *Eight Tips on Classroom Routine and Management*, consider the following questions:

1. How can classroom routines and management become a natural part of our mathematics learning?

2. How can you keep all students accountable for working and learning, even when you are not present?

3. What are your favorite tips from this video that you want to be sure to implement?

Video 6.2 Eight Tips on Classroom Routine and Management

Smoothly run classrooms facilitate learning, whereas chaotic or disorganized classrooms can lead to confusion and frustration that prevent freedom to learn. In this chapter, we have seen various procedures and structures to move students in and out of groups, monitor group work, and encourage students to work together in groups as well as take responsibility for their learning. Having specific structures in place allows for maximum effort and time to be spent on the most important thing of all—learning.

FREQUENTLY ASKED QUESTIONS

Q: How can you have groups work together when your room is very small?

A: Many times, space limits the desk or table arrangements, but even the smallest rooms can facilitate groupings. For example, if desks are already in pods, those become set spaces for groups to meet. If desks are in pairs, two desks at a time can be rotated 180 degrees to make a group of four desks with the pair of desks behind them. Other times, desks do not need to be moved at all, but rather students may choose to sit together on the floor, under a table, in a corner, or wherever. Space should never be the determining factor as to whether pairs or small groups are used for differentiation.

Q: Do you accept late work?

A: I do. I know it is a challenge keeping up with the paperwork, but I always try to remember that the learning is what is important. I would rather have students do the work of learning than adhere to rules that just didn't work in a particular case. I usually gave my students "OOPS!" passes (about two per quarter) that they could use for late assignments without any type of penalty. Sometimes life interrupts, and they couldn't get the work done that night. I know I didn't always get papers graded on the timeframe my students wanted.

Keepsakes and Plans

What are the keepsake ideas from this chapter, those thoughts or ideas that resonated with you that you do not want to forget?

Classroom Routines—Grouping:

1.

2.

3.

Classroom Routines—Directions:

1.

2.

3.

Classroom Routines—Monitoring:

1.

2.

3.

Classroom Routines—Flex Time:

1.

2.

3.

Based on my keepsake ideas, I plan to:

1.

2.

3.

CHAPTER SEVEN

STEP BACK

TOOLS FOR ASSESSING AND EVALUATING IN A DIFFERENTIATED CLASSROOM

Most of us love the process of planning lessons and being in the classroom with the kids. Planning for differentiation is completely dependent on knowing our students well, determining the best entry points and strategies for learning for each lesson, and making sure students are progressing as planned. In this chapter, you will find the following:

Assessment For, Of, and As Learning

Principles to Develop Assessments

Designing Effective Assessments

Frequently Asked Questions

Keepsakes and Plans

I remember my first year of teaching mathematics. I couldn't wait to give a test or quiz so I could take them home and grade them. Yes, I'm serious. I thought all of my students would receive an A or a B on the test. After all, my lessons had gone well. My students asked questions in class, and most did their homework (it was a long time ago). Surely all my students would be able to perform with 80 percent mastery or above. And then I graded the tests. I couldn't understand it. There were students earning Cs or Ds and even some who failed. What had I done wrong? How could I have not realized this? The answer is very simple. I taught. I didn't assess. The most beautifully designed lessons, implemented well in a growth-mindset learning environment, may still not produce the desired results if we are not keeping track of exactly which students are succeeding, which are struggling and making progress, and which are completely lost. Continual assessment needs to be *part of* teaching . . . they're inseparable.

ASSESSMENT FOR, OF, AND AS LEARNING

As a new teacher, I thought assessment and evaluations were synonymous in the life of a student. Assessments in my mind were the same as the items that I used to create points for my grade book, which were basically homework assignments, tests, and quizzes. We now have a much more robust view of assessment that benefits students. Assessment is no longer about evaluating students and assigning a grade but much more about helping students understand their own learning progress, informing next steps for learning and instruction, and determining the summary of learning at the end of the unit.

Assessment should provide a wide view of a student's learning progression through a unit. It begins with determining what students know, understand, and are able to do in regard to the upcoming unit before any instruction. This includes assessing for the essential prerequisite knowledge as well as the upcoming learning. It continues with monitoring each student's learning throughout the unit in a moment-by-moment fashion and concludes with determining the accumulation of content knowledge and understanding at the end of the unit. Throughout the unit, students self-evaluate their progress, what strategies are working for them, and what their next steps should be. In essence, this is the meaning of assessment—from preassessment to formative assessment to summative assessment and even the students' self-assessment.

Balance is the key when considering assessment design in a differentiated classroom. Assessments should be balanced between differentiated tasks where students are able to best show what they truly know, understand, and are able to do and tasks that are more traditional in format. Furthermore, whether in your state or district mathematics is assessed with paper and pencil or on a computer, it is important to provide students the opportunities to use the same formats that will be used on high-stakes testing.

A second aspect of balancing assessment is that assessment needs to be a consistent and ongoing look at student learning throughout a unit. It should be a "picture of the entire forest" rather than a "picture of a tree." In other words, conclusions should never be based on a single measure, a single type of measure, or sporadic measurements.

"Assessment *for* learning, assessment *of* learning, and assessment *as* learning" are now frequently used in developing a compete picture of assessment. Assessment *for* learning accentuates the use of information by the teacher to plan instruction that will benefit and move students to the desired learning outcomes for the unit. It also includes student self-assessment that enables students to reflect on their current strengths in regard to the upcoming unit, areas for growth, and ability to set learning goals for themselves. When we assess our students for their interests and learning profiles (see Chapter 2), we are using assessments for learning as this information informs us as to the best ways to reach and hook our students. Preassessment for each unit provides readiness information prior to the start of a unit. Because these assessments are meant to provide information about how to design specific instruction, they are not graded.

Assessments *of* learning, on the other hand, are summative in nature. They are to measure the degree to which students have reached the learning goals of the unit.

Assessments *as* learning integrate the assessment process into instruction and learning. It has the goal of letting both the teacher and the student know the progress toward the learning goal. They show the areas in which the student is strong and is working toward mastery, areas in which progress is needed, or areas in which there is no progress. Formative assessments are assessment *as* learning.

Make a list of the assessments you typically use throughout a unit. Next to each assessment, make a note as to whether it is *for (f)*, *of (o)*, or *as (a)* learning. What conclusions can you draw from your list? What goals will you set?

PRINCIPLES TO DEVELOP ASSESSMENTS

As you plan your unit or lesson, you are thinking about appropriate assessments. No matter what type of assessment you are going to create, first and foremost use your unit's KUD to guide the construction. Not all of the KUDs will be on every assessment— prioritizing which learning objectives will be included on the specific assessment, as well as how students will demonstrate their level of knowledge and understanding of the objectives, is the "big idea" of assessment design. Preassessments and summative assessments should be planned before instruction begins, and instruction follows the assessment plan. Formative assessments are embedded within the instruction plan and can be designed during the specific lesson planning. The details on how to use the KUD to guide the assessment design are included in the specific assessment sections later in this chapter.

Once the specific goals based on KUDs are established, the following are guiding questions to help design the specific assessment:

1. What strategies and structures can I use to best allow my students to demonstrate what they truly know, understand, and can do? Should the specific assessment be more traditional in format (paper and pencil) or online? Should it be a blend?

2. Should the assessment be differentiated and, if so, how?

3. How will I organize the assessment? Should the assessment escalate in challenge? Should it be organized by skill or topic? Should it be organized with a skills (Know) section and an explanation and conceptual (Understand) section?

4. What will I do with the information? Assessment information is valuable for so much more than grades. We tend to think of only using the information from preassessments and formative assessments for next-step instruction, but summative assessment data also let us know about how students are ready to move on to the next unit with confidence, which skills and understandings might need to be reinforced to move on, and which students might need to have some kind of remediation as they move on.

5. How will I keep track of the information?

6. How will students take action on their assessment information?

Before discussing the specifics for each type of assessment, consider one more form that can be used for any type of assessment: authentic performance assessment.

Authentic performance assessment creates a scenario in which students grapple with a real-world situation, come to a decision of some kind, and create an explanation or report with mathematical defense as evidence of learning. Authentic performance assessments are sometimes summative and can take the form of a project or larger task, but they can also be short formative assessments that are part of class instruction. Authentic performance assessments can even be posed as a preassessment to see how students reason about the application of the knowledge and understandings of the upcoming unit. Figure 7.1 gives an example of a formative authentic performance assessment for sixth- or seventh-grade geometry.

Often authentic performance assessments are summative in nature. Because these tend to be time-consuming and extensive, the task can be given at the start of the unit and can be worked on by students throughout the unit, as opposed to being given a large task at the end of the unit and needing many days for completion. The example in Figure 7.2 could be given at the beginning of an eighth-grade statistics or an Algebra 1 linear functions unit. As students progress through different topics throughout the unit, they can work on appropriate areas for their performance assessment. Figure 7.2 gives an example of an extensive summative authentic performance assessment of bivariate data, linear functions, scatterplots, and lines of best fit.

FIGURE 7.1

PAINTING DAY

Standard	Solve real-world and mathematical problems involving area, surface area, and volume.
Know	• Area formulas. • Surface area is a sum of individual areas of polygons found on the faces and bases of a polyhedra.
Understand	• Three-dimensional shapes are built from two-dimensional shapes. • Area covers and surface area wraps (volume fills and perimeter surrounds). • Only like things can be added or subtracted.
Do	• Apply area formulas to a real-world context. • Apply addition and subtraction of area in a real-world context.

For All:

I really want to have our classroom painted, but the district tells me it will cost too much money. They say I can paint it, if I pay for it. Since I am a broke teacher, I need your help to determine just how much this is going to cost.

Your task is to determine how much paint will we need and how much it will cost. You will write up a proposal with your findings, including diagrams with your measurements to help explain how your cost was determined.

Don't forget—we won't paint over the windows or the door, so do not include those. I also want to paint my stacking cubes (inside and out) where I store my books and stuff behind my desk so they match.

Thank you for your help!

Authentic Performance Task: Top Tier	The guy at Home Depot says I shouldn't use the same paint on the walls as on my stacking cubes. He says to use the enamel interior paint on the walls since it is a classroom and will clean easily. It costs $33.23 and covers about 350 square feet per gallon. On the cubes he recommends a less expensive paint. It will cost $28.97 and covers between 250 and 400 square feet per gallon. I think it will be very cool to paint geometric shapes on the wall with the paint I use for the cubes. I want to paint a huge circle with diameter of a yard (seventh grade) and miscellaneous quadrilaterals and triangles. Please sketch your cool geometry shape wall in your diagram and calculate the paint needed for the shapes.
	Tax where I live is 8.6%. That adds up, so don't forget to include it in your estimate.

Authentic Performance Task: Mid-Tier	The guy at Home Depot says to use the enamel interior paint on the walls since it is a classroom and will clean easily. It costs $33.23 and covers about 400 square feet per gallon. I think it will be very cool to paint geometric shapes on the wall with the paint I use for the cubes. I want to paint a circle (seventh grade) and miscellaneous quadrilaterals and triangles. Please sketch your cool geometry shape wall in your diagram and calculate the paint needed for the shapes. I'll use a cheaper paint on those and want to buy only what I need. The prices for that paint are $28.97 per gallon or a quart is $15.74 but only covers 100 square feet. Don't forget to add tax of 8.6%.
Authentic Performance Task: Lower Tier	The guy at Home Depot says to use the enamel interior paint on the walls since it is a classroom and will clean easily. It costs $33.23 and covers about 400 square feet per gallon. I think it will be very cool to paint geometric shapes on the wall with the paint I use for the cubes. I want to paint a circle (seventh grade) and miscellaneous quadrilaterals and triangles. Please sketch your cool geometry shape wall in your diagram and calculate the paint needed for the shapes. I'll use a cheaper paint on those and want to buy only what I need. The prices for that paint are $28.97 per gallon or a quart is $15.74 but only covers 100 square feet. Don't forget that you can find the area formulas you need on our Area Foldable or in the back of your book. When you work with π for this project, you will need to substitute 3.14 so you can calculate in terms of money. Don't leave π in the area this time. If you want a graphic organizer to help, just let me know. Don't forget to add tax of 8.6%.

Scoring Guide:	Points
Diagrams of walls, doors, and windows with dimensions	/4
Diagrams of geometric shapes	/2
Correct calculations of area(s)	/10
Correct calculations of paint needed	/2
Correct calculations of cost	/2
Written proposal with complete explanations of cost	/5
Total Points	/25

FIGURE 7.2

PROVE IT TO ME!

Standards	Construct and interpret scatterplots for bivariate measurement data to investigate patterns of association between two quantities. Describe patterns such as clustering, outliers, positive or negative association, linear association, and nonlinear association.
	Know that lines are widely used to model relationships between two quantitative variables. For scatterplots that suggest a linear association, informally fit a straight line, and informally assess the model fit by judging the closeness of the data points to the line.
	Use the equation of a linear model to solve problems in the context of bivariate measurement data, interpreting the slope and intercept.
Know	• Vocabulary: scatterplots, clustering, outliers, line of best fit, frequency, relative frequency, association
	• Positive or negative association in graphs
	• Linear association in graphs
	• Nonlinear association in graphs
	• Two-way tables
	• Relative frequency is the number of observations of a given type divided by the total number of observations.
Understand	• Data can be represented and analyzed in different ways.
	• Patterns in visual representations of data show important information about what is being
	o Researched
	o Analyzed
	o Questioned
	o Discovered
	• Functions can be used to model and analyze data.
Do	• Create a scatterplot with given data.
	• Interpret different types of patterns.
	• Construct a frequency table summarizing data collected from the same subject.
	• Fit a line of best fit when appropriate and use this to interpret rate of change or predicted values.

	• Describe type of association of data based on a scatterplot.
	• Defend a choice of representation for data and analysis.
	• Explain how functions can be used with data.

For all tasks:

Change is everywhere. Temperatures, populations, income, crime rates, pollution levels, stock prices, and so on, change. Sometimes change in one area affects another. For example, as the population changes in your hometown, the incidence of violent crime might change as well. You have already compiled a list of real-world changes that you believe may be linear and you have heard others' ideas as well.

You will now analyze a situation involving bivariate data that is happening in our world and make recommendations based on your findings. You may select an issue to research or two aspects that you believe are related such as time spent on social media per day and grade point average to determine correlation or causation.

You will take on the role of a professional involved in researching or gathering bivariate data on your area of interest. Examples of data analyst roles might include scientists, financial analysts, teachers, school principals or psychologists, or other professional positions required to gather and analyze data to make decisions or predictions.

Finally, you will have to put together a final report and presentation defending your research or data collection, conclusions, and the mathematics supporting your claims. Your presentation and report should be from the perspective of the professional you chose to represent.

(Note: The performance assessment is predominately interest differentiation as students choose their bivariate data and whether they will research a world situation or conduct their own survey to gather data.)

Part 1: Outline	Write a brief outline of your project, including
Date Due	• The issue being researched or data being gathered
_____	• The variables
	• How you expect to obtain the data needed (a minimum of _____ data points are required)
	• Your prediction about the data (what you expect to learn from the data)
	• _____ possible conclusions you might draw from this result
	(Note: The blanks in the number of data points and conclusions are left open so that the number can be determined based on the difficulty of the topic and the readiness of the student.)

(Continued)

FIGURE 7.2 (Continued)

Part 2: Research Date Due _____	Locate a source (or sources) to find the information you need. <ul><li>Identify the sources and record all of the data points you will be using, OR write your survey questions and describe your sampling technique. What data will you gather, and how will you display them?</li><li>Compile and graph the data on a poster to be used in a presentation.</li><li>Sketch a regression line for the data.</li><li>Find the equation of a line of best fit.</li><li>Write a brief summary interpreting the change in your project. For example, what does the slope of the regression line represent in your study?</li></ul>
Part 3: Conclusions Date Due _____	You will develop a list of at least ____ possible conclusions that you have reached based on your data. These conclusions must be specific. For example, "There will be over 5,000 murders in Phoenix in the year 2027" rather than "Murders will go up." You must be able to justify the numbers at which you arrive. (Note: The blank is filled in by teacher and student agreement based on the data being gathered and the readiness of the student.)
Part 4: Peer Critique Date Due _____	In groups of three to five, you will present your study data, graph, and conclusions. Each member of the group will critique all other members' presentations. You will rate each other on a 1 (very poor) to 5 (very good) scale in the following categories: <ul><li>Relevant, real data</li><li>Mathematical accuracy</li><li>Reasonableness of model (scatterplot, line of best fit)</li><li>Validity of conclusions</li><li>Attractiveness of poster and overall presentation</li></ul>
Part 5: Presentation Date Due _____	(Note: This is an optional section for the teacher because project presentations often take so much time and are generally not as beneficial as other types of presentations.) You will present your issue to the entire class as you did to the small group. You will choose one of your conclusions from Part 3 and defend this conclusion to the class using your data. You presentation must include the mathematics of your research and conclusions.

For the topic you are currently teaching in mathematics, make a list of all possible scenarios and professionals who use the skill or concept. This list can help give ideas and provide the roles and situations for a performance assessment. Use this list to sketch the initial idea for an authentic performance assessment. Would your idea be a preassessment, a formative assessment, or a summative assessment?

Please remember that no matter how you design your assessment, and whether it is differentiated by readiness, interest, or learning profile, the essential learning being assessed does not change.

DESIGNING EFFECTIVE ASSESSMENTS

When designing differentiated assessments, remember that whether differentiated or not, the purpose of the assessment needs to remain the focus. Any assessment strategy you currently use can be differentiated by readiness, interest, or learning profile.

DIFFERENTIATING ASSESSMENT FOR LEARNING: PREASSESSMENT

Assessment *for* learning informs teachers and students of where they are as they enter a new unit of learning. Preassessing a unit is essential if we are to determine how to most effectively provide the appropriate support and challenge for our students. Preassessment does not necessarily mean a pretest. You might try to use other forms to gather information rather than a test format for finding out what your students already know or don't know, or about what they might have misconceptions. Chapter 2 gives several examples of formats for preassessment.

In designing an effective preassessment, consider the following:

- The Know and Understand from the unit design. Isolate the most important skills, formulations, processes, and the undergirding understandings that make sense of the knowledge.

- The Do list that describes what students will be able to do as a result of both knowing and understanding the content of the unit. This will help guide the formation of the specific task or questions used in the preassessment.

- The prerequisite learning in order to be successful. List the essential prerequisite skills coming into the unit. Be sure that you think about what is truly essential—what do students need to know and understand in advance to be successful with the new unit?

These points will provide the content for the preassessment. The next group of considerations is the structure and possible differentiation of the preassessment. With a preassessment, the goal is to find out where students are in relation to the upcoming unit. To do this, the structure of the task should not prevent students from being able to show what they know and understand.

- What structures will best allow students to demonstrate their current knowledge and understanding?

- Should the preassessment be differentiated? If so, how?

  o Readiness—Provide a word bank to stimulate key vocabulary and ideas and allow multiple methods for explanation, including pictures, modeling, or oral explanations with scaffolded examples.

  o Interest—Provide options for students to choose how to show their learning. Give several questions to assess a given learning objective and allow students to choose which one or two they want to complete. Another interest differentiation would be to provide multiple formats, such as traditional mathematical work, models, sketches, multiple representations, or explanations, from which students can choose.

  o Learning profile—Design assessment tasks according to one of the learning profile structures (see Chapter 4). Allow students to choose which format to use.

A final consideration in planning the preassessment is when to give it. Often teachers begin their units with preassessment. However, to effectively use the information from the assessment, it should be given several days in advance to allow the information to be analyzed and to plan the start of the unit accordingly. If the preassessment is given as the first step in the new unit, there is no time to analyze and plan. You are already starting. In addition, if the preassessment is given as a whole-class discussion (as is often the case when developing a Know–Want to know–I have Learned chart or other whole-class structure), the information often shows what the most vocal or most advanced students know rather than specific information about each student. Be sure that whatever preassessment you choose to give, individual students are responsible for showing what they truly know.

Figure 7.3 shows a Preassessment Planning Template.

Specific strategies and examples of preassessment are given in Chapter 2 and are included there as a method for assessing for students' readiness.

Using Preassessment Information

Preassessment data are used to determine the best methods of beginning a unit. These data will predominantly be about your students' readiness in relation to the upcoming unit. As such, how you begin will depend on what your information reveals.

To begin to make sense of your data, sort the students' work into piles showing significant differences in relation to demonstration of the KUDs. This may take some different tries to determine the *significant* differences. It might be easy to see which students have mastered the prerequisite information and which have not, or which students already know some of the strategies that are upcoming in the unit and which have no clue. This might sound straightforward, but we also know there could be students who are approaching mastery in some areas but not in others, or students who are able to solve specific types of problems but are not able to explain mathematically the meanings of the operations and/or properties involved, why the process is correct, or why their answers are reasonable. Certainly, we will see students who can correctly use a process to solve a "naked number" problem or graph a function, for example, but then cannot transfer their knowledge to a contextual application. Sorting and resorting students' work along different criteria will give a full picture of the entry points of all of your students.

With the full picture of where students are in relation to the beginning of the unit, the first few days can be planned. Begin with the initial concepts and overview of the unit. All students

Consider It!

- How have student differences been apparent as you begin new units of study? How have you previously addressed these differences at the start of a unit?

- What are the advantages of giving a preassessment several days before the unit begins (during the previous unit)? What are the disadvantages?

FIGURE 7.3

PREASSESSMENT PLANNING TEMPLATE

Unit Title _____

Date _____

From the unit design, list the specific **Know, Understand,** and **Do** that need to be assessed.

Know	
Understand	
Do	

Based on the content of the unit, what essential knowledge/skills and understanding should students *already* have in order to be successful in this unit?

Know	
Understand	

What structures, designs or strategies will best access students' learning?

Possible structures, designs or strategies for the assessment	

Does the preassessment need to be differentiated? If so how, and for whom?

How?	Differentiation	For Whom? (list names)
Readiness		
Interest		
Learning Profile		

 The full template can be downloaded at resources.corwin.com/ everymathlearner6-12.

should participate in this discussion or activity to develop common vocabulary, concepts, and direction. The next task will most likely be differentiated according to the preassessment data. Consider various stations or tasks to develop the first skill or concept in your unit. For students who have already demonstrated proficiency, design a related task, interest application, or a processing task that asks students to explain the "how and why" of the objective. This strategy for planning can continue to be used as the unit develops but will be based on more current and accurate formative assessment.

DIFFERENTIATING ASSESSMENT AS LEARNING: CHECKS FOR UNDERSTANDING, THE FORMATIVE ASSESSMENT PROCESS, AND STUDENT SELF-ASSESSMENT

Most often, assessment *as* learning is referred to as "ongoing assessments." These broad terms encompass many moments in daily instruction, from simple checks for understanding, to engagement in a full formative assessment process that provides students with feedback, to students' self-evaluations. What these three types of assessments have in common is that they occur throughout the unit and let both the teacher and students know how students are progressing with their learning.

Checks for Understanding

Checks for understanding provide the teacher with information about where the students are in the moment. They can be formal or informal. Figure 7.4 provides several descriptions of checks for understanding.

Anything that happens in a classroom can and should serve as a check for understanding—even simply paying attention to the types of questions and comments students make. The trick is to keep track of the information you are observing for each student.

The Formative Assessment Process

Formative assessment is the area of assessment often discussed because of its importance in learning. It is so important that it has reached the status of initials: FA! However, the interpretation of just what is formative assessment is sometimes dependent on the school, district, or book you are reading. The term *formative assessments*

FIGURE 7.4

CHECKS FOR UNDERSTANDING

Strategy	Example
Signals	Signals can be anything from thumbs up, down, and sideways; fist of five with 0 = no clue, 1 = just beginning, 2 = a little bit, 3 = pretty good, 4 = strong, and 5 = I can teach this; windshield checks have students compare their understanding to a windshield covered in mud, splatted by bugs, somewhat spotty, or crystal clear. Another signal can be red, yellow, and green cups or paper tents signaling whether the students are full steam ahead, getting stuck, or completely stopped. Signals can be used before, during, or after a specific problem. If before, ask who thinks they know what this problem means and how to start. If after, ask how students did, and if during, use the signal as a device to provide help.
Exit or Entry Cards	Exit or entry cards have no more than three questions posed specifically related to the day's lesson (exit card) or the previous lesson or homework (entry card). Teachers can use exit cards to assess how well students understood the lesson and then group students accordingly in readiness groups when beginning the next day's lesson. Entry cards can be sorted into readiness groups as well. Entry or exit cards are completely flexible. They can be anything from sample questions, a written explanation of a process or concept, or a "find the error" type of task. One type of exit card often used is a 3-2-1 card that asks the following: Three tips for solving the problems we did today are . . . Two connections I can make between the problems and big ideas are . . . One question I still have is . . .
White Boards	White boards are used for students to hold up individual work or short answers to specific questions that could include vocabulary, true/false, or always, sometimes, and never style questions. White boards can also be used as a means for groups to report out after discussing a problem. The "scribe" should change within the group with each problem. Another way to use white boards in class is to have students sit back-to-back and, when both partners have finished working, turn and compare their work. This adds an element of fun to the process. The partners work out any differences in their work, compare solution paths, and discuss any other points of interest. The teacher monitors and records the pairs' solutions and paths.
Any Written Work	Recording evidence of learning from written work or groups' conversations can serve as checks for understanding as long as the information is recorded. It can be recorded in check sheets against standards or learning objectives, on index cards in a card file or a flipchart, or on electronic devices.

has been used to describe purchased, standardized tests administered at prescribed intervals; benchmarks created by a district team; quizzes and homework; and various other descriptors or tools. For our purposes, though, formative assessment has a broader definition. It is the process of evaluating anything that occurs in the classroom that will give the teacher insight into students' mathematical understanding, provide specific feedback to students on which they will take action, and allow teachers to make instructional choices in response to student understanding.

John Hattie (2012) suggests that the effect size of providing feedback to students is 0.75, which puts it in about the top 10 influences on achievement. However, the effect size of engaging in a formative assessment process (or formative evaluation, as Hattie calls it), which involves using assessment data *as* learning and provides students *with* feedback, has a walloping 0.9 effect size.

So if we are to think of formative assessment as more of a process (Popham, 2011) than a task, to be effective,

- specific and timely feedback must be provided to students,

- students must be actively involved in their own learning and take action on the provided feedback,

- teachers react to and make adjustments to the teaching trajectory based on their professional noticing and assessment data,

- students must self-assess and take steps or set goals to improve, and

- teachers must recognize the effect that assessment has on motivation and the self-esteem of students (Wiliam, 2011).

Furthermore, formative assessment can be formal or informal, graded or not graded.

In order for a formative assessment to have the fullest effect on learning that it can have, feedback and students taking action on the feedback must be a priority. In addition, not just any feedback will do. Several qualities determine if the feedback being given will be effective (Tomlinson & Moon, 2013; Wiggins, 2012; Wiliam, 2011). Figure 7.5 gives the criteria and descriptions of effective feedback.

Consider It!

What separates a formative assessment and a check for understanding? What are the benefits of each in a lesson?

FIGURE 7.5

FEEDBACK CRITERIA

Characteristic	Description
Understandable	Feedback needs to be provided in such a way that the student understands what is meant. Be sure students understand any shorthand notations or academic vocabulary that might be written. If providing verbal feedback, ask the student to echo back what he or she is hearing or to ask you a follow-up question.
Specific and Focused	Students need to know precisely what to do to improve, and feedback should enable students to persevere with the mathematical task. For example, "Be careful" or "Close!" may not be clear to the student as to where he or she needs to attend. "You have several arithmetic errors" and "Watch the labeling of your graph" are more specific and understandable without providing the correction to errors. Feedback should be focused on the learning objectives to keep a narrowed intent on improvement.
Accurate	It is possible to give students feedback that is not accurate because the mistake a teacher assumes a student is making is not actually the reason for the error. Be sure to find out why an error occurred by asking "Explain what happened at this step" when giving immediate feedback. Be sure that the feedback provided will help students understand the mathematical task or devise a corrected solution pathway.
Frequent and Timely	Feedback needs to be provided as "in the moment" as possible. You are the best provider of feedback, but student-to-student feedback should be taught and encouraged as part of the mathematical practices and discourse. As you circulate through the room, listen for these conversations and affirm or correct the feedback being given. Be sure to not stay more than 19 seconds with any group of students in order to keep circulating and offering feedback that is timely. (Kanold, 2016)
Action Oriented	Feedback should enable students to take the next step in understanding and completing the mathematical task. It should be explicit enough for students to take action without doing the work for the student.
Differentiated	Feedback can be used to stretch students' learning when appropriate or can be used to help students get "unstuck." Some questions and prompts may be preplanned and are called "advancing questions," to help students move beyond and extend their mathematical understandings and skill, and "assessing questions," to help students move forward when they are stuck (Kanold & Larson, 2012). In addition, different models, manipulatives, representations, and suggestions may be offered as feedback based on how students best make sense of the mathematical content.

As described earlier, the formative assessment process has one of the largest impacts on student learning of anything we do in the classroom. James Popham (2011) states that "recent reviews of more than four thousand research investigations highlight that when the (formative assessment) process is well-implemented in the classroom, it can essentially double the speed of student learning, producing large gains in students' achievement. At the same time, it is sufficiently robust so different teachers can use it in diverse ways and still get great results with their students" (p. 63).

When planning for formative assessment, consider the following:

- The specific K, U, and/or D on which the lesson is focused. Lessons may be about building a specific skill, so the focus will only be on specific Know targets from the unit design. Other times, they may be concept-building lessons or a combination. The formative assessment will target the lesson's learning objective.

- How will effective feedback be given to students? Who will provide it? Will you circulate among students to provide feedback, will feedback be given from peers, or will there be a combination of both?

- When will time be provided for students to take action on the feedback? Will it be simultaneous with the feedback? Given as homework?

When engaging in the formative assessment process, the best source for uncovering student learning on which to provide feedback is to employ tasks that are high level and multifaceted.

Chapter 3 describes how to "teach up" to ensure these types of tasks. In addition, all of the strategies and activities in Chapter 4 can be used as formative assessments. Figure 7.6 shows a student's work on a complex task.

FIGURE 7.6

STUDENT WORK ON AREA

The Fencing Task

Ms. Brown's class will raise rabbits for their spring science fair. They have 24 feet of fencing with which to build a rectangular rabbit pen in which to keep the rabbits.

- If Ms. Brown's students want their rabbits to have as much room as possible, how long would each of the sides of the pen be?

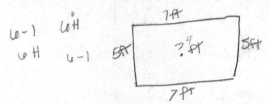

- How long would each of the sides of the pen be if they have only 16 feet of fencing?

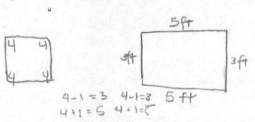

- How would you go about determining the pen with the most room for any amount of fencing? Organize your work so that someone else who reads it will understand it.

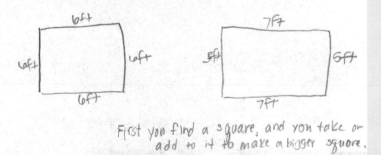

Problem Source: Stein, Smith, Henningsen, & Silver, 2009, p. 2. Student work © Abigail Williams.

What feedback would you give the student (Figure 7.6) on her work? List what you would ask and suggest for her next steps.

Using Ongoing Assessment Information

Once again, ongoing assessment data are used to help teachers and students evaluate what the next learning steps should be. In an algebra class, students were working with rational exponents and translating between exponential and standard numeric forms. Based on an exit card, the teacher determined that some students had mastery of rational exponents (Group 1). There were students who either correctly translated with integer exponents but not with other rational exponents or correctly translated with fractional exponents but did not correctly interpret a negative exponent, but not both (Group 2). Some students confused or did not correctly translate the majority of rational exponents (Group 3). Figure 7.7 shows the tasks given to groups of students based on their exit cards.

FIGURE 7.7

NEXT STEPS WITH RATIONAL EXPONENTS

Group	Task
Group 1	Students were asked to explain why the steps for translating rational exponents worked and how they could either be remembered or could be recovered if they were not remembered. They were given a choice of the following: • Design a step-by-step problem example with explanations for each type of rational exponent, followed by "tips to remember" and "if you do forget. . . ." • Create a "Visual Guide to Rational Exponents" with pictures and diagrams to explain each type of exponent. On the left page are examples and steps visually, and on the opposing right page are the tips and what to do if you forget.

(Continued)

FIGURE 7.7 (Continued)

	• Compose a rap or jingle to remember and explain how to work with rational exponents. • Make a cheat sheet for an upcoming quiz on rational exponents. Include every type of rational exponent we have encountered as well as the mathematics behind the process, how to remember what to do with each type, and what to do if you do forget on the quiz. As an additional bonus and challenge, a list of equations with rational exponents was provided to see if students could logically move beyond translation to solving the equations. This was optional but highly encouraged.
Group 2	Students were paired with mixed strengths—one student who is strong with integer exponents (Student A) with a student strong in fractional exponents (Student B). They teach each other from their strength and practice together translating all rational exponent problems. The task is structured as follows: • Student A teaches Student B the role of a negative sign with exponents. • Student B practices problem set with integer exponents. • Student B teaches Student A how to handle fractional exponents translating to roots. • Student A practices a problem set with fractional exponents. • Both students alternate being "Hands and Brain" where the brain tells the hands what to write on a mixed practice set of all rational exponents. • As a conclusion, students craft a mathematical explanation as to why rational exponents mean what they do and how to remember each type.
Group 3	These students began with the teacher for a reteach on rational exponents. The reteach began by reviewing operations with whole-number exponents, especially division and a power raised to another power as these would be important to understand rational exponents. The teacher then emphasized the role of a negative in an exponent and why fractional exponents are really roots by using the laws of exponents, which they had just reviewed. They were then asked to work in pairs on the Group 2 assignment.

All students were able to reach the required standard of translating between rational exponents and standard numerical representation, and most were able to explain the mathematical reasoning undergirding the representations. Many students were able to move beyond converting between the representation to solving equations.

Student Self-Assessment

One area of assessment that is often overlooked is having students assess their own learning. In fact, students often do not think about their learning as they are learning but often feel that you either get it or you don't (see growth mindset in Chapter 5) and are surprised by their quiz or test scores. Student self-reflections can be just about anything from rating their effort and success on a specific skill from 0 to 5 or marking specific problems with a ! to represent that they feel certain they are correct, a ? to represent that they think they are correct but are not really sure, or an X to describe that they tried but are pretty sure they aren't correct. Journal prompts and other writing opportunities (exit cards, reflection questions on homework, tasks, quizzes, or tests) are very appropriate as a means for students to self-reflect on how things are going. Figure 7.8 gives examples of possible self-reflection tools for individuals as well as groups.

FIGURE 7.8

STUDENT SELF-REFLECTION TOOLS

Description	Tool
A) Class Self-Assessment, My Math Today	My Math Today NAME: _____ PERIOD_____ 0 = did not do 2 = did most of the time 1 = did but just barely 3 = did consistently **In class today, I chose to** **SCORE SELF:** ☐ Pay attention throughout class 0 1 2 3 ☐ Take notes thoroughly 0 1 2 3 ☐ Participate actively in class 0 1 2 3 ☐ Ask questions (in or after class) 0 1 2 3 ☐ Work effectively in my group or with my partner 0 1 2 3 **To continue learning, I choose to** **SCORE SELF:** ☐ Spend more time on homework and use notes 0 1 2 3 ☐ Study a little each night 0 1 2 3 ☐ Ask for extra practice on a current topic or to review a basic skill 0 1 2 3 ☐ Preview/read the next section in the textbook 0 1 2 3 ☐ Compare/read class notes 0 1 2 3 ☐ Other: _____ 0 1 2 3 STUDENT SIGNATURE: _____ My Math Today

(Continued)

FIGURE 7.8 (Continued)

B) Individual Goal Setting	

Individual Goal Setting

My goal(s) for this semester are

1. _____

2. _____

3. _____

To accomplish this I will need to

1. _____

2. _____

3. _____

So this week I will

1. _____

2. _____

3. _____

Checkpoint: On a scale of 0–5, how did I do on my goals for this week?

	Monday	Tuesday	Wednesday	Thursday	Friday
Goal 1					
Goal 2					
Goal 3					

C) Group Self-Assessment

Group Self-Assessment

Name of Students on Team: _____

Criteria	Not	OK	Yes	Awesome
1. We stayed on task.	0	1	2	3
2. We respected whoever was speaking by not interrupting and by valuing what was shared.	0	1	2	3
3. We helped one another.	0	1	2	3
4. We asked clarifying questions if we didn't understand or agree.	0	1	2	3
5. We ensured that all members understood and were actively participating.	0	1	2	3
6. Our team excelled by				

_____

_____

7. We could do better as a team on the following areas next time:

_____

_____

8. Additional comments

_____

_____

NAME: _____ **PERIOD** _____

D) Self-Reflection Following Assessment	

Student Self-Reflection Following Formal Assessment

Please review and reflect on your assessment and then fill in the following information

I did well and know and understand thoroughly:	I did okay, but do not thoroughly know or understand:	I do not know or understand:

I still need to work on	To do so I will

I worked carefully and checked my work and answers on these problems:	I worked carefully OR checked my answer on these problems:	I didn't really check anything, I just did these problems:

To be a better test taker next time, I will

The full tools can be downloaded at resources.corwin.com/everymathlearner6-12.

Assessments *for* and *as* learning are largely differentiated. Throughout the unit, we are concerned that students learn the mathematics content fully, in whatever manner will best work for them. Sprinkled throughout the unit should be standardized assessments that model any high-stakes test the students may encounter and to measure student progress strictly against the standards. If you are planning an authentic performance assessment as a summative assessment for the unit, there should be more standardized formative assessments throughout the unit because the summative assessment is nonstandard. If, however, you are planning a traditional test for the summative assessment, use more differentiated nonstandard formative assessments throughout the unit.

DIFFERENTIATING ASSESSMENT OF LEARNING: SUMMATIVE ASSESSMENT

Summative assessments usually occur at the end of a unit, but any cumulative assessment can be regarded as a summative assessment. These may be mid-unit quizzes or other assessments, district or quarterly benchmark exams, or any other assessment that evaluates students' progress at a particular point in time. Summative assessments can be in the form of a paper-and-pencil assessment, a presentation, or an authentic performance assessment. The key to designing a valuable summative assessment is that it remains true to the learning goals of the unit as determined by the unit's standards and KUD. When designing a summative assessment, be sure to

- Reflect the same importance of the learning goals on the assessment as in the unit. On the summative assessment, the number of items relating to a particular standard or K, U, or D should be in the same proportion as the instruction and tasks throughout the unit.

- The depth of the questions or tasks on an assessment should be at the same level of cognitive demand as throughout the unit and as specified by the standard. I know a few teachers who believe that "being rigorous" means giving exceedingly difficult assessments. On the other hand, I know teachers who give relatively easy summative assessments so that students do not struggle too much. Neither of these is the correct stance. The rigor and depth of complexity (not difficulty) of the assessment is determined by the standard.

- If differentiated applications, strategies, or methods were used throughout the unit, they should also be reflected in the assessment.

Consider It!

What are the pros and cons of differentiating a summative assessment? What are the possible concerns or constraints?

Summative assessments may be differentiated by readiness, interest, and learning profile as well, but carefully.

Readiness differentiation should allow students to show what they know, understand, and are able to do. Readiness differentiation strategies could include the following:

- Including multiple representations and solution paths for equal value

- Providing manipulatives, reference tools, and so on, as needed, or space on a test designated as sketches or drawings to simulate a manipulative

- Providing oral or pictorial mathematical explanations

- Giving a word bank to stimulate thinking

- Scaffolding questions with some parts filled in

- Formatting a test with larger print and more writing space

Interest and learning profile differentiation on a summative assessment may include the following:

- Having a section on a test that is required for all students, but also providing a bank of questions and point values and allowing students to choose problems to acquire a certain number of points

- Giving a choice of the applications for a topic on which to be assessed

- Providing choices in format for the assessment: traditional paper and pencil, creating a presentation or lesson on the topic, creating a test and answer key, or "designing" a textbook chapter on the topic

- Designing authentic performance assessments that allow for multiple roles or products

TIP FOR ELL/SPECIAL EDUCATION STUDENTS

Be sure that any Individualized Education Plan (IEP) or 504 accommodations are strictly followed when designing assessments. For ELL learners, consider providing a word bank with diagrams to help students write explanations, or allow other methods for explanation such as pictures or demonstrations. Record instructions and questions in the students' native language if possible, or use models, pictures, and/or gestures to help students understand the tasks and expectations.

To guarantee the validity of the summative assessment, no matter the design or differentiation, ensure that the same learning targets are being assessed in the same proportion and at the same depth of knowledge on every version.

CONCLUSION

Assessments are to be a way of determining students' progress toward the learning goals as established by the unit's standards and corresponding KUD. Assessment allows us to make "next-step" decisions about assessment. Differentiated assessments allow us to truly determine what students know, understand, and are able to do based on the content and not on the structure by which we ask them to perform. These same assessments should serve as a method of reflection for our students as they also self-assess and determine their own next steps in learning.

The structure or design of an assessment is not as critical as the content that it assesses. Almost any strategy can be used for preassessments, checks for understanding, and formative assessments. Mathematical summative assessments most often tend to be paper and pencil, presentation, or an authentic performance assessment.

Finally, do not confuse grading and assessing. Assessments inform instruction for both the teacher and the student. Grades merely record some form of percentage or other measure of proficiency at a given point in time.

FREQUENTLY ASKED QUESTIONS

Q: Is it fair if tests are differentiated?

A: Assessments, including tests, are to measure what students know, understand, and are able to do in regard to specific learning targets at a specific point in time. The structure of the test or assessment should not restrict the students' ability to show their learning. In some ways, differentiated assessments are more fair than nondifferentiated. With that understanding, it is also important to realize that part of mathematics is the ability to write and solve problems. There are times when paper-and-pencil assessments are the appropriate measure and other options should not be used. In the same way, not all assessments need to be differentiated, but neither should all assessments be exactly the same for all students all of the time.

Q: What about grading?

A: The first principle of grading in a differentiated classroom (in fact, in all classrooms) is that not everything should be graded. Students should not rely on a grade as motivation in order to complete tasks. Grades tend to shut down intrinsic motivation and also end learning. There is ample research evidence on the importance of feedback over grades for learning (O'Connor, 2009; Reeves, 2015; Wiggins, 2012). With that established, for most of us, grades are a necessary evil, so it is important to grade against the learning targets regardless of the specific task or differentiation. The most consistent strategy for this is to design a rubric based on the mathematical expectation. If desired, a nominal number of points could be assigned for the quality and neatness of the work or individual requirements of a specific task.

Keepsakes and Plans

What are the keepsake ideas from this chapter, those thoughts or ideas that resonated with you that you do not want to forget?

Assessment for, of, and as Learning:

1.

2.

3.

Principles to Develop Assessments:

1.

2.

3.

Designing and Using Preassessments (for Learning):

1.

2.

3.

Designing and Using Ongoing Assessments (as Learning):

1.

2.

3.

Designing and Using Summative Assessments (of Learning):

1.

2.

3.

Based on my keepsake ideas, I plan to:

1.

2.

CHAPTER EIGHT

CLOSE UP

A WEEK IN THE LIFE OF A DIFFERENTIATED MATHEMATICS CLASSROOM

The goal of this book has been to bring the various pieces and the process of differentiating mathematics instruction together for you, step-by-step, into a cohesive and doable endeavor. But what does it look and sound like once all the pieces are in place?

In this chapter, you will find the following:

A Look Into a Week in a Middle School Classroom

A Look Into a Week in a High School Classroom

Advice From the Field

The content chosen for this chapter was selected for its transferability. Working correctly with integers is fundamental to all future work with equations and functions. A focus on solving linear equations begins in sixth grade and builds in skill and principles through every grade and course throughout high school. In an advanced algebra course, students use their prior knowledge and understanding to work with polynomials, radical and rational equations, and functions.

A LOOK INTO A WEEK IN A MIDDLE SCHOOL CLASSROOM

OPERATING ON INTEGERS

Joshua Christopher, a seventh-grade teacher, is planning his unit on integers and integer operations. Mr. Christopher builds his unit by focusing on the group of standards addressed throughout the unit—especially the Know, Understand, and Do (KUD) he developed with his grade-level team for the unit. He understands the importance of developing understanding with his students, particularly the concept of a negative sign meaning "opposite," and plans to begin the unit slowly to solidify that understanding. Mr. Christopher believes that he will be able to move more quickly through the operations with integers if students fully understand and can transfer this understanding. He develops lessons by using resources and activities he already has as well as finding new resources online.

The standards make it appear that this unit is primarily about computation, but Mr. Christopher is aware of the importance of being able to accurately calculate and explain the role of integers as his students move forward in algebra and especially with solving equations. Because of this knowledge, he will build time for students to experiment with the operations of integers through two primary models: the number line and two-color counters. He plans to have his students gain experience through working with integer models and having them recognize and summarize the patterns they see. This summarization will become the source of the "rules" or procedures for operating with integers, rather than giving students the steps for solving integer problems and having them practice them, as more traditional textbooks and approaches have done in the past.

FROM UNIT TO LESSON PLAN

As Mr. Christopher begins the unit, he knows from his preassessment and earlier conversations that some of his students do not remember any discussions of integers from sixth grade, their descriptive role in the world, or how to order or place them on the number line. Some students can discuss positive and negative numbers in context and can place them on a number line, but they confuse the ordering of negative numbers. Another smaller group of students is fluent with describing positive and negative numbers, placing integers on the number line, and ordering integers, but none of the students in class have an understanding of negative as "opposite" or any experience with operations of integers. As Mr. Christopher makes initial plans for the unit, he begins with the standards, KUDs, and possible assessments on the unit-planning document. Figure 8.1 shows the unit plan for Mr. Christopher's unit.

Mr. Christopher uses his Math Planning Calendar to sketch out his daily lessons for the unit, which will last approximately 3 weeks. He begins his lesson planning by planning the daily big ideas and skills for the unit, as well as some of the activities that he has that will fit with each day's objectives. He plans to differentiate

---

FIGURE 8.1

"OPERATING ON INTEGERS" UNIT PLAN

Unit Title: **Operating on Integers**

Standards Addressed (from Common Core State Standards, NGO and CCSSO, 2010):

Understand that positive and negative numbers describe quantities having opposite values and directions on the number line.

Apply and extend previous understandings of addition and subtraction to add and subtract rational numbers (*integers only in this unit*); represent addition and subtraction on a horizontal or vertical number line diagram.

Apply and extend previous understandings of multiplication and division and of fractions to multiply and divide rational numbers (*integers only in this unit*).

By the end of the unit, what will students come to . . .

(Continued)

FIGURE 8.1 (Continued)

Know	Understand	Be Able to Do
Vocabulary: absolute value, integer, negative, number system, opposite, positive, zero pair	A negative in mathematics always means "the opposite."	Model integers and integer operations in different ways
The layout of a number line	Any number is a member of one or more number systems, and each number system has clearly defined properties including operations.	Apply and compute operations with integers
How to model integers and integer operations with two-color counters and number lines		Explain the relationships between positive and negative numbers
Notation of absolute value and integers	Mathematical operations apply to and follow the same patterns within our number systems and mathematical disciplines.	Apply integers to and solve real-world situations
How to add, subtract, multiply, and divide integers		

Preassessment Ideas:

Frayer Times Four: **Vocabulary**: 16 problems (5 + 3; 5 + (–3); –5 + 3; –5 + (–3). This pattern with addition is repeated with subtraction, multiplication, and division); **Short answer**: Describe what a negative means in mathematics and how you can see this meaning on a number line, in operations, and anywhere else. **Representations**: Show any methods, pictures, or rules that you know about working with integers.

Summative Assessment Ideas:

You are a Target store manager in charge of balancing your store's inventory and budget. You will calculate a month's inventory purchasing and sales using your knowledge of integers (since for the IRS everything rounds to the nearest dollar). You will give a monthly summary including your balance sheet and written explanation of the balance to your boss.

Formative Assessment Ideas:

Guided practice, independent practice, classroom observations, exit cards, modeling, mini-quiz over addition/subtraction and multiplication/division

Resources:

Number lines, two-color counters, chart paper (construction paper), markers

 The full unit plan can be downloaded at resources.corwin.com/everymathlearner6-12.

each day's lesson from the day's goal and/or topic, as well as any information from prior lessons that informs decisions about what his students need to best move forward in learning. His initial planning calendar is shown in Figure 8.2.

FIGURE 8.2

OPERATING ON INTEGERS PLANNING CALENDAR

Math Planning Calendar

Unit: Operating on Integers

Duration: 3 weeks

Monday	Tuesday	Wednesday	Thursday	Friday
10/10 What is opposite, and why do I care? Intro Integers / Number Systems Number line, two-color counters, absolute value and zero pairs	10/11 Thinking about addition Part 1 – Real-world contexts, model with number lines and counters	10/12 Thinking about addition Part 2 – Number lines and counters, Integer War Patterns if time	10/13 Thinking about addition Part 3 – Number lines and counters, Finding Patterns and Efficiency Nod and trade if time	10/14 Thinking about subtraction Part 1 – "Pick Up, Put Down" Using Addition to Understand Subtraction. If time, begin number lines and counters
10/17 Thinking about subtraction Part 2 – Number lines and counters, "Adding the Opposite," Subtraction Integer War, finding the patterns	10/18 Adding and subtracting integers – mixed practice with contexts and naked number problems	10/19 Assessment addition and subtraction Challenge: How do you think adding and subtracting integers applies to other rational numbers?	10/20 Thinking about multiplication Part 1 – Real-world contexts, Opposites of Opposites, Frog and Hop game	10/21 Thinking about multiplication Part 2 – Real-world contexts, making sense with counters and repeated addition, Finding the patterns
10/24 Properties of operations and integers and interesting patterns	10/25 Thinking about division – Using multiplication to make sense of division, counters, finding patterns	10/26 Assessment multiplication and division	10/27 Mixed practice – all operations and problem solving	10/28 Summative Authentic Performance Assessment

 The completed calendar for this unit and a blank planning calendar can be downloaded at resources.corwin.com/everymathlearner6-12.

Throughout the unit, Mr. Christopher will reinforce two primary tools for integers: the number line and two-color counters. These tools not only will serve to represent integers but also will be used to build the conceptual understanding involved with operating on integers and provide a method for students to discover the steps or "rules" of integer operations on their own. Students can also use these tools as strategies for solving integer problems as they grow in their knowledge and fluency. He plans to use counters and number lines as he introduces concepts and skills but will make sure that they are tools for understanding only and thus will not pressure students to become facile with them if they are not proving to be helpful to develop understanding and fluency. Along with using these concrete strategies to model integer operations, he will also continue to reinforce the essential understandings for the unit through modeling, differentiated activities, questioning, and discourse.

Another constant throughout the unit, and in fact daily in Mr. Christopher's mathematics class, is the Standard for Mathematical Practice (SMP) 3, constructing viable arguments and critiquing the reasoning of others. Mr. Christopher does not list this on every lesson plan as he realizes that it is the most common component of his daily mathematics class.

The understanding that a negative sign in mathematics means opposite is the primary emphasis to reinforce why integers operate in the manner they do. This understanding will be built into conversations every day and exemplified by using the "opposite direction" on the number line, or "opposite sides" of the two-color counters. He knows that this foundational understanding about negatives and integers in general will be important throughout his students' mathematics career.

DAILY PLANNING—DAY 1

Mr. Christopher draws on his preassessment information to decide how to best begin the unit. He wants to start the unit slowly to build a solid concept of positive and negative integers as opposites. This first day of the unit will be spent making sense of the terms *positive* and *negative* through contexts and building foundations for opposites and zero pairs. He will also introduce the two tools, number line, and two-color counters and ask students to use both representations to construct zero pairs. The standards for mathematical practice in this lesson will concentrate on SMP 4 (models), SMP 5 (tools), SMP 6 (precision with vocabulary and notation), and SMP 8 (patterns of adding integers).

FIGURE 8.3

DAY 1 LESSON PLAN

Operating on Integers Lesson Plan – Day 1

Date: 10/10

Standards:
Understand that positive and negative numbers are used together to describe quantities having opposite directions or values.

Highlighted Standards for Mathematical Practice:
SMP4: Model with mathematics.
SMP5: Use appropriate tools strategically.
SMP6: Attend to precision.
SMP8: Look for and express regularity in repeated reasoning.

Know:

- Vocabulary: absolute value, integer, negative, number system, opposite, positive, zero pair
- The layout of a number line
- How to model integers and integer operations with two-color counters and number lines
- Notation of absolute value and integers

Understand:

- A negative in mathematics always means "the opposite."
- Any number is a member of one or more number systems, and each number system has clearly defined properties including basic operations.

Be Able to Do:

- Model integers and integer operations in different ways
- Explain the relationships between positive and negative numbers

Whole Class:

1. Ask students to find a partner and brainstorm everything they can think of that has to do with the words "positive" and "negative." It does not have to be limited to math—it can be in their lives, other subjects, or anything at all they can think of. To record their ideas, choose one of the following (interest differentiation):

- Make a bulleted list
- Draw pictures
- Create a word splash
- Make a two-column table (+ and –)
- A record of your choosing other than "we'll just remember."

Finally summarize, how can you explain the relationship between positive and negative? (Get students to the point of understanding they are opposite.)

(Continued)

FIGURE 8.3 (Continued)

2. Discussion and Notes:

- Numbers can also be positive and negative—and we just decided that this describes an opposite. So what is the opposite of 12? (–12) What is the opposite of –6? (6) In math, when you see a negative sign, you can think opposite. We will keep coming back to that idea.

- We describe situations with positive and negative numbers. For example, when you lose points on a test, you see "minus 1" which is written as –1. That is also a "negative 1." If you give me $5, I gained money and can write it as +5. Give several examples and ask students the number to describe the situation.

- Introduce Integers
  - Any number can be positive or negative, except for 0, which we say is neither positive—or negative.
  - Positive and negative whole numbers and zero make up "integers." Give examples of positive and negative numbers and have students say yes or no for integer.
  - All positive and negative whole numbers and fractions, and zero, are called rational numbers—we'll talk about those next unit.

Note: With modeling below, show the notation of absolute value, negative numbers with parentheses as needed, and that we are really adding opposite numbers as an equation.

- Models for Integers
  - Number line (work in definition of absolute value here)
  - Two-color counters
- Zero Pairs
  - Model with contexts
  - Model on number line
  - Model with counters

Small Group:

Groups of 3 (choice of partners): Hands, brain, and pencil activity. After each specific task, roles rotate so with each task students have a different job.

1. Model absolute values—brain tells hands what to do or write, pencil records the notation
   a. Show an absolute value of 4 on number line (repeat twice to get both possibilities)
   b. Show an absolute value of 8 with counters (repeat twice to get both possibilities)
2. Model making a zero and record the equation.
   a. With a number line model, brain tells hands how to draw to make a zero pair with addition (repeat three times to have all students experience all three roles)
   b. With two-color counters, brain tells hands how to draw to make a zero pair with addition (repeat three times to have all students experience all three roles)
3. As a group, come up with an explanation of how to "make zero." You must use the three vocabulary terms: absolute value, positive, and negative.

The majority of Mr. Christopher's students are able to describe real-world situations that can be described by integers, a concept developed in sixth grade, so he decides not to set up the opening paired activity of generating ideas and associations with the terms *positive* and *negative* in great detail. To give students flexibility and creative control of the task, he has students pick the partners with whom they will want to work and offers a choice of how they will share their thinking:

- Make a bulleted list
- Draw pictures
- Create a word splash
- Make a two-column table (+ and –)
- A record of your choosing other than "we'll just remember"

He warns his students that no matter which format they choose, they only have approximately 8 minutes to complete their task and be ready to share some of their thoughts.

As students share their examples and thinking about positives and negatives, a variety of experiences such as "getting a gift" as positive but "losing money" as negative are suggested. Relationships and friendships are described as both positive and negative. A few students describe that numbers "above" zero are positive but "below" zero are negative. When Mr. Christopher asks them to explain what they mean by above and below, several explanations, including "bigger" and "more," come out, but eventually the class agrees that it means greater and less than. One student suggests that it can be above and below if you have a thermometer that goes up and down. Mr. Christopher uses that opportunity to introduce number lines, both vertically and horizontally, even though he had not planned to do so at this time in the lesson.

To conclude this introduction of the lesson, he asks students to write on whiteboards an integer that would describe the following:

- Climbing up three steps
- Climbing down seven steps
- Losing $10
- A temperature drop of 4°
- Going up a mountain 400 feet in altitude
- Can you think of other examples to challenge the class?

When Mr. Christopher asks how students described the relationship between positive and negative, most students have already decided that they are opposites. Some students say "pro and con" or "good and bad." Other descriptions easily led to the conclusion that positive and negative can be described as opposites.

Following this foundational discussion, Mr. Christopher gives his class brief notes for their mathematics notebooks. He starts with the understanding that in mathematics, a negative means opposite. He asks his students if this was true, what would negative numbers be the opposite of? As students respond positive numbers, Mr. Christopher draws a number line on which to show "opposite" numbers. As he plots opposite numbers (e.g., 2 and –2) that were suggested by students, he has students describe how far (the distance) each number was from zero. He uses this exercise to define absolute value and shows students the notation for absolute value, $|2| = |–2|$. As students suggest pairs of numbers, he asks why no one has suggested a pair of fractions. He then shows $\pm\frac{1}{2}$ on the number line. He explains that fractions also have opposite values, and those values, along with zero which is neither positive nor negative, form the rational number system. However, in this unit, students would only be working with integers, which are positive and negative whole numbers and zero. This serves as the introduction to vocabulary that will continue to build throughout the unit with natural usage.

To lead into the concluding activity, Mr. Christopher asks students to consider a few scenarios and what would happen as a result, such as the following:

- Climb up three steps then go down three steps
- Lose $5 and find $5
- Turn halfway around to face the back wall, then turn halfway again . . . and again and again

He then asks students to think about how integers might be added to have a sum of zero. Finally, he introduces both the number line and two-color counters as tools for adding integers. Figure 8.4a provides a look at how Mr. Christopher introduces the use of a number line, and 8.4b shows two-color counters.

FIGURE 8.4

INTRODUCING NUMBER LINES AND TWO-COLOR COUNTERS

	Visual	Explanation
a) Number Line	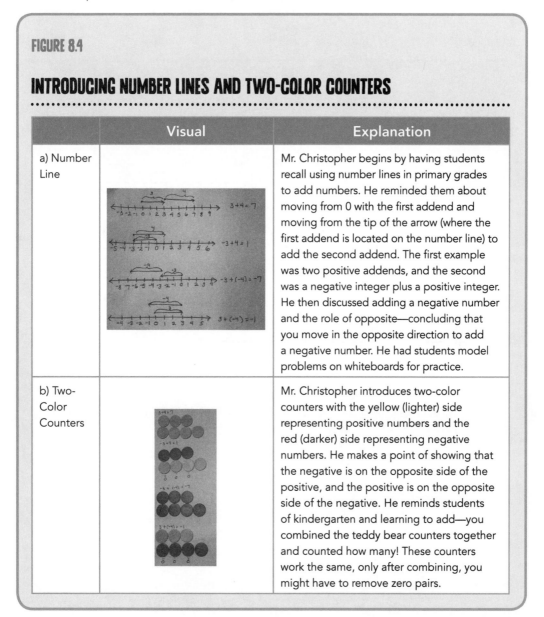	Mr. Christopher begins by having students recall using number lines in primary grades to add numbers. He reminded them about moving from 0 with the first addend and moving from the tip of the arrow (where the first addend is located on the number line) to add the second addend. The first example was two positive addends, and the second was a negative integer plus a positive integer. He then discussed adding a negative number and the role of opposite—concluding that you move in the opposite direction to add a negative number. He had students model problems on whiteboards for practice.
b) Two-Color Counters		Mr. Christopher introduces two-color counters with the yellow (lighter) side representing positive numbers and the red (darker) side representing negative numbers. He makes a point of showing that the negative is on the opposite side of the positive, and the positive is on the opposite side of the negative. He reminds students of kindergarten and learning to add—you combined the teddy bear counters together and counted how many! These counters work the same, only after combining, you might have to remove zero pairs.

Mr. Christopher uses the end of class for a "hands, brain, and pencil" activity summarizing the learning from the day. Students get into groups of three, with one person being the "hands" who can only do what the brain tells him or her to do. Another student is the "brain" who can only communicate, as a brain has no hands. The third student is the "pencil," who records the mathematical notation for what the hands and brain are completing. Students rotate roles after each problem. Figure 8.5 shows the Getting to Zero task, and Figure 8.6 shows a completed task.

FIGURE 8.5

GETTING TO ZERO

Our group: _____

Getting to Zero

Directions: For each section, rotate who will be the hands, who is the brain, and who is the pencil. Initial each round who is in the different roles.

Modeling Absolute Value

1. _____ Hands   _____ Brain   _____ Pencil

   a. Use a number line to show an absolute value of 4.   Notation (Write it in math)

   ← —————————————————————→   _____

   _____ Hands   _____ Brain   _____ Pencil

   b. Use a number line to show an absolute value of 4   Notation (Write it in math)
      a different way.

   ← —————————————————————→   _____

2. _____ Hands   _____ Brain   _____ Pencil

   a. Use two-color counters to show an absolute value of 4.   Notation (Write it in math)
      Draw the counters below.

                                                                _____

_____ Hands   _____ Brain   _____ Pencil

b. Use two-color counters to show an absolute value of 4.   Notation (Write it in math)
   Draw the counters below.

_____

Modeling Zero

1. _____ Hands   _____ Brain   _____ Pencil

   a. Use a number line to show a sum of 0.   Notation (Write it in math)

   _____

   _____ Hands   _____ Brain   _____ Pencil

   b. Use a number line to show a different sum of 0.   Notation (Write it in math)

   _____

   _____ Hands   _____ Brain   _____ Pencil

   c. Use a number line to show a third sum of 0.   Notation (Write it in math)

   _____

2. _____ Hands   _____ Brain   _____ Pencil

   a. Use two-color counters to show a sum of 0.   Notation (Write it in math)
      Draw the counters below.

   _____

   _____ Hands   _____ Brain   _____ Pencil

   b. Use two-color counters to show a different sum of 0.   Notation (Write it in math)
      Draw the counters below.

   _____

   c. Use two-color counters to show a third sum of 0.   Notation (Write it in math)
      Draw the counters below.

   _____

3. As a group, come up with an explanation of how to "make zero." You must use the three
   vocabulary terms: absolute value, positive, and negative.

Getting to Zero can be downloaded at resources.corwin.com/
everymathlearner6-12.

As students work on Getting to Zero, Mr. Christopher monitors all groups to see if they are understanding the concept of zero pairs, can work with both of the tools to represent addition of integers, and are correctly recording the notation involved with absolute values and integers. When Mr. Christopher notices any kind of mistake, he redirects students with a question so that students can make corrections in the moment. For example, in the student work in Figure 8.6, students do not write the absolute value signs, so had resulting equations such as –4 = 4. When Mr. Christopher asks how that can be true, the students correctly explain the concept of absolute value but do not know how to write it. Mr. Christopher asks them to check their notes to see if they can find how to write the notation of absolute value. The students then correct their work.

FIGURE 8.6

STUDENT WORK ON GETTING TO ZERO

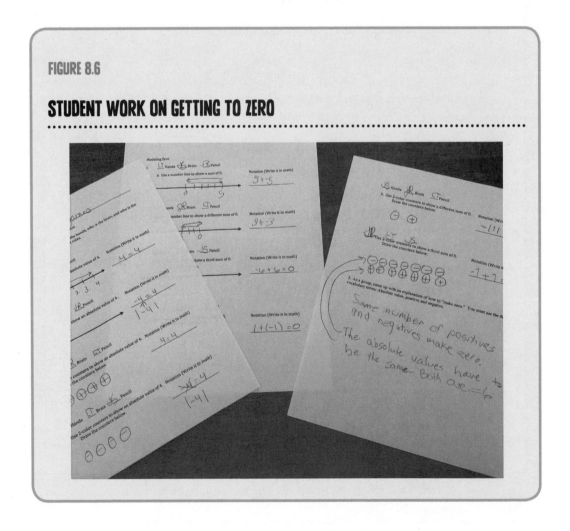

To conclude the lesson, Mr. Christopher asks his students to individually complete an exit card giving two examples of making a zero:

1. Use a number line model and write the resulting equation.
2. Draw two-color counters and write the resulting equation.

DAILY PLANNING—DAY 2

After observing students' work and reviewing the individual exit cards from Day 1, Mr. Christopher recognizes the following:

- All students know that zero pairs could be formed by an "equal number" of positives and negatives and can model adding to zero with both the two-color counters and the number line.

- Notation is very sloppy for all but two students, including not using absolute value bars and not using parentheses to enclose a negative number as a second addend. Other students put positive numbers in parentheses when they are the second addend.

- The role of absolute value in forming zero pairs is not explicitly understood. No student explicitly explained that if the absolute value of a negative number equaled the absolute value of a positive number, they would create a zero pair and sum to zero. Mr. Christopher wonders if this is an important understanding or if the knowledge that pairing one positive and one negative results in a zero pair is sufficient for building the concept of adding integers. He will work in the concept of absolute value as he talks to students and listens to students' explanations but does not believe he will formally assess for it.

Day 2 will build on the previous day by using the concept of zero to add integers. The same tools will be used to model addition of integers to lay the groundwork for students to recognize the patterns of adding integers and generalize these patterns to discover the "rules" or procedures for adding integers. He expects the patterns and generalization to emerge toward the end of the third day of the unit and be formalized on the fourth. The standards for mathematical practice in this lesson will concentrate on SMP 1 (perseverance and reasoning), SMP 2 (quantitative reasoning), SMP 4 (models), SMP 5 (tools), and SMP 8 (patterns of adding integers).

Mr. Christopher begins math class by highlighting several of the students' explanations of adding integers from yesterday's Getting to Zero activity. He reads three different explanations, one that explains how to use a number line to show addition to zero, one that explains how to use the two-color counters to add to zero, and a third that describes more generally how to be sure that the negative value is the same as the positive value to add together. He asks his class to compare and contrast the three explanations. The class concludes that the same "amount" of negative and positive needs to be added to have a sum of zero and that the general explanation is the strongest of the three because it describes addition, not the use of a tool to add. Mr. Christopher takes the opportunity to discuss what students mean about the "value" or "amount" of positive and negative. Could they explain that mathematically? Students go back to the model explanations, such as "the number of positive and negative counters is the same" or that "the distance in the positive and the negative directions on the number line is the same." He asks the students to tell him what we call the distance on the number line from zero, and following their response of absolute value, he asks them to practice in pairs explaining how to add to zero using the term *absolute value* in their explanation. This natural progression that arose from his students' discourse allows Mr. Christopher to address the vocabulary precision of including absolute value in the students' explanations.

To conclude the whole-class opening, Mr. Christopher quickly reviews the notation of absolute value and enclosing a negative number in parentheses when it is the second addend and why these symbols are necessary. For example, he contrasts an example of student work from the day before showing $-4 = 4$ and $|-4| = |4|$. Second, he shows $4 + -4$ and $4 + (-4)$. Students conclude that the notation of mathematics makes things easier to see and understand. From the examples and conversations, Mr. Christopher concludes that he does not need to review the use of the number line or two-color counters at this time.

Mr. Christopher plans to introduce integer addition through real-world contexts just as he did the previous day with the meaning of integers. He has created three sets of real-world problems with which he wants his students to wrestle. To transition into the activity, he asks his students if they think all integer addition problems will have a sum of zero. He asks them to brainstorm and suggest the kind of addition problem that would have a positive sum or a negative sum. He then models the setup for a one-word problem and asks students to use a number line or counters to find the answer:

> Bad news! I owe my friend $5.00. Good news! I just found $8.00 in my wallet! How much money will I have after I pay back my friend? Use integers to answer the question!

Based on his observations of how his students solve this problem on whiteboards, yesterday's activities of representing contexts with integers and the Getting to Zero task, and prior knowledge of his students, he gives his students a colored sticky note. Students will be allowed to work alone, find a partner, or form a group of three of their choosing by finding partners with the same color sticky note as their own.

> Yellow group: Given contexts that build up to three addends, write equations and use tools as needed to solve. In the final two problems, use two-digit integers to limit the use of the tools as an added stretch and challenge.

> Blue group: Begin with representing contexts with an integer value. Next, given contexts, write equations and use models to solve. Partners can float to the teacher (green) group as needed.

> Green group: Begin with representing contexts with an integer value. Next, given contexts, write equations and use models to solve. Students will work with the teacher to begin, then alone, in pairs, or in triads as they are ready.

Mr. Christopher does not expect even his top students to be able to solve the most challenging problems, but has also learned that they often surprise him with what they already know or can figure out. For this reason, he includes problems that he would not expect them to be able to complete to stretch and challenge his advanced mathematics students.

To monitor the groups as they work, he plans to work with the green group to get them started with specific steps and problems, believing that they will be able to work together after two examples to complete the problems giving an integer for specific contexts. These are the same type of problems as began the class yesterday. While the students in the green group complete the problems,

FIGURE 8.7

INTEGERS DAY 2 EXIT CARD

Solve the following problem:

The average temperature in Minneapolis in the winter is about 19° Fahrenheit (which is –7° Celsius). One very cold day, the temperature was 25° below the average (Fahrenheit). What was the temperature that day?	
Make Sense: Diagrams or number line	Notation: Write it in math
Final solution:	

Mr. Christopher will circle the room to be sure all groups understand their directions and have begun. He will repeat this process, modeling a problem with the green group and getting them started to work on the next problem and then checking on other groups. In addition, Mr. Christopher puts responsibility on students to monitor their learning, and students can float in and out of the "teacher" group as they feel need.

Mr. Christopher closes his lesson by bringing all of his students together to discuss the "yippees" (what went well) and "yikes" (what was a challenge and stretched you) for adding integers. He has prepared an exit task that follows the same format as the word problems that the groups have completed but with more challenging numbers. He wants to see how each of his students will attack the problem and if they are becoming more efficient with using their tools. Figure 8.7 shows the exit card for the lesson.

Figure 8.8 shows the lesson plan for Day 2.

FIGURE 8.8

DAY 2 LESSON PLAN

Operating on Integers Lesson Plan – Day 2

Date: 10/11

Standards:
Understand that positive and negative numbers are used together to describe quantities having opposite directions or values.

Apply and extend previous understandings of addition and subtraction to add and subtract rational numbers (integers only in this unit); represent addition and subtraction on a horizontal or vertical number line diagram.

Highlighted Standards for Mathematical Practice:
SMP1: Make sense of problems and persevere in solving them
SMP2: Reason abstractly and quantitatively
SMP4: Model with mathematics
SMP5: Use appropriate tools strategically
SMP8: Look for and express regularity in repeated reasoning

Know:

- Vocabulary: absolute value, integer, negative, number system, opposite, positive, zero pair
- The layout of a number line
- How to model integers and integer operations with two-color counters and number lines
- Notation

Understand:

- A negative in mathematics always means "the opposite."
- Mathematical operations apply to and follow the same patterns within our number systems and mathematical disciplines.

Be Able to Do:

- Model integers and integer operations in different ways
- Apply integers to and solve real-world situations

Whole Class:

1. Highlight great explanations of adding to zero from yesterday's group task #3.
2. Review vocabulary and notation with whiteboards
3. Review zero pairs (adding to zero) with number lines and two-color counters on whiteboards. Ask if anyone is beginning to prefer a method yet.
4. Will everything always equal zero when you add integers? What do you think? Can you give an example when it wouldn't equal zero? Introduce and model context problems.

(Continued)

FIGURE 8.8 (Continued)

Small Groups

Readiness differentiation based on exit card and small group observations:

1. Given contexts that build up to three addends, write equations and use models as needed to solve. Work with a partner or alone as preferred.

2. Begin with representing contexts with an integer value. Next, given contexts, write equations and use models to solve. Work with partners. Partners can float to teacher group as needed.

3. Begin with representing contexts with an integer value. Next, given contexts, write equations and use models to solve. Students with teacher to begin, and are released to work in pairs or triads as they are ready.

Whole-Class Discussion:

1. Yippees and yikes—what went well, what didn't go well, what do we still need to work on?

2. Pros and cons of the number line and two-color counters? Any preference?

Exit Card:

Describe a situation that could be represented by a sum of −15

Describe a situation that could be represented by a sum of +10

Solve the following problem:

The average temperature in Minneapolis in the winter is about 19° Fahrenheit (which is −7° Celsius). One very cold day, the temperature was 25° below the average (Fahrenheit). What was the temperature that day?	
Make Sense: Diagrams or number line	Notation: Write it in math
Final solution:	

Formative Assessment: Small group work monitoring, Yippees and yikes

Check for Understanding: Small group sheets, exit cards

 The entire week's daily lesson plans and blank lesson planning templates can be downloaded from resources.corwin.com/ everymathlearner6-12.

DAILY PLANNING—DAY 3

When planning for Day 3 of the unit, Mr. Christopher reviews his students' individual written work from the previous day, including the word problems and the exit card, as well as his anecdotal records from the unit thus far. He finds the following:

- All of his students are able to use either a number line or counters to model the word problems.

- Three of his most advanced students find a way to use the counters more effectively for two-digit numbers by drawing a large circle with the integer of the smaller absolute value in it, matching it with a large circle with the opposite integer in it and then additional circles to total the integer. Figure 8.9 shows their work.

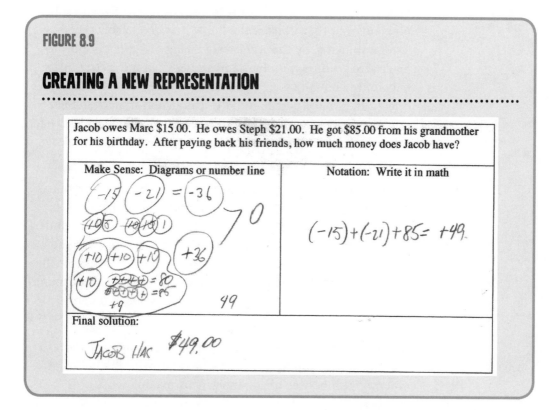

FIGURE 8.9

CREATING A NEW REPRESENTATION

Jacob owes Marc $15.00. He owes Steph $21.00. He got $85.00 from his grandmother for his birthday. After paying back his friends, how much money does Jacob have?

Make Sense: Diagrams or number line	Notation: Write it in math
	$(-15)+(-21)+85= +49$

Final solution:

JACOB HAS $49.00

- Most students can solve their word problems, although Mr. Christopher believes that some are dependent on their group mates and cannot replicate the thinking on their exit card task. Many students rely on solving the word problems from reasoning about the context (especially with money problems) rather than with integers.

For this lesson, Mr. Christopher will have students practice adding integers using the tool or tools of their preference, if any. They will play a game of Integer War to practice many problems with an element of fun. The game will help the class generate a long list of addition problems, which will lead to recognizing patterns and generalizing the steps for adding any two integers. The standards for mathematical practice in this lesson will concentrate on SMP 1 (perseverance and reasoning), SMP 2 (quantitative reasoning), SMP 4 (models), SMP 5 (tools), and SMP 8 (patterns of adding integers).

To begin the lesson, Mr. Christopher asks his students to discuss the problem solving from the day before. He asks them to reflect on how the context helped students solve the problems, and if it made things more difficult for them, how so? Some students express frustration with having to keep using the tools to solve problems, but they don't really know how else to solve them. Several students say that they were trying to figure out how to make zero with the numbers and seeing what is left over instead of counting out all of the counters or making huge number lines. A few additional students think this is a good strategy but are not sure how to do it. Mr. Christopher has the students who had solved the money problem in Figure 8.8 explain their thinking.

Mr. Christopher explains that they will be playing a game that involves adding integers, and so he wants to be sure everyone is very comfortable finding sums with either the number line or two-color counter methods. He practices several problems and asks two students to come model each problem, one with the number line and one showing the two-color counters under the document camera. The remaining students work on whiteboards so that Mr. Christopher could check each student's progress.

He concludes the time by saying that by the end of class, he hopes everyone will be much closer to not needing the tools to add any longer, and by tomorrow, he is fairly sure that almost everyone will be able to add integers by making sense of the numbers.

Mr. Christopher then introduces the game of Integer War. Students play with a deck of cards with face cards removed. The red cards represent negative numbers, and the black cards represent positive numbers. Each player will turn up two cards simultaneously and add his or her cards, and the player with an absolute value closest to zero wins all of the cards. In case of a tie, or war, the tied players count three cards face down and then turn two additional cards up to add. The winner gets all of the cards involved in the round. Figure 8.10 shows the Integer War directions and accountability sheet.

FIGURE 8.10

INTEGER WAR

Integer War!

Dealing The Cards

Deal out an equal number of playing cards to each player. (If you are playing with an odd number of players, put any extra cards face down in the center of the desk. The player who wins the first round takes the extra cards.)

The Play

Each player turns up two cards. Black cards (clubs and spades) are positive face values, and the red cards (diamonds and hearts) are negative face value. Aces count as 1. For example, the 3 of hearts counts as −3 and the 5 of clubs counts as +5.

Each player adds his or her two cards together. The player closest to zero (think absolute value!) gets all of the cards. If it is a tie, it's WAR!

War

In case of a war, each player puts 3 cards face down, then turns up the next 2 cards. Add these cards, and the player closest to zero gets all of the cards.

Winning

The player who gets all of the cards wins!

Work

You will need to show your work! For every two cards you turn up, record the equation and your answer. You should have a list of problems and answers by the time you finish your game!

Player 1   Player 2

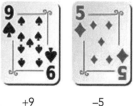

+9   −5   =   +4   −7   −1   =   −8

Player 1 wins because |4| is closer to zero than |-8|

(Continued)

FIGURE 8.10 (Continued)

Integer War!

Record your equations here!

Card 1	Card 2	Equation and Sum	Absolute value of sum

The Integer War directions and accountability sheet can be downloaded at resources.corwin.com/everymathlearner6-12.

As students play Integer War, Mr. Christopher circulates among the students, watching to see how students are solving problems and providing feedback. He makes notes about which students are still using tools and which tools they prefer. He also encourages students to reason about the numbers as to what happens when you are adding same-sign numbers and making a zero if signs are different and figuring out what is left over. Some students begin to make that leap while others keep using the tools. Two groups of students are able to add the digits 1 through 10 quickly, and so Mr. Christopher challenges these students to play double-digit Integer War, turning over four cards representing two double-digit integers with the first card (tens place) representing the sign of the integer. Mr. Christopher addresses readiness differentiation as needed as his students play the game and use or do not use tools as they desire, and he addresses learning profile by providing the variety of tools for students to choose. Figure 8.11 shows one student's work as she played.

FIGURE 8.11

PLAYING INTEGER WAR

Mr. Christopher calls his students back together to close the lesson. He divides his whiteboard into four quadrants: Positive + Positive, Positive + Negative, Negative + Negative, and Negative + Positive. He specifically has the Positive + Positive and Negative + Negative on the left side of the board and the Positive + Negative and Negative + Positive on the right. He wants his students to see the patterns more clearly by grouping problem types in this way. Each student fills in one problem in each of the quadrants from their Integer War sheet. Mr. Christopher asks his students to look at the groups of problems and see if they can find any patterns in the addends and sums.

The first observation is that positive plus positive always gives a positive answer. When asked why this makes sense, a student responds, "It is just the same addition as we've been doing since kindergarten. Nothing is different." Following this is the observation that "negative plus negative is the same, only negative." When pressed to explain more, the student comes to the conclusion that you add the absolute values of the addends, and the sum remains negative. Mr. Christopher asks his students to imagine using a number line or counters and describe what happens when you add two negative numbers. Why would adding the absolute values of the numbers and making the sum negative work? Students quickly realize the sum of two negative numbers gets "more negative" just like adding two positive numbers gets "more positive."

This left the more challenging problem of adding integers with opposite signs. Students observe that some sums were positive and other negative, and Mr. Christopher follows this comment by asking if they can recognize a pattern based on the signs of the addends and the sign of the sum. Students quickly realize that the sign of the addend with the greater absolute value determines the sign of the sum. One student suggests that you could subtract the absolute values and use the sign of the addend with the greater absolute value. Toward the end of class, Mr. Christopher challenges his students to consider the pattern for adding integers with opposite signs and if they see a pattern justifying why the pattern is reasonable or works. This challenge is given in addition to practicing integer addition problems for homework.

Figure 8.12 shows Mr. Christopher's lesson plan for Day 3.

FIGURE 8.12

DAY 3 LESSON PLAN

Operating on Integers Lesson Plan – Day 3

Date: 10/12

Understand that positive and negative numbers are used together to describe quantities having opposite directions or values.

Apply and extend previous understandings of addition and subtraction to add and subtract rational numbers (integers only in this unit); represent addition and subtraction on a horizontal or vertical number line diagram.

Highlighted Standards for Mathematical Practice:
SMP1: Make sense of problems and persevere in solving them
SMP2: Reason abstractly and quantitatively
SMP4: Model with mathematics
SMP5: Use appropriate tools strategically
SMP8: Look for and express regularity in repeated reasoning

Know:

- Vocabulary: absolute value, integer, negative, number system, opposite, positive, zero pair

- The layout of a number line

- How to model integers and integer operations with two-color counters and number lines

- Notation

Understand:

- A negative in mathematics always means "the opposite."

- Mathematical operations apply to and follow the same patterns within our number systems and mathematical disciplines.

Be Able to Do:

- Model integers and integer operations in different ways

Whole Class:

1. Discuss the addition context problems from yesterday. How did having stories (situations/contexts) help in solving the problems? How did it make things more difficult or challenging?

2. Today we are going to practice adding integers. Let's practice a few together. Have two students come up to the board to model the number line method and two-color counter method for solutions for each problem. The rest of the students work at their desks with the model they prefer and hold up final solutions on whiteboards.

(Continued)

FIGURE 8.12 (Continued)

3. We are going to play Integer Addition War today. Explain rules and show accountability sheet.

Partner Work (partners by choice):

Play Integer Addition War

Circulate as partners play and check accountability sheet—challenge some students to play double-digit addition war if ready.

Whole Class:

Post a long list of addition equations on the board. Challenge students to see if they can recognize any patterns in the types of integers being added and any shortcut methods they might see from the patterns.

Formative Assessment/Check for Understanding: Whiteboard answers during whole-class opening, Integer War accountability sheets.

The entire week's daily lesson plans and blank lesson planning templates can be downloaded from resources.corwin.com/everymathlearner6-12.

DAILY PLANNING—DAY 4

Thursday's lesson will be a formalization of adding integers and having students recognize and use the procedures involved with adding any two integers. Mr. Christopher knows from experience that often students will learn steps for adding integers, and seem to use and know them well, but then will confuse steps as soon as they learn multiplication. For this reason, he has moved very slowly and has students experience various strategies and representations to make sense of the numbers and not just memorize a set of steps or rules. As Mr. Christopher plans for the day's lesson, he reviews his records and the students' Integer War sheet. He sees the following:

- Fourteen students are adding single-digit addition correctly without using tools.

- Five students are not getting correct sums for their problems.

- Three students are adding double-digit integers correctly using a sketch of their own making.

- The remaining nine students are finding correct sums using the tools, with most using the two-color counters over the number line.

The standards for mathematical practice in this lesson will continue to concentrate on SMP 1 (reasoning to make sense of the "rules" of integer addition), SMP 2 (quantitative reasoning), SMP 4 (models), SMP 5 (tools), and SMP 8 (patterns of adding integers).

Mr. Christopher begins class by reviewing any questions over the answers for the homework problems. He wants to continually reinforce why the sums make sense based on the addends and not a list of steps. He lets students know that his goal is not that his students will always have a bag of two-color counters with them to solve problems or need to sketch a number line! He wants students to envision a mental model of these tools as needed to make sense of their answers as they work. He reviews that when addends have the same sign, the absolute values of the addends can be added, and the sign of the addends is also the sign of the sum. He asks three students to explain why that pattern is correct making sense of the numbers or drawing on a mental model.

Mr. Christopher then asks his students if anyone has come up with more ideas as to how to add integers with opposite signs. One student says that he used the two-color counters to make sense of the sign of the sum. She says that as she made and removed zero pairs, the remaining counters would be the sign of the addend with the greater absolute value because there would be more of them. Everyone agrees that would be why the sign of the sum is determined that way. Another student builds on that reasoning and says, "After you remove the zero pairs, you have the difference between the absolute values—the extras. That is what subtraction does."

Mr. Christopher asks his students to form groups of four and come up with two sentences. One sentence will explain a shortcut for adding two integers with the same signs, and the other sentence is to explain a shortcut for adding two integers with opposite signs. The only requirement is that they use correct mathematical vocabulary. All groups report their sentences, and the class votes on the following shortcuts for adding integers:

1. If both addends have the same sign, add their absolute values and use the sign of the addends in the sum.

2. If the addends have different signs, subtract their absolute values, greater minus lesser, and use the sign of the greater absolute value in the sum.

Mr. Christopher introduces stations for the next 30 minutes of class. His students are to use station work as Mr. Christopher tries to incorporate stations weekly if possible. Students are required to complete two stations of their choosing but can complete more if they are able. He says that he will try to bring the stations back at another point in the unit. The stations, differentiated by interest, are as follows:

M—Math Games—Play Integer Addition War or double-digit integer addition depending on the challenge level you want. OR Play Integer Four in a Row.

A—Alone Time—Complete an integer addition worksheet.

T—Take a Chance—Given a scenario of a week in the life of a compulsive shopper, model the income and expenditures through addition of integers and give a final balance.

H—Hmmmm—Using a guided task sheet, try to figure out how subtraction of integers might work.

Figure 8.13 shows Integer Addition Four in a Row. Since Integer Four in a Row is a new game for the students, Mr. Christopher explains the rules. There are two paper clips on the addend strip

FIGURE 8.13

INTEGER ADDITION FOUR IN A ROW

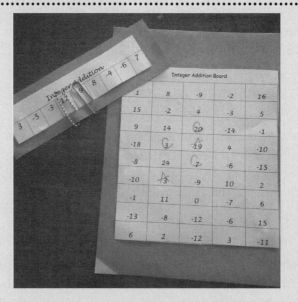

 The Integer Addition Four in a Row game and record sheet can be downloaded at resources.corwin.com/everymathlearner6-12.

of integers. On your turn, you may move one of the paper clips only, add the two addends, and mark the sum on the board with your initial. The second player takes his or her turn in the same way, moving only one paper clip and marking the sum on the board with his or her initial. The winner is the player who gets four squares in a row, horizontally, vertically, or diagonally.

Students are asked to try to use the class shortcut methods, rather than using the tools. However, if students wanted to check their answers by using these tools or are very uncertain how to use the shortcuts, they could use the tool of their choice. Every activity has an accountability sheet to record their work and thinking.

Mr. Christopher observes the choices students are making and monitors their addition strategies. To conclude class, he has designed an individual synthesizing task differentiated by learning profile. Students will explain how to add integers, being sure to include the following:

- Vocabulary—absolute value, integer, negative, positive, zero pair
- An explanation of the "shortcuts" and why they work
- Four examples minimum—one each of Positive + Positive, Positive + Negative, Negative + Positive, and Negative + Negative
- Bonus: show models to explain the "shortcuts"

Choose one of the following formats for your explanation:

- A written explanation
- Picture book–style explanation (very visual with pictures, few words)
- Write a letter to a friend who missed this lesson and explain everything to him or her
- Prepare a lesson teaching how to add integers that I can use in the future
- Another idea that you have as long as you check with me first

Students are told not to try for perfection because time is short, and Mr. Christopher wants to see what they understand before beginning subtraction of integers tomorrow. Some students ask to finish it for homework, and Mr. Christopher allows them to do this but takes pictures of their work thus far so that he can review their work overnight.

Figure 8.14 shows the lesson plan for Day 4.

Operating on Integers Lesson Plan – Day 4

Date: 10/13

Standards:
Understand that positive and negative numbers are used together to describe quantities having opposite directions or values.

Apply and extend previous understandings of addition and subtraction to add and subtract rational numbers (integers only in this unit); represent addition and subtraction on a horizontal or vertical number line diagram.

Highlighted Standards for Mathematical Practice:
SMP1: Make sense of problems and persevere in solving them
SMP2: Reason abstractly and quantitatively
SMP4: Model with mathematics
SMP5: Use appropriate tools strategically
SMP8: Look for and express regularity in repeated reasoning

Know:

- Vocabulary: absolute value, integer, negative, number system, opposite, positive, zero pair

- The layout of a number line

- How to model integers and integer operations with two-color counters and number lines

- Notation

Understand:

- A negative in mathematics always means "the opposite."

- Mathematical operations apply to and follow the same patterns within our number systems and mathematical disciplines.

Be Able to Do:

- Model integers and integer operations in different ways

- Apply and compute with integers

Whole Class:

1. We ended yesterday discussing possible patterns that we saw when adding integers. Let's look at our list again and see the patterns more slowly. Why do the patterns make sense?

2. Develop "rules" for adding integers.

Small Group MATH Rotations (Interest differentiation: choose two stations, 15 minute rotations):

M – Math Games – Play Integer Addition War and double-digit integer addition depending on the challenge level you want. OR Play Integer Four in a Row.

A – Alone Time – Complete an addition of integers worksheet.

T – Take a Chance – Given a scenario of a week in the life of a compulsive shopper, model the income and expenditures through addition of integers and give a final balance.

H – Hmmmm . . . . Using a guided task sheet, try to figure out how subtraction of integers might work.

Closure Activity: Learning Profile Differentiaton

Students explain how to add integers being sure to include

- Vocabulary – positive, negative, zero pair, integer
- An explanation of the "rules" and why they work
- Four examples minimum – one each of pos + pos; pos + neg; neg + pos; neg + neg
- Bonus: show models to explain the "rules"

Choose one of the following formats for your explanation:

- A written explanation
- A picture book–style explanation (very visual with pictures, few words)
- Write a letter to a friend who missed this lesson and explain everything to him or her
- Prepare a lesson teaching how to add integers that I can use in the future
- Another idea that you have as long as you check with me first

Formative Assessment: Station work
Check for Understanding: Closure activity

 The entire week's daily lesson plans and blank lesson planning templates can be downloaded from resources.corwin.com/everymathlearner6-12.

DAILY PLANNING—DAY 5

The final lesson of the week will be to begin integer subtraction. There will be 2 days spent solely on subtracting integers, with a third day dedicated to reviewing combined addition and subtraction. The 2 days of subtraction will follow a much abbreviated version of the 4 days for addition, with students involved in games and modeling of subtraction to make sense of the process. At the end of the second day, Mr. Christopher expects that his students will have made the connection that subtracting integers is equivalent to adding the opposite integer as the second addend. Today his students will spend time playing another card game that will involve summing cards in the hand and discarding cards and finding a new total. The game involves both addition and subtraction, but students will be able to play the game using addition. The standards for mathematical practice in this lesson will concentrate on SMP 2 (quantitative reasoning), SMP 5 (tools), SMP6 (attend to precision), and SMP 8 (patterns of subtracting integers).

Figure 8.15 shows the lesson plan for Day 5.

DAY 5 LESSON PLAN

Operating on Integers Lesson Plan – Day 5

Standards:
Understand that positive and negative numbers are used together to describe quantities having opposite directions or values.

Apply and extend previous understandings of addition and subtraction to add and subtract rational numbers (integers only in this unit); represent addition and subtraction on a horizontal or vertical number line diagram.

Highlighted Standards for Mathematical Practice:
SMP2: Reason abstractly and quantitatively
SMP5: Use appropriate tools strategically
SMP6: Attend to precision
SMP8: Look for and express regularity in repeated reasoning

Know:

- Vocabulary: absolute value, integer, negative, number system, opposite, positive, zero pair
- The layout of a number line
- How to model integers and integer operations with two-color counters and number lines
- Notation

Understand:

- A negative in mathematics always means "the opposite."
- Mathematical operations apply to and follow the same patterns within our number systems and mathematical disciplines.

Be Able to Do:

- Model integers and integer operations in different ways
- Apply and compute with integers

Whole Class:

1. Review some of the addition explanations from closure yesterday. Transition to the idea of subtraction.

2. Model "Pick Up, Put Down" game. So far, this game will be played thinking only about adding the values of each new hand but will record both addition and subtraction equations.

Small group activity:

With partners or triads, "Pick Up, Put Down"

Ask groups if they can recognize any kind of pattern with subtracting integers as compared to adding integers.

Whole Class:

1. What patterns or relationships did you see between adding and subtracting integers?

2. Model subtraction with number line, making sure that movement on the number line is defined by a negative sign, meaning opposite (that is, subtracting a positive number moves the opposite way from adding, and subtracting a negative number moves the opposite way from subtracting a positive, or the opposite of the opposite of adding).

3. Model subtraction with counters showing how to add zero pairs if you need to subtract a positive or negative that is not available to "take away."

4. Practice with blocks of numbers to show that subtraction is really "adding the opposite."

   e.g. $8 + (-4)$ and $8 - 4$; $4 + (-9)$ and $4 - 9$; $3 + 4$ and $3 - (-4)$; and so on.

Closure (Differentiated by Readiness): All: How would you explain the relationship of adding and subtracting integers? Give examples and use at least one of the models (number line or counters). Use any format you like to make your explanation understandable even to your parents.

Challenge: What is the role of adding zero pairs with counters when subtracting? When do you need to do that? Solve: $3 - (-5) =$

On track: How can you explain why subtracting a negative number is just like adding the absolute value of the number? Solve: $3 - 5 =$

Struggling: Which model for subtracting do you like the best so far, and why? Solve: $3 - 5 =$

Formative Assessment – "Pick Up, Put Down" worksheets

Check for Understanding: Closure activity

 The entire week's daily lesson plans and blank lesson planning templates can be downloaded from resources.corwin.com/everymathlearner6-12.

Mr. Christopher begins his class by asking students to reflect on adding integers. What is going well for them and what is still a little bit of a challenge? Most students are feeling confident about addition but admit that they need more practice to add greater integer values and become faster at using their class shortcuts for addition without using any of the tools. Mr. Christopher highlights several of the students' addition summaries from the previous day, enjoying sharing examples of all four formats that had been chosen.

He continues explaining that the students will play one more game today, still using addition. It is called Pick Up, Put Down. The game is played with a deck of cards with the face cards removed, with red cards representing negative integers and black cards representing positive integers. Directions: Begin with dealing a hand of three cards to each player. The remaining cards are placed in a stack face down as the draw pile. The top card of the draw pile is flipped face up to start the discard pile. Black cards represent positive numbers, and red cards represent negative numbers. In the table, students record the total value of their initial hand. For each turn, the players draw a card from either the draw pile or the top card in the discard pile. They record the "picked up" card in their table, record the equation that represents what was added, and write the new total value of the hand. The player then discards a card from his or her hand into a discard pile face up. The student records the "put down" card in the table, the equation that represents what was subtracted, and the final value of the hand. The player with the hand with a sum closest to zero after five rounds is the winner.

Mr. Christopher checks in with each pair or triad of students as they play. He is careful to check that all students are recording the "put down" move equation as a subtraction problem and also checks the accuracy of the equations and solutions for each of their moves. As students are finishing their games, he prompts the class to start looking at the subtraction problems they recorded to see if there are any surprises or patterns.

Mr. Christopher brings his class back together to discuss the surprises and patterns that students see. He divides his whiteboard into four quadrants labeled Positive – Positive, Positive – Negative, Negative – Negative, and Negative – Positive, similar to what

Figure 8.16 shows Pick Up, Put Down being played.

he had done for addition the previous day. He has students write any equations they have that match each quadrant on the board. When asked for surprises or patterns, students respond with the following:

- There doesn't seem to be any reasoning about the difference. Sometimes it is positive and sometimes it is negative.

- All the answers of positive minus negative are positive, and all the answers from negative minus positive are negative. (Mr. Christopher asks the student what you call the answer to a subtraction problem, then repeats the observation using "differences" instead of answers.)

- With the negative minus a positive, if you add the absolute values of the numbers and make the difference negative, it works.

- With positive minus positive, it's what we've always done. But sometimes you have to subtract a bigger . . . greater number. So I think about what would subtract to zero, then how much more needs to be subtracted. Like the first one . . . 3 – 5. If you have 3 – 3, it's zero. But you still have to subtract two more, so it's like zero minus two. So the difference is –2.

- With negative minus negative, you can subtract the absolute values and then you get the absolute value of the answer. Difference. But I don't know how to figure out if the difference is positive or negative.

Mr. Christopher says that everyone's observations are very helpful, but he doesn't want to have to try to remember four different shortcuts for subtracting integers. He asks the students who chose the Hmmmm station the day before, Thinking About Subtracting Integers, if they had come to any decisions or had a hint to get everyone starting to think about a general pattern for subtraction. Following some of their observations to which he does not reply yes or no, he asks students to consider some pairs of problems to see if there is a connection. He shows students how to model the subtraction problems with two-color counters, leaving the number line model for the next class on Monday. He asks students to consider the following:

- 4 – 3 and 4 + (–3)

- 7 – (–3) and 7 + 3 (for this example, he modeled how to add zero pairs with the counters in order to subtract)

- –3 – (–8) and –3 + 8

He then asks students to volunteer pairs of problems if they think they see a pattern. After several more pairs, he asks the students to pair up and share the secret to subtraction as they understand it so far. Mr. Christopher waits until all students can explain that you can change the subtraction to addition and make the second addend the opposite sign of the number in the subtraction problem (subtrahend) in their own way. He then practices a few more problems to see if they could change the notation correctly.

Mr. Christopher explains to the students that the only reason this will work is because addition and subtraction have a cool relationship—they are opposite operations (which is why you can add the opposite integer when subtracting), but they are also inverse operations, which the students will use a little later when they solve algebraic equations. He also told his students not to worry too much about this now, because they will continue to discuss what this means.

To close class, Mr. Christopher has a tiered exit card for his students. However, because he has not been able to use the number line model for subtraction, the original "walking" tier is not appropriate. He changes that in the moment. He asks all students to respond to the first prompt and challenges the students to choose the most challenging prompt they feel they can correctly answer based on the "Running, Jogging, and Walking" prompts as follows:

All Students: How would you explain the relationship of adding and subtracting integers? Give examples and use at least one example using counters. Use any format you like to make your explanation understandable even to your parents.

Running: How can you explain why subtracting a negative number is just like adding the absolute value of the number? Solve: $3 - (-5) =$

Walking: What is the role of adding zero pairs with counters when subtracting? When do you need to do that? Solve: $3 - (-5) =$

Walking: How does thinking about subtracting to zero help you solve a positive minus a positive problem? Use $3 - 5$ to explain your thinking, and solve the problem.

As Mr. Christopher observes his students' working on the exit card, he encourages some students to choose a more challenging second prompt if he felt they had chosen too easy a level. He wishes his students a great weekend and tells them they will pick up with subtraction again on Monday.

A LOOK INTO A WEEK IN A HIGH SCHOOL CLASSROOM

BEYOND LINEAR—WORKING WITH POLYNOMIALS

Abigail Tory is teaching a second-year high school algebra course (Algebra 2) and is planning a polynomial unit. The unit begins with the arithmetic of polynomials, most of which should be review for her students, and the new material, such as expanding binomials using Pascal's triangle, should be an easy extension of their prior knowledge. Following operations with polynomials,

Ms. Tory will transition into polynomial functions and modeling real-world data with polynomial functions. She believes that reminding students of how they first simplified linear expressions, then solved linear equations, and finally represented and interpreted linear functions in earlier grades will help students see the progression of content in this unit.

Ms. Tory believes that this unit can be built upon her students' prior knowledge and understanding of both solving equations and representing, interpreting, and modeling with functions. Therefore, her preassessment data and knowledge of her students' Algebra 1 memory and success play a large part in her planning. She already recognizes the students who are flexible and fluid with algebraic manipulation and function representation, those who struggle in one area or the other, and those who need reinforcement with all prior information.

Ms. Tory will use the essential understandings to link and connect the various topics and skills in the unit. While there are numerous standards included in the unit, they are connected through only four understandings. It will be critical that students see all of the connections through the understandings and not treat the different topics and skills as something unique to fully integrate the learning and store it into memory. Through this, students should be able to extend, transfer, and apply the learning into various representations and contexts.

FROM UNIT TO LESSON PLAN

Ms. Tory begins to plan her unit by creating a unit plan and a tentative calendar. The unit plan lists the standards on which the unit is built. She unpacks these standards into the Know, Understand, and Do (KUD) and lists these in a table. The KUD will guide her daily instructional decisions. Finally, Ms. Tory lists possible assessment ideas in the unit plan, including a preassessment for the unit to be given several days in advance, daily formative assessments and checks for understanding, and items she might want to include in a summative assessment. Figure 8.17 shows Abigail Tory's unit plan, which she titles "Beyond Linear: Working With Polynomials."

Once the unit plan is completed, Ms. Tory sketches out on a calendar the topics, number of days, and preliminary learning tasks for the unit. She checks to be sure that all of the standards are addressed and the KUD is established and connected in these initial plans. The planning calendar is seen in Figure 8.18.

FIGURE 8.17

BEYOND LINEAR: WORKING WITH POLYNOMIALS UNIT PLAN

Unit Title: Beyond Linear: Working With Polynomials (Algebra 2)

Standards Addressed (from Common Core State Standards, NGO and CCSSO, 2010):

Polynomial Arithmetic:

- Understand that polynomials form a system analogous to the integers, namely, they are closed under the operations of addition, subtraction, and multiplication; add, subtract, and multiply polynomials.
- Rewrite simple rational expressions in different forms; write $a(x)/b(x)$ in the form $q(x) + r(x)/b(x)$, where $a(x)$, $b(x)$, $q(x)$, and $r(x)$ are polynomials with the degree of $r(x)$ less than the degree of $b(x)$, using inspection, long division, or, for the more complicated examples, a computer algebra system.
- Know and apply the Remainder Theorem: For a polynomial $p(x)$ and a number a, the remainder on division by $x - a$ is $p(a)$, so $p(a) = 0$ if and only if $(x - a)$ is a factor of $p(x)$.

Polynomial Equations:

- Know there is a complex number i such that $i2 = -1$, and every complex number has the form $a + bi$ with a and b real. (*Review from last unit*)
- Use the relation $i2 = -1$ and the commutative, associative, and distributive properties to add, subtract, and multiply complex numbers. (*Review from last unit*)
- Solve quadratic equations with real coefficients that have complex solutions. (*Review from last unit*)
- Use the structure of an expression to identify ways to rewrite it. *For example, see x4 – y4 as (x2)2 – (y2)2, thus recognizing it as a difference of squares that can be factored as (x2 – y2)(x2 + y2).*
- Explain each step in solving a simple equation as following from the equality of numbers asserted at the previous step, starting from the assumption that the original equation has a solution. Construct a viable argument to justify a solution method.
- Prove polynomial identities and use them to describe numerical relationships. *For example, the polynomial identity (x2 + y2)2 = (x2 – y2)2 + (2xy)2 can be used to generate Pythagorean triples.*

Polynomials Functions:

- Use function notation, evaluate functions for inputs in their domains, and interpret statements that use function notation in terms of a context.
- Graph polynomial functions, identifying zeros when suitable factorizations are available and showing end behavior.
- Identify zeros of polynomials when suitable factorizations are available, and use the zeros to construct a rough graph of the function defined by the polynomial.
- Graph functions expressed symbolically and show key features of the graph (by hand in simple cases and using technology for more complicated cases).

By the end of the unit (new learning), what will students . . .

(Continued)

FIGURE 8.17 (Continued)

Know	Understand	Be Able to Do
Vocabulary: binomial expansion, complex conjugates, complex numbers, continuous functions, degree, end behaviors, even function, factor by grouping, intervals, Fundamental Theorem of Algebra, imaginary numbers, odd functions, Pascal's triangle, polynomial and polynomial functions, relative (local) maximums and minimums, Rational Root Theorem, Remainder Theorem, repeated differences (finite differences), repeated solution, symmetry, synthetic division, Determining degree of polynomial, and polynomial equation from a table of values. Strategies for operations with polynomials (e.g. lattice multiplication and division; long division; synthetic division) Remainder Theorem Rational Root Theorem Fundamental Theorem of Algebra Binomial expansion using Pascal's triangle How to identify key component of a polynomial graph	Polynomials are very similar to integers. Arithmetic with polynomials works in the same ways as arithmetic with integers. They are closed in addition, subtraction, and multiplication, just as are integers. (Algebra is grown up arithmetic.) Polynomial functions follow all of the same general patterns as any other functions with parent functions, transformations, domain and range, representations, etc. Polynomial functions are used to model, analyze, and make predictions in many real-world situations. Defining an imaginary number, i, explains many mathematical anomalies including polynomial functions without a Real zero, and defines roots for polynomial functions whose graphs do not cross the x-axis.	Identify polynomials and polynomial functions. Operate on polynomials using multiple strategies. Rewrite simple rational expressions using inspection and long division. Use Pascal's triangle to expand binomials. Explain how operating on polynomials is like operating on integers. Apply the factor and remainder theorems to factor or evaluate polynomials. Prove polynomial identities and find Pythagorean triples. Graph polynomials and identify key features. Factor polynomials using multiple methods. Compare and contrast strategies used with polynomials (operations, expansion, factoring, evaluating, etc.).
Analyzing a polynomial to sketch its graph $i^2 = -1$ Cycles of imaginary numbers		Find all zeros of a polynomial function, including imaginary zeros.

Not all roots of a function are real. Some roots of a function can occur multiple times. How to determine rational roots for a polynomial function		Explain how a polynomial function has the same number of roots as its degree even though some graphs appear to have fewer or no roots. Apply polynomials in real-world contexts in order to analyze, solve, or make predictions concerning the situation.

Preassessment Ideas:

Quick Write: What do you know about polynomials? (Provide word bank with all vocabulary in unit.) Fill in categories:

Operations (give problems to complete, and ask for multiple strategies)

Representations

Finding zeros

Analyzing a graph

Review: Complex number review problems

Summative Assessment Ideas:

Chapter test

Authentic Performance Assessment: Choose an application for polynomial modeling: Roller Coasters, Engineering Packaging, Research various tables of data that are modeled by a polynomial – Scatterplot, fit a polynomial model and interpret the results, Create a Game to practice operations and graphing polynomials, Write a "Do-It-Yourself Polynomials" book.

Formative Assessment Ideas:

Exit cards, homework, class activities, discourse, quiz, and quest

 The full plan can be downloaded at resources.corwin.com/ everymathlearner6-12.

Throughout the unit, Ms. Tory plans to relate the current learning to students' prior learning. To introduce new information, such as the rational root theorem, she will connect to prior information by having a "Been There, Done That" section of notes and activities that make the connection explicit. This should help students as they extend their understanding of solving equations and functions. The following lessons focus on the first full week of the unit, beginning with a concept attainment activity on polynomials, extending to a new method to recognize polynomial functions from a table.

FIGURE 8.18

BEYOND LINEAR: WORKING WITH POLYNOMIALS CALENDAR

Math Planning Calendar

Unit: Beyond Linear: Working with Polynomials

Duration: 4 weeks

Monday	Tuesday	Wednesday	Thursday	Friday
10/24 Discovering polynomials – Concept Attainment Intro – Cutting Pizzas? – Roll Dice, build polynomial, table, etc. – Vocabulary?	10/25 Working with polynomials: Review the stuff we know – Addition / subtraction review – Algebra tiles – Define terms with "what" and "how many" – Multiplication (algebra tiles and binomial distributive) – Analogous to the integers	10/26 More multiplying polynomials – Area / box models – Lattice – Distributive property – Binomial expansion and Pascal's triangle	10/27 Dividing polynomials algebra tiles Inverse Lattice Long Division If time: Begin or introduce practice stations	10/28 Practice, Practice, Practice – Paired worksheet with common answers (required for all) – Stations on add/sub; mult; div – Closing: LP summarization on operations
10/31 Synthetic Division Introduce remainder theorem Factoring as division Factor Patterns	11/1 Applying factoring patterns to Pythagorean triples Operations quiz	11/2 More factoring Solving for 0 Introduce Ps and Qs (Rational Root Theorem)	11/3 Solving polynomial equations	11/4 Graphing – End Behaviors – Zeros and roots – Transformations – Degrees and roots
11/7 Stations – Division with Ps and Qs (long or synthetic) – More factoring practice – Equation solving with real solutions – Graphing	11/8 Modeling with polynomials (interest differentiation to choose the modeling context)	11/9 QUEST!! – Arithmetic – Remainder Theorem – Graphing – Interpreting models	11/10 More graphing . . . – Imaginary roots – Complex numbers – Quadratics with imaginary factors (review)	11/11 Fundamental Theorem of Algebra and Descartes's rule of signs

11/14	11/15	11/16	11/17	11/18
More graphing practice and analyzing graphs of polynomials	More modeling with polynomials	Stations (choose 2) – Review operations – Review graphing – Review solving equations – Review complex numbers – Review factoring – Finish modeling applications	Game day to review for test	Unit test

DAILY PLANNING—DAY 1

After Ms. Tory sketched out her unit on a planning calendar, she designed more specific lesson plans. She did this by looking at the unit plan and selecting the specific standards and KUD that pertain to the lesson.

Ms. Tory begins the polynomial unit by asking her students if they remember hearing the word *polynomial*. All students agree that they have heard it, but some admit that they probably don't remember exactly what it means. Ms. Tory tells them that this is a great unit because there is very little new information. In fact, everything that they will be learning and with which they will be working is based on things they have already learned, and so each day is going to feature a segment called "Been There, Done That!" Each class period, the "Been There, Done That" segment will remind students of what they already know and understand to connect the day's topic. Today's "Been There, Done That" is to remember what a polynomial is. To do so, Ms. Tory has a concept attainment activity, called What Is a Polynomial (see Figure 8.20), that provides examples and nonexamples of polynomials. She asks her students to find a partner, inspect the examples, and come up with three statements as to what is a polynomial.

Figure 8.19 contains the lesson plan for Day 1.

FIGURE 8.19

DAY 1 LESSON PLAN

Beyond Linear: Working With Polynomials Lesson Plan – Day 1

Date: 10/24

Standards:

Understand that polynomials form a system analogous to the integers, namely, they are closed under the operations of addition, subtraction, and multiplication; add, subtract, and multiply polynomials.
Use the structure of an expression to identify ways to rewrite it.

K: Vocabulary: degree, end behaviors, polynomial and polynomial functions, relative (local) maximums and minimums, repeated (finite) differences
    Determining degree of polynomial, and polynomial equation from a table of values

U: Polynomials are very similar to integers. Arithmetic with polynomials works in the same ways as arithmetic with integers. They are closed in addition, subtraction, and multiplication, just as are integers. (Algebra is grown up arithmetic.)

D: Identify polynomials and polynomial functions.

Highlighted Standards for Mathematical Practice:
SMP1: Make sense of problems and persevere in solving them
SMP2: Reason abstractly and quantitatively
SMP7: Look for and make use of structure.
SMP8: Look for and express regularity in repeated reasoning.

Whole Class:

1. Concept Attainment activity on "Are" and "Are Not" polygons

2. "Make three statements you can conclude about polygons"

3. Reinforce vocabulary – polynomial, degree, function

4. A cool new identifier for a polynomial function – examine tables and differences

5. Review tasks and have students find partners within their chosen tasks (encourage students to "go for it" as needed).

Paired activity based on tiered tasks:

- Cut the Cake
- Trying Tables
- Polynomial or Not?

Ms. Tory compiles her students' statements about polynomials to form a working definition of "a finite expression with some combination of variables, exponents and constants, but the exponents must be a whole number and there cannot be division by a variable. Graphs of polynomials are continuous (smooth and connected)." Through the conversation, Ms. Tory also lists key vocabulary that will be needed for the day's activity, including "degree, continuous, expression, term, and whole number exponent."

To transition to the next paired activity, she has her students discuss some of the representations on the activity and targets the tables. She asks students if they can tell if a table of values would fit their description or not without graphing. The students respond that the tables have to be defined at every value to be a polynomial function. Ms. Tory responds that from the examples, she can understand why they say that. But that is not the only criteria. For example, sine and cosine graphs are defined everywhere but are not polynomial. To explore further, she uses the second table on the sheet and asks students to decide if it is linear or not. This is a quick and easy conversation as the students express in various ways that there was not a constant rate of change. Ms. Tory uses this to lead into discovering that polynomial functions will eventually have a constant difference. If a table of values never reaches a constant difference, then it is not a polynomial function. She then asks if the students can determine the function that produced the table from the values. When students determined that the function was $y = x^2 - 2$, Ms. Tory asks if they think there is a connection between the degree of the function and the number of times it takes to get to a constant difference in the table. She has students whisper to a partner their hypothesis and say they will continue to work on

FIGURE 8.20

POLYNOMIAL CONCEPT ATTAINMENT

What Is a Polynomial?

These ARE Polynomials	These ARE NOT Polynomials

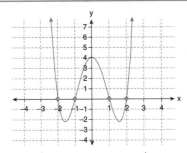

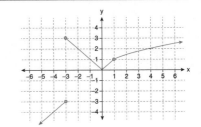

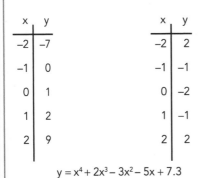

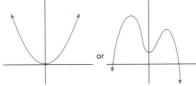

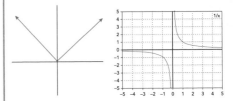

x	y
−2	−7
−1	0
0	1
1	2
2	9

x	y
−2	2
−1	−1
0	−2
1	−1
2	2

x	y
−2	−5/2
−1	−2
0	und.
1	2
2	5/2

x	y
−1	und.
0	0
1	1
4	2
9	3

$$y = x^4 + 2x^3 - 3x^2 - 5x + 7.3$$

$$y = 2.7x^5$$

$$y = 5 \qquad y = \frac{-3}{4}x^{31} + 3x - 1$$

$$y = x^2 + x^{2/3} + 3$$

$$y = \frac{x^3 + 2x^2 - x + 1}{x - 2}$$

$$y = \sqrt{x} \qquad y = \sqrt[3]{x} + 4$$

$$y^2 = x$$

Write three sentences that describe what makes a polynomial, a polynomial.

 The Concept Attainment Activity can be downloaded at resources.corwin.com/everymathlearner6-12.

this in the next activity. Figure 8.21 shows Ms. Tory's work on the whiteboard that facilitated the class conversation.

Ms. Tory introduces the next activity where students will explore patterns in tables to determine if they are polynomial functions or not. This is a tiered activity, and she has her students work in predetermined partners from her appointment clocks (see Chapter 6) based on readiness. The top-tier activity, called Cut the Cake, is self-directed and not only leads students to discover the constant finite difference of a polynomial function but also explores how to find the exact function first from a system of equations and then from the finite differences. The middle-tier activity, Trying Tables, is also self-directed, exploring the finite differences from a table of values. Students then use the constant differences to find values of the functions. The final tier, Polynomial or Not?, guides students through thinking about the finite differences and how they apply to the degree of the function. Figure 8.22 shows Cut the Cake, Figure 8.23 shows Trying Tables, and Figure 8.24 shows Polynomial or Not?

Ms. Tory circulates through the room, visiting each pair as they work. She believes the tiers she created are appropriate because

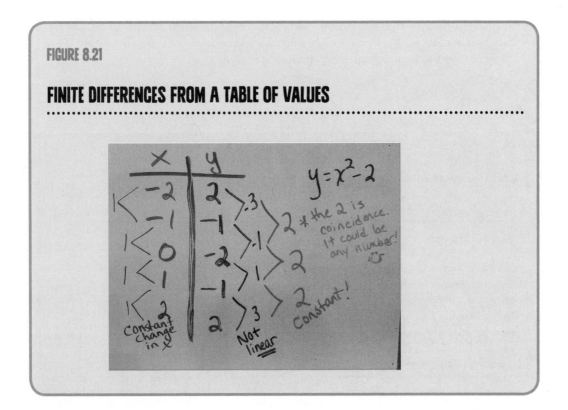

FIGURE 8.21

FINITE DIFFERENCES FROM A TABLE OF VALUES

no pair of students feels their task is too easy, nor does any pair complete their activity too quickly. She begins her monitoring of students with the pairs of students working with the Polynomial or Not? activity, to be sure that each pair of students understands the directions and are able to begin. She next visits the Cut the Cake students to be sure that they have "cut the cake" correctly and have built the first table of values without error, knowing that if this is completed incorrectly, the rest of the activity will be affected. She then checks in with the Trying Tables groups to be sure that they are moving along well. After checking in with every pair of students, she is able to move more freely through the classroom, working with students as she is needed and observing the students with whom she has concerns. As she monitors progress, she makes note of whom she wants to present their work based on

---

FIGURE 8.22

TIER 1: CUT THE CAKE

Cut the Cake

Kadi the crazy pastry chef decided that she wanted to cut her cakes into as many pieces with the fewest cuts as possible. She didn't even care that it would cause pieces that were irregular in size and shape. She began cutting cakes in the following manner:

Record the maximum number of pieces Kadi can get for each number of cuts.

Number of cuts	0	1	2	3	4
Number of pieces					

Kadi (being a math enthusiast) wanted to determine if her new way of cutting cakes was a polynomial function. She decided to see how the number of pieces was changing by looking at the differences.

1st Differences

2nd Differences

Is the function linear? _____   How do you know?

Is the function quadratic? _____   How do you know?

What is the maximum number of cake pieces you can obtain by making five cuts? _____
Explain how you figured this out.

Kadi thought this was way cool! She decided to play with quadratic functions some more! If the first numbers in each row are 1, 1, and 1 respectively, what is the quadratic relationship? (See hints below if needed!)

$$f(x) = ax^2 + bx + c$$

x	0	1	2	3	4
y = f(x)	1				

1st difference: _____ 1 _____   _____   _____   _____

2nd difference: _____ 1 _____   _____   _____

Hints for steps:
1. The function is quadratic. What does that tell you about the 2nd difference?
2. Try to fill in the 1st differences.
3. Try to fill in the y-values or f(x) in the chart.
4. Think about the quadratic relation, $f(x) = ax^2 + bx + c$. If x = 0, what does y or f(x) equal? Where is this in the table?
5. If x = 1, what does y equal? If x = 2, what does y equal?

6. Can you use step 5 to find a system of equations to solve for a and b?

(Continued)

FIGURE 8.22 (Continued)

If the first numbers in each row are –2, 3, and 4 respectively, what is the quadratic relationship?

$$f(x) = ax^2 + bx + c$$

x	0	1	2	3	4
y = f(x)	–2				

1st difference: 3 _____ _____ _____ _____

2nd difference: 4 _____ _____ _____

Kadi wondered why this worked, and if it could be made easier. She noticed the systems were the same both times except for the constants. She used the same process with only the algebraic symbols.

$$f(x) = ax^2 + b + c$$

x	0	1	2	3	4
y = f(x)	c	a + b + c	4a + 2b + c		

1st difference: a + b _____ _____ _____ _____

2nd difference: _____ _____ _____

Fill in the rest of the chart. What is always on the 2nd difference line? _____

How could this be used to find the quadratic function equation given the first values in each row?

The ever-curious (but still crazy) Kadi questioned if this would work for cubic functions as well!

$$f(x) = ax^3 + bx^2 + cx + d$$

x	0	1	2	3	4	5
$y = f(x)$	13	17	27	55	113	213

1st difference:

2nd difference:

3rd difference:

Find the cubic function for this table of values. If you like, do the next problem first.

Can you generalize for any cubic function?

$$f(x) = ax^3 + bx^2 + cx + d$$

x	0	1	2	3	4	5
$y = f(x)$						

1st difference:

2nd difference:

3rd difference:

The Cut the Cake answer key can be downloaded at resources.corwin .com/everymathlearner6-12.

FIGURE 8.23

TIER 2: TRYING TABLES

Trying Tables

Polynomial functions can appear to be difficult to discover from a table of values unless you know a cool pattern that emerges.

Part 1

Use repeated (finite) differences and see what happens.

1. This is a cubic polynomial function.

x	y
−2	15
−1	1
0	−1
1	−3
2	−17

    How many times did you have to find a difference before the differences showed a constant change?

2. This is a quadratic polynomial function.

x	y
−2	2
−1	−2
0	−4
1	−4
2	−2

    How many times did you have to find a difference before the differences showed a constant change?

3. This is a fifth degree polynomial function.

x	y
−3	−311
−2	−47
−1	1
0	1
1	1
2	49
3	313
4	1201

How many times did you have to find a difference before the differences showed a constant change?

What can you conclude about the degree of a polynomial function and the number of times it takes to get to a constant difference?

This process is called either repeated difference or finite differences. Explain why both names would be appropriate.

Part 2

You have now discovered a pattern for determining if a table is a polynomial table or not. Decide whether each of the following tables is a polynomial function or not. Explain how you know.

1.

x	y
−4	und.
−3	13
−2	6.5
−1	2.33
0	0.25
1	0.2
2	2.1667
3	6.1429
4	20.111

2.

x	y
−3	−4.442
−2	3.26
−1	−2
0	0
1	2
2	3.26
3	4.44

Part 3

You can use repeated differences to find the value of functions as well.

1. Find as many repeated differences for the following cubic function as possible. Note that the table is drawn horizontally, so the differences will go down the page instead of to the right.

(Continued)

FIGURE 8.23 (Continued)

x	1.3	2.3	3.3	4.3	5.3	6.3
y	2.197	12.167	35.937	79.507		

Knowing that it is a cubic function, what should the values on the bottom row (third differences) be? Fill them in.

Next, use the values on the third row to fill in the values on the second row (second differences).

Repeat this process to find the first differences.

Finally, fill in the missing values in the table.

2. Use finite differences to find the missing values in the function table.

x	−3	−2	−1	0	1	2	3	4
y	18	−13	−10	−3	2			

Not everyone has completed this activity. Please explain:

1. How can you determine from a table of values if a function is a polynomial function or not, and if it is, the degree of the function.

2. How can using finite differences help find missing values in a function table, if the function is polynomial?

 The Trying Tables activity can be downloaded at resources.corwin .com/everymathlearner6-12.

FIGURE 8.24

TIER 3: POLYNOMIAL OR NOT?

Polynomial or Not?

Polynomial functions can appear to be difficult to discover from a table of values unless you know a cool pattern that emerges.

Part 1

Use repeated (finite) differences and see what happens.

1. This is a cubic polynomial function.

Note: The x-values are changing constantly (by 1 in this table), so the process of finite differences will work.	

x	y				
−2	15	−14			
−1	1	−2			
0	−1	−2			
1	−3	−14			
2	−17				

How many times did you have to find a difference before the differences showed a constant change?

2. This is a quadratic polynomial function. Find the first and second differences.

x	y
−2	2
−1	−2
0	−4
1	−4
2	−2

How many times did you have to find a difference before the differences showed a constant change?

(Continued)

FIGURE 8.24 (Continued)

3. This is a fifth degree polynomial function.

x	y
−3	−311
−2	−47
−1	1
0	1
1	1
2	49
3	313
4	1201

How many times did you have to find a difference before the differences showed a constant change?

What can you conclude about the degree of a polynomial function and the number of times it takes to get to a constant difference?

This process is called either repeated difference or finite differences. Explain why both names would be appropriate.

Part 2

You have now discovered a pattern for determining whether a table is a polynomial table or not. Decide whether each of the following tables is a polynomial function or not. Explain how you know.

1.

x	y
−4	und.
−3	13
−2	6.5
−1	2.33
0	0.25
1	0.2
2	2.1667
3	6.1429
4	20.111

Explain your conclusion:

2.

x	y
−3	−4.442
−2	3.26
−1	−2
0	0
1	2
2	3.26
3	4.44

Explain your conclusion:

3.

x	y
−4	137
−3	18
−2	−13
−1	−10
0	−3
1	2
2	23
3	102
4	305

Explain your conclusion:

You can also use a horizontal table and the same process.

4.

x	−2	1	0	1	2	3
y	−11	1.5	4	5.5	3	3.5

(Continued)

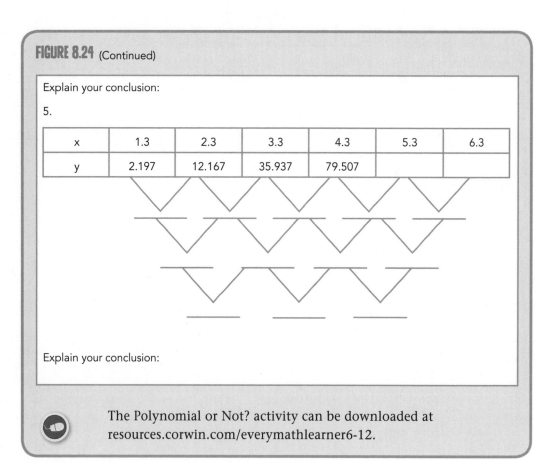

FIGURE 8.24 (Continued)

Explain your conclusion:

5.

x	1.3	2.3	3.3	4.3	5.3	6.3
y	2.197	12.167	35.937	79.507		

Explain your conclusion:

The Polynomial or Not? activity can be downloaded at resources.corwin.com/everymathlearner6-12.

completeness of understanding, quality of explanation, and a chance to have students present who do not often present. As she makes this determination, Ms. Tory asks the partners if they will be willing to present their work and gives them a chance to practice what they will say before going to the front of the class.

After students have finished their tasks, Ms. Tory calls the class back together as a whole. The tasks have been designed to build on each other, and so she asks the partners presenting Polynomial or Not? to share their process, one problem that is challenging, and their conclusions. She listens for the primary conclusion of this task to be that tables can be used to determine if a function is a polynomial function or not and its degree if it is. Following the presentation, she asks if anyone else who has done the same task can add to the conclusions. She repeats this process with Trying Tables next, knowing that the added component of understanding would be that not only can tables determine polynomial and degree, but the process of repeated differences can help you find missing values in a table without knowing the exact polynomial function.

Finally, the presentation from Cut the Cake adds the understanding that the exact polynomial function can be found if the first values in the table and each successive difference are known.

To conclude class, Ms. Tory has her students complete the following exit card: How can you determine from a table of values if a function is a polynomial function or not? How can you determine the degree of the function if it is polynomial? What other cool things will a table allow you to find for a polynomial function?

DAILY PLANNING—DAY 2

After observing students' work and reviewing the individual exit cards from Day 1, Ms. Tory identifies the following:

- All students can explain that if the differences in a table of values eventually reach a constant difference, it is a polynomial function.

- Some students repeat the differences until they reach a constant difference of zero and so concluded that the degree of the polynomial was one greater than what it actually was.

- Some students working with Trying Tables are not able to use the concept of common differences to find missing values independently.

- All students correctly explained that the number of times it took to reach a constant difference was equal to the degree of the polynomial (although there is some confusion about how many differences are needed as mentioned in the second bullet). No students have explored this prior to this lesson, and many comment that it is an easier way to work with tables to decide what kind of function it is. Many students who completed the Cut the Cake exercise state that it is helpful to have a specific pattern to find the function equation instead of trying to find a pattern from the table when it is a challenging function rule.

Ms. Tory is not concerned about some of the challenges she sees in the different activities, as Day 1 was to pique students' interest and have all students working appropriately and making initial connections.

The second day of the unit will continue to build on students' prior knowledge and be a review of the polynomial operations of addition, subtraction, and multiplication. Ms. Tory anticipates that students will be able to add and subtract without problem, and most will be able to multiply two binomials using the distributive property, which they learned in previous years as "FOIL." She wants to take the time today to build all students' confidence in working with polynomials as well as to lay the foundation for the understanding that polynomials form a system that is analogous to integers.

Ms. Tory gives her students a four-problem warm-up: one expression involving addition and subtraction of polynomials to simplify, a multiplication problem involving two binomials, a multiplication problem with three binomials, and a multiplication problem with a binomial and a trinomial. She wants to see if her students are completely comfortable and have multiple strategies to solve these problems. If this is the case, Ms. Tory will move ahead on her calendar to Day 3 and explore multiple methods for multiplication and Pascal's triangle. However, she is convinced that if students need a day of review of basic skills with polynomials for greater confidence and comfort, it will be worth the time. As expected, most students are able to simplify the expression, although some still make mistakes with like terms involving more than one variable or exponent, and others make computational mistakes with integers. She is surprised that many students make errors with multiplying the two binomials, and almost none have strategies for anything other than the multiplication of two binomials. Based on her observations of the warm-up, Ms. Tory proceeds with her lesson plan.

To begin Day 2, Ms. Tory tells her students that today is all about "Been There, Done That!" There is nothing brand new today, and it is all about being very sure that they can perform the basic operations with polynomials before getting more complex with division and factoring. She next posts the tables from Cut the Cake showing the algebraic differences of quadratic and cubic polynomials and asks two students who had completed the task yesterday to explain how the differences are found. Students are able to discuss substitution, evaluation, and combining like terms in their explanations. She tells her students that she thought that she would ask them to work on quartic and quintic solutions, but as she starts the quartic solutions, she realizes that even she doesn't want to do that much hand work! Instead, she has another idea to think about combining like terms.

Ms. Tory brings out algebra tiles for the students. Some grumble that they used those in middle school and don't need them now. She answers, "Been There, Done That!" and then explains that they won't be used a lot, but she has always found that seeing the visual tools often helps to make sense of strategies as well as clarifying common misconceptions when working with polynomials. In fact,

FIGURE 8.25

DAY 2 LESSON PLAN

Beyond Linear: Working With Polynomials Lesson Plan—Day 2

Date: 10/25

Standards:

Understand that polynomials form a system analogous to the integers, namely, they are closed under the operations of addition, subtraction, and multiplication; add, subtract, and multiply polynomials

Highlighted Standards for Mathematical Practice:
SMP1: Make sense of problems and persevere in solving them
SMP2: Reason abstractly and quantitatively
SMP5: Use appropriate tools strategically
SMP6: Attend to precision
SMP7: Look for and make use of structure
SMP8: Look for and express regularity in repeated reasoning

K: Vocabulary: degree (like terms), define "term" by the "what" and "how many"

Strategies for operations with polynomials

U: Polynomials are very similar to integers. Arithmetic with polynomials works in the same ways as arithmetic with integers. They are closed in addition, subtraction, and multiplication, just as are integers. (Algebra is grown up arithmetic.)

D: Operate on polynomials using multiple strategies.

Explain how operating on polynomials is like operating on integers.

Whole Class:

1. Review the algebraic repeated differences from yesterday, and add tables already filled in for 4th and 5th degrees. Discuss how the differences were found.

2. Ask students to brainstorm how they know which terms to combine of find differences of when simplifying expressions. How does this relate to adding and subtracting polynomials?

3. Introduce stations -

Stations: Students are required to do a minimum of one activity in addition/subtraction and one with multiplication.

Algebra Tiles: Practice addition, subtraction, and multiplication with algebra tiles. Goal is to reinforce like terms with symbolic notation (e.g., and) and set up the area model (or box method) for multiplication.

(Continued)

FIGURE 8.25 (Continued)

Roll a Problem: Addition and Subtraction

Roll a Problem: Multiplication

Game Station: Polynomial Memory

Nike: Just Do It! Worksheet station

Closure: In what ways are working with polynomials and integers alike? Sticky note post up and grouping to summarize

Individual/formative assessment: Practice sheets

 The entire week's daily lesson plans and blank lesson planning templates can be downloaded at resources.corwin.com/everymathlearner6-12.

she plans to use them to introduce some new strategies the next 2 days as well. She asks her students to work with her to review their use as one of the stations uses them for sketching addition, subtraction, and multiplication.

As Ms. Tory reviews the use of algebra tiles, she emphasizes the difference between $x + x$ and $x \cdot x$. She reminds students that addition combines and counts a total of like things, so $x + x$ means that there are two x-tiles, and multiplication creates an area, so $x \cdot x = x^2$. She shows the difference in the tiles and tells her students that no one should make the mistake of $x + x = x^2$ or $x \cdot x = 2x$! Figure 8.26 shows the algebra tile difference between $x + x$ and $x \cdot x$.

She also reviews multiplication of polynomials with the algebra tiles, knowing that it will lead to tomorrow's area or lattice model as well as factoring and division. She discusses with her students the limitations of not being able to model beyond first- and second-degree polynomials because of the tiles but reinforces they are used to more deeply understand the concept and not as much for solving complex problems.

Ms. Tory lets her students know that today is all about their choices (interest differentiation) and practice. They may work alone, with a friend, or up to three people in a group. Students can choose the stations they want to do, as long as they show that they have added, subtracted, and multiplied polynomials. Ms. Tory asked students to complete at least two of the stations along with the

ALGEBRA TILES: $X + X$ VERSUS $X \cdot X$

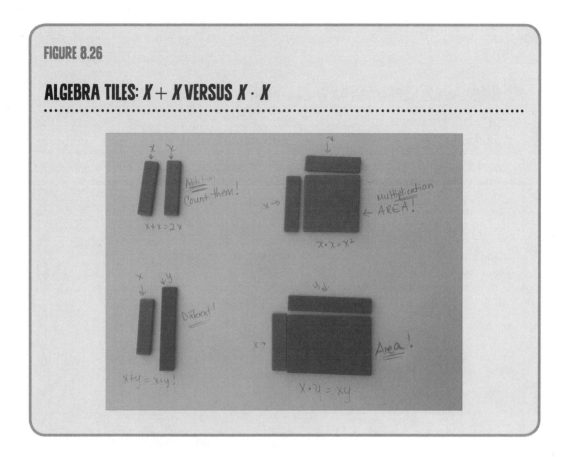

"Nike—Just Do It" station, which is required for all students. That worksheet and an exit card would be collected at the end of class. The other stations are for fun and practice. Figure 8.27 explains the four stations.

Ms. Tory is careful to watch her students at work at the various stations. She corrects sign errors that are made, sometimes as an oversight and other times from not being secure with integer operations. Some students are still making exponent errors when multiplying or not paying attention to exponents when determining like terms. She reinforces to the students the need to attend to precision and even reminds them of SMP 6—attend to precision!

At the end of the class time, Ms. Tory asks her students to pair with a partner they have not worked with yet this week. She asks them to share their roses (things that were wonderful) and thorns (things that stuck a little) from working with polynomials. She next asks them to discuss the similarities and differences between working with polynomials and working with integers in addition,

FIGURE 8.27

POLYNOMIAL ARITHMETIC REVIEW STATIONS

Station	Explanation
Algebra Tile Practice	Station using and sketching algebra tiles with simplifying expressions and multiplying polynomials. Students reflect on similarities and differences of adding, subtracting, and multiplying integers and polynomials.
Roll-a-Problem for addition and subtraction	Roll dice and draw cards to build problems to solve on a template. 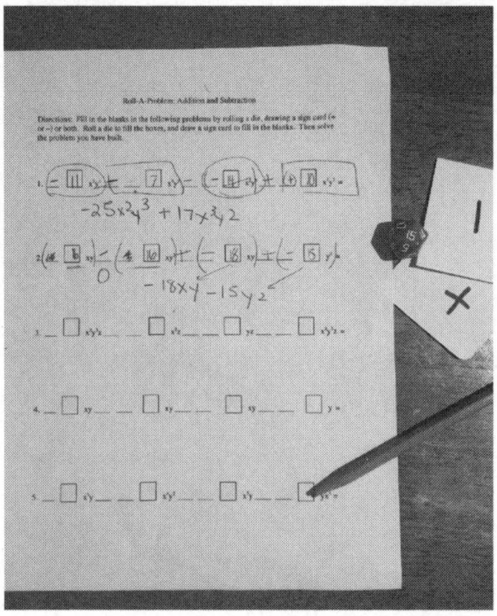
Roll-a-Problem for multiplication	Roll dice and draw cards to build problems to solve on a template. 

Polynomial Memory	Play a memory game with polynomial problems and solutions to match. 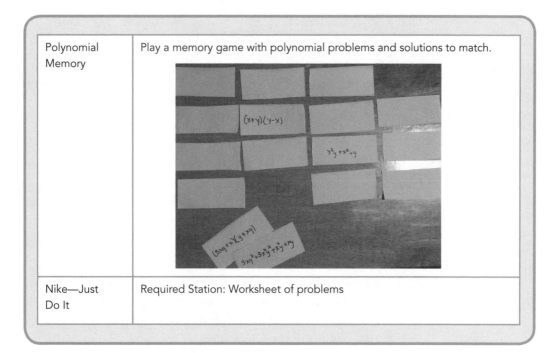
Nike—Just Do It	Required Station: Worksheet of problems

subtraction, and multiplication. Ms. Tory adds that this will be their exit card ticket for the day, so take advantage of time to talk to each other and gain ideas.

Class ends as students finish their exit card prompts and turn in both the exit card and "Nike—Just Do It" worksheet. On the way out the door, students pick up a practice sheet, primarily on multiplication and a few polynomial addition and subtraction problems, for homework.

DAILY PLANNING—DAY 3

Ms. Tory reviews her students' work from the operations worksheet and exit card and finds that her students are able to add polynomials without problem, other than careless errors. Her students easily multiply two binomials using distribution as expected, and 12 students are able to use distribution to multiply polynomials other than binomials. She realizes the following:

- Subtraction is still more confusing than adding polynomials for five students, who continue to make sign errors.

- Multiplying beyond distributing two binomials (students still referred to this as FOIL) is problematic for a little more than half of the class.

- Eight students remember how to use standard algorithm multiplication for multiplying a trinomial and a binomial.

- No students appear to have any strategy beyond distributive property for multiplying polynomials other than the few who were able to use the standard algorithm.

- Students' explanations on the exit cards comparing integers and polynomials are clear for all students in using the coefficients of the terms in the same ways that integers are used in operations. Many say that the coefficients follow the same integer rules as just using integers. This is the first step for what Ms. Tory was hoping to see because it shows that her students are making the connection to prior knowledge when operating with polynomials and not trying to learn "a new thing."

- Students do not consider exponent or integer rules when multiplying polynomials in their explanations, and as expected, no students talk about closure of polynomials, as that had never been discussed.

The warm-up on the board as students come into class are arithmetic problems, including expanding multidigit numbers and multiplying using either lattice or box method and expanding exponential notation into multiplication of repeated factors. These simple problems will be used to transition into alternate methods of polynomial multiplication and binomial expansion. She notices that most students do not know the box or area model for multiplication, and approximately half of the class knows how to use lattice multiplication. This causes Ms. Tory to revise the order in the "Been There, Done That!" practice by moving the standard algorithm first followed by the alternative methods that will require direct instruction.

To begin class, Ms. Tory asks her students to choose a partner and sit in chairs back-to-back with their whiteboards, markers, and erasers. She lets students know that they will begin with the "Been There, Done That!" problems so they can see how the same processes also apply to multiplying polynomials. She explains to the students that they will each work the problems on their whiteboards, and when both are ready, they will turn around and compare their work. She begins with triple-digit by double-digit standard algorithm multiplication, warning students to keep the problem on one side of their whiteboards because they would put a second problem next to it. Almost all students are able to complete this without problem, and so Ms. Tory then asks the students to

Figure 8.28 shows Ms. Tory's lesson plan for Day 3.

DAY 3 LESSON PLAN

Beyond Linear: Working With Polynomials Lesson Plan—Day 3

Date: 10/26

Standards:
Understand that polynomials form a system analogous to that of integers, namely, they are closed under the operations of addition, subtraction, and multiplication; add, subtract, and multiply polynomials.

Use the structure of an expression to identify ways to rewrite it.

Prove polynomial identities and use them to describe numerical relationships.

Highlighted Standards for Mathematical Practice:
SMP2: Reason abstractly and quantitatively
SMP5: Use appropriate tools strategically
SMP6: Attend to precision
SMP7: Look for and make use of structure
SMP8: Look for and express regularity in repeated reasoning

K: Strategies for operations with polynomials (e.g., lattice multiplication)
Binomial expansion using Pascal's triangle

U: Polynomials are very similar to integers. Arithmetic with polynomials works in the same ways as arithmetic with integers. They are closed in addition, subtraction, and multiplication, just as are integers. (Algebra is grown-up arithmetic.)

D: Operate on polynomials using multiple strategies.
Use Pascal's triangle to expand binomials.
Explain how operating on polynomials is like operating on integers.

Whole Class:

1. Back-to-back whiteboard review of multiplication
   a. Double-digit multiplication using lattice and box methods
   b. Binomial multiplication with distributive property (FOIL for most)
   c. Triple-digit multiplication with standard algorithm
2. Introduce methods of multiplication with polynomials with back-to-back practice
   a. Distributive Property (quick because already know binomial. Show trinomial)
   b. Area or box / Like lattice when you add diagonal boxes
   c. Standard algorithm (if time permits)

3. Show binomial raised to a power
   a. $(a + b)^2$ – they do on white boards using whatever method
   b. $(a + b)^3$ – take solution from a. (above) and multiply again

(Continued)

FIGURE 8.28 (Continued)

  c. Show products of $(a + b)^4$ and $(a + b)^5$
  d. See what patterns students recognize in the products based on the powers
  e. Pascal's triangle

Menu Planner
(Work alone or with one partner; finish as homework)

Main Course: Please complete:

- Practice sheet with multiplication using various strategies and Pascal's triangle practice – Do last so it can be homework if needed.
- Choose a "Fill-It" card to solve.

Side Dish: Math Game. Choose one to play:

- Cut-and-Paste Multiplication Match
- Build-a-Problem Multiplication of Polynomials
- Multiplying Polynomials Build-a-Square

Dessert: If time, you may:

- Create a word problem that involves multiplication of polynomials
- Play another game

Exit Card: Which method for multiplying polynomials do you like best and why?

  1. Multiply $(x^3 + x^2 – 3x + 5)(x^2 + 9x + 2)$
  2. Expand $(x – 2)^5$

How does multiplying polynomials relate to multiplying integers?

Formative Assessment/Check for Understanding: Practice sheets and record sheet from game that is chosen.

 The entire week's daily lesson plans and blank lesson planning templates can be downloaded at resources.corwin.com/everymathlearner6-12.

use the exact process on polynomials, multiplying a trinomial and a binomial next to the numeric multiplication. Figure 8.29 shows one student's whiteboard with the standard algorithm.

Ms. Tory next models lattice multiplication and has her students try the process on their whiteboards. Figure 8.30 shows examples of lattice multiplication using whole numbers.

Ms. Tory decides not to proceed with the area or box model of multiplication, as no students knew that model, and she does not want to cause any confusion. She does not feel that it will contribute to further understanding of polynomial multiplication and so decides to move into polynomial multiplication using

FIGURE 8.29

STANDARD ALGORITHM OF MULTIPLICATION

. . . .

$$
\begin{array}{r}
3\overset{2}{2}5 \\
47 \\
\hline
2275 \\
1300 \\
\hline
15{,}275
\end{array}
$$

$$
\begin{array}{r}
x^2 + 3x + 2 \\
x - 4 \\
\hline
-4x^2 - 12x - 8 \\
x^3 + 3x^2 + 2x \\
\hline
x^3 - x^2 - 10x - 8
\end{array}
$$

FIGURE 8.30

LATTICE MULTIPLICATION

. . . .

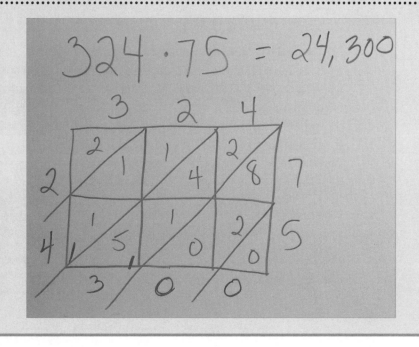

$324 \cdot 75 = 24{,}300$

a modified lattice method that follows the lattice method with whole numbers. Figure 8.31 shows an example of polynomial multiplication using this method.

FIGURE 8.31

LATTICE METHOD FOR POLYNOMIAL MULTIPLICATION

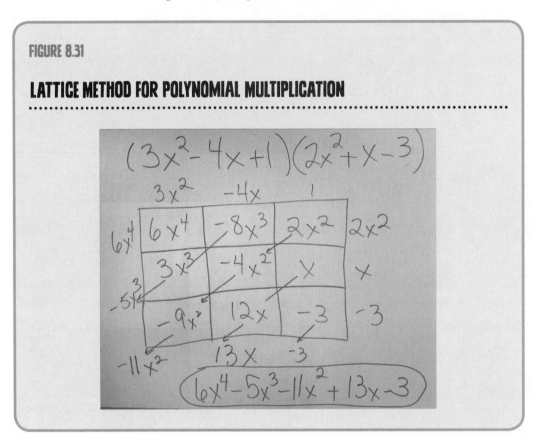

After several back-to-back practices with multiplication, Ms. Tory is ready to move on to the final topic of the day: binomial expansion using Pascal's triangle. To begin, Ms. Tory has her students show the factor expansion of $(x + 1)^1$, $(x + 1)^2$, $(x + 1)^3$, and $(x + 1)^4$. After showing the expansions, she asks her students to do the multiplication for the binomials to a power. She posts the answers as follows:

$$x + 1$$
$$x^2 + 2x + 1$$
$$x^3 + 3x^2 + 3x + 1$$
$$x^4 + 4x^3 + 6x^2 + 4x + 1$$

Ms. Tory then adds the fifth and sixth expansions and asks students if they notice any patterns.

$$x^5 + 5x^4 + 10x^3 + 10x^2 + 5x + 1$$
$$x^6 + 6x^5 + 15x^4 + 20x^3 + 15x^2 + 6x + 1$$

The first observation is that the exponents on the variable go down by one on each term. Another student notices the symmetry of the coefficients. Ms. Tory explains that this is the expansion pattern that will work with any binomial. She then asks if anyone would like to continue to multiply out all the binomials when computing an expansion. Of course, all the students say no. Ms. Tory knows that all of her students need to know how to expand a binomial using Pascal's triangle and exponent patterns and that no student currently knows how to do this. Because of this, she chooses to give direct instruction and have her students practice in pairs as she gives directions.

Ms. Tory tells her students that for the final 20 minutes of class, they will begin a Polynomial Menu Planner. In the menu, they have two required pieces (main dish), but they might want to save the practice sheet for the end, and it can be their homework if needed. The middle section (side dish) has a choice of three options, and if they have time and want extra practice, there is a dessert (optional) menu. To encourage her students to try the optional items, Ms. Tory lets her students know that their word problem could possibly find its way on an assessment if they write a very creative one. Figure 8.32 shows the Polynomial Menu Planner.

FIGURE 8.32

POLYNOMIAL MENU PLANNER

· ·

Menu Planner
(Work alone or with one partner; finish as homework)

Main Course: Please complete:

- Practice sheet with multiplication using various strategies and Pascal's triangle practice – Do last so it can be homework if needed.
- Choose a "Fill-It" card to solve.

Side Dish: Math Game. Choose one to play:

- Cut-and-Paste Multiplication Match
- Build-a-Problem Multiplication of Polynomials
- Multiplying Polynomials Build-a-Square

Dessert: If time, you may:

- Create a word problem that involves multiplication of polynomials
- Play another game

With 8 minutes left of class, Ms. Tory gathers the students back together to ask for questions or concerns. She gives them an exit card with two problems:

1. Multiply $(x^3 + x^2 - 3x + 5)(x^2 + 9x + 2)$
2. Expand $(x - 2)^5$

DAILY PLANNING—DAY 4

Ms. Tory now plans to move on to division of polynomials. This will be important as the class moves to completely factoring a polynomial using the rational root theorem. Today's lesson is designed to relate polynomial division to polynomial multiplication, as well as to relate division to the long division students learned in fourth grade.

FIGURE 8.33

DAY 4 LESSON PLAN

Beyond Linear: Working With Polynomials Lesson Plan – Day 4

Date: 10/27

Standards:
Understand that polynomials form a system analogous to that of integers, namely, they are closed under the operations of addition, subtraction, and multiplication; add, subtract, and multiply polynomials.

Rewrite simple rational expressions in different forms; write a(x)/b(x) in the form q(x) + r(x)/b(x), where a(x), b(x), q(x), and r(x) are polynomials with the degree of r(x) less than the degree of b(x), using inspection, long division, or, for the more complicated examples, a computer algebra system.

Use the structure of an expression to identify ways to rewrite it.

Highlighted Standards for Mathematical Practice:
SMP2: Reason abstractly and quantitatively
SMP3: Construct viable arguments and critique the reasoning of others
SMP5: Use appropriate tools strategically
SMP7: Look for and make use of structure
SMP8: Look for and express regularity in repeated reasoning

K: Strategies for operations with polynomials (e.g., lattice multiplication and division; long division)

U: Polynomials are very similar to integers. Arithmetic with polynomials works in the same ways as arithmetic with integers. They are closed in addition, subtraction, and multiplication, just as are integers. (Algebra is grown-up arithmetic.).

D: Operate on polynomials using multiple strategies.

Explain how operating on polynomials is like operating on integers.

Pair Activity:
Create a Fact Family!
- Numeric multiplication/Division
- Algebraic multiplication/Division (show multiplication—cubic product minimum)

Whole Class:
- How do fact families help?
- Would you rather multiply or divide? Why?

Using Multiplication to Divide
- Algebra Tiles
- Lattice/Area

Partner Activity
Create a problem and trade
      (Use Lattice/Area to multiply, then give division problem on opposite side)

Do It Again—Long Division
- Numeric
- Algebraic

What if the divisor is not a factor?
- Numeric
- Algebraic

Learning Profile Differentiation—Operation Comparison Project

We have been saying that working with polynomials is not that different from working with integers. It is now your job to explain what this means. Choose your method:
1. Create a Venn diagram with integers and polynomials
2. Make a tip sheet for how to preform operations on polynomials. Be sure to relate each operation to integers first and then to the polynomials.
3. An opposing page book showing the four operations—with the left page showing the operations with integers and the right page showing the operations with polynomials.

No matter which option you choose, be sure that you include

- clear steps for the various methods and operations
- direct and specific comparisons and examples for each operation with integers and with polynomials
- a conclusion determining whether working with polynomials is more alike or more different than working with integers

Formative Assessment/Check for Understanding: Class observations; Operation comparison project.

Closure: Class vote: Is working with polynomials more like or more different from working with integers?

 The entire week's daily lesson plans and blank lesson planning templates can be downloaded at resources.corwin.com/everymathlearner6-12.

Following yesterday's lesson, the students in Ms. Tory's class

- Multiply polynomials using both the lattice and standard methods

- Can generate Pascal's triangle and understand how the values correlate to the coefficients of the terms in a binomial expansion

- Are able to expand a binomial, but some students are making errors in the expansion by not correctly applying ascending or descending exponents to the terms as needed or by forgetting to multiply Pascal's value to the combined variable terms. This will take additional practice that Ms. Tory plans to build in through the rest of the unit in spiral review and stations.

Day 4 begins with a "Been There, Done That!" warm-up asking students to create two fact families involving multiplication and division: one using numbers and the other using polynomials. As class comes together, various students share their polynomial fact families. Ms. Tory explains that today's lesson focuses on dividing polynomials and that they will do it with two different methods just as they used two different methods for multiplication of polynomials. In fact, just like with their fact families, the methods will be the inverse process for the lattice method and the standard algorithms.

To begin, students complete a multiplication of polynomials using the lattice method and Ms. Tory reminds them that this is another "Been There, Done That!" Students begin by multiplying $(x^2 + 2x + 1)$ $(x + 3)$ on their whiteboards. As students work on the problem using the lattice method, she asks what the related division statement would be. Ms. Tory uses $(x^3 + 5x^2 + 7x + 3) \div (x + 3)$.

Ms. Tory asks her students to not do anything with their problems quite yet in order to show them with algebra tiles what they are about to do. To model the concept, she demonstrates multiplying $(2x + 3)(x-1)$ with the algebra tiles. Once the product is built on the inside of the area, she removes one of the factors of tiles from across the top. This now shows $(2x^2 + x - 3) \div$ $(x-1)$. She asks her students to talk about how they would figure out the missing factor. This is the same process they will be using with the lattice method.

Ms. Tory now asks her students to carefully erase the top polynomial from their lattice ($x^2 + 2x + 1$) and the terms that are in each of the cells of their boxes. This leaves the setup of the lattice, the product ($x^3 + 5x^2 + 7x + 3$) along the outside of the box, which is now the dividend, and one factor down the right side of the box, which is now the divisor. It is now set up to use as division. Figure 8.34 shows the setup of the division problem using the lattice method.

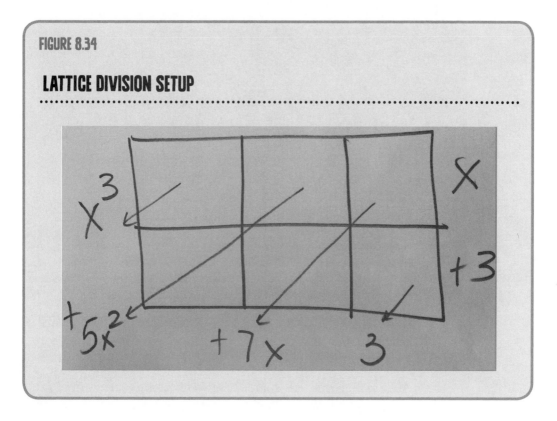

FIGURE 8.34

LATTICE DIVISION SETUP

Ms. Tory works through the inverse process of using the lattice to determine the missing factor, or quotient. She explains that just like finding a product using the lattice method, you find the missing factor or quotient by thinking about filling in cells that will combine diagonally to add to specific terms in the dividend. Figure 8.35 shows a completed division problem using the lattice method with color-coded steps.

Students practice in pairs, with one partner multiplying factors using the lattice method and then giving the related division problem to his or her partner to divide. This method allows students to practice multiplication and division, as well as

FIGURE 8.35

LATTICE POLYNOMIAL DIVISION

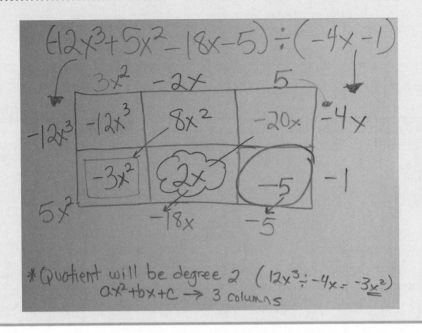

provides the correct answer for the division problem. If students disagree on an answer, Ms. Tory checks to see if there was an error that they did not spot.

After each partner has completed two division problems (four complete rounds), Ms. Tory brings students back together to work on the second method for polynomial division: long division. Ms. Tory uses the "Been There, Done That!" approach and asks her students to do a long division problem ($7,875 \div 21$) on one side of their whiteboard and compare with a partner. She has one student come up and explain every thought and every step of the long division process. Ms. Tory explains that this will be the exact same thought process and steps for long division with polynomials. Next to their long division problem, students follow Ms. Tory's model of $(2x^3 + 7x^2 + 5x - 10) \div (x + 2)$. Figure 8.36 shows the long division problems side by side.

To conclude the division practice, Ms. Tory introduces one more side-by-side set of problems involving remainders. She reminds students that their "Been There, Done That!" with remainders

FIGURE 8.36

LONG DIVISION

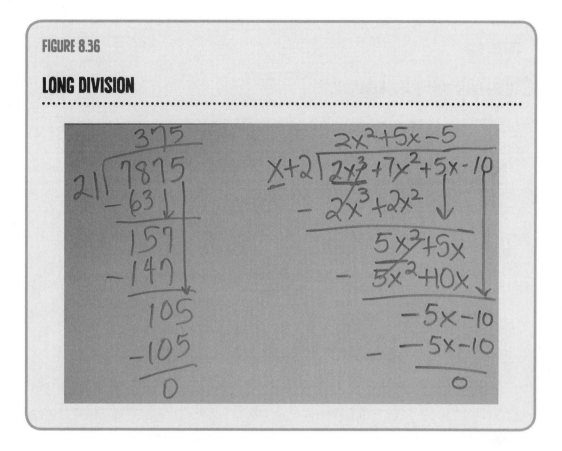

was to write the quotient with the remainder as a fraction, the remainder becomes the numerator of the fraction and the divisor the denominator. The same will be true with polynomial division. Figure 8.37 shows the side-by-side problems with a remainder.

To conclude the series of lessons, Ms. Tory wants her students to compare operating on polynomials with operating on integers. She has prepared three options from which students will choose based on Sternberg's triarchic theory that are analytical, practical, and creative. Students can continue to work on this project for homework. Figure 8.38 shows the task that will summarize the 4 days of the unit thus far.

Most students are able to finish their comparison project or come very close before the end of class, and so Ms. Tory brings the students together at the end of class to have a vote as to whether working with polynomials is more similar to or different from working with integers. She has several different students defend their positions as class closes.

FIGURE 8.37

LONG DIVISION WITH REMAINDER

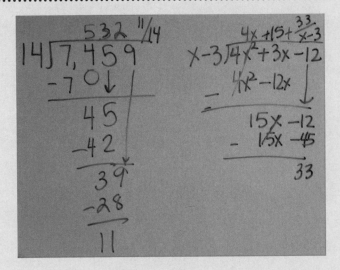

FIGURE 8.38

OPERATIONS COMPARISON PROJECT

Polynomial Operations Comparison Project

We have been saying that working with polynomials is not that different from working with integers. It is now your job to explain what this means. Choose your method:

1. Create a Venn diagram with integers and polynomials.

2. Make a tip sheet for how to perform operations on polynomials. Be sure to relate each operation to integers first and then to the polynomials.

3. An opposing page book showing the four operations—with the left page showing the operations with integers and the right page showing the operations with polynomials.

No matter which option you choose, be sure that you include the following:

- Clear steps for the various methods and operations

- Direct and specific comparisons and examples for each operation with integers and with polynomials

- A conclusion determining whether working with polynomials is more similar to or different from working with integers

DAILY PLANNING—DAY 5

Ms. Tory has planned differentiated stations based on readiness today to have students review and solidify all polynomial operations. She knows that having these skills as automatically as possible will help on Monday when she reviews factoring as division, leading to the rational root theorem and synthetic division to determine factors of polynomials with a degree higher than 2. These stations will also serve as review for an upcoming quiz.

Figure 8.39 Shows the Day 5 lesson plan.

FIGURE 8.39

DAY 5 LESSON PLAN

Beyond Linear: Working With Polynomials Lesson Plan – Day 5

Date: 10/28

Standards:

Understand that polynomials form a system analogous to that of integers, namely, they are closed under the operations of addition, subtraction, and multiplication; add, subtract, and multiply polynomials.

Use the structure of an expression to identify ways to rewrite it.

Prove polynomial identities and use them to describe numerical relationships.

Rewrite simple rational expressions in different forms; write $a(x)/b(x)$ in the form $q(x) + r(x)/b(x)$, where $a(x)$, $b(x)$, $q(x)$, and $r(x)$ are polynomials with the degree of $r(x)$ less than the degree of $b(x)$, using inspection, long division, or, for the more complicated examples, a computer algebra system.

Highlighted Standards for Mathematical Practice:

SMP2: Reason abstractly and quantitatively
SMP3: Construct viable arguments and critique the reasoning of others
SMP5: Use appropriate tools strategically
SMP6: Attend to precision
SMP7: Look for and make use of structure
SMP8: Look for and express regularity in repeated reasoning

K: Strategies for operations with polynomials (e.g., lattice multiplication)

Binomial expansion using Pascal's triangle

U: Polynomials are very similar to integers. Arithmetic with polynomials works in the same ways as arithmetic with integers. They are closed in addition, subtraction, and multiplication, just as are integers. (Algebra is grown up arithmetic.).

(Continued)

D: Operate on polynomials using multiple strategies.

Use Pascal's triangle to expand binomials.

Explain how operating on polynomials is like operating on integers.

Small Group MATH Stations (Readiness differentiation: Color-coded activities at each station):

M – Math Modeling – Use operations with polynomials to model and solve scenarios

A – Alone Time – Complete a worksheet on repeated differences, operations and binomial expansion

T – Take a Chance – Thinking about polynomial division: what about factoring? Do I really need the variables?

H – Hmmmm . . . How would you answer the following challenging questions?

 The entire week's daily lesson plans and blank lesson planning templates can be downloaded at resources.corwin.com/ everymathlearner6-12.

Ms. Tory has color-coded blue and red activities at each station for two different readiness levels, and she gives students a red, blue, or purple strip of paper as they enter the room. She tells the students that at each station are two tasks, a red and a blue. If they have one of those colored pieces of paper, they are to do those tasks. If they have purple, they may choose red or blue but must do at least one of each color in completing the stations. The students will move through four stations in any order, spending as much time as they need at each station. The stations are as follows:

M—Math Modeling—Use operations with polynomials to model and solve scenarios. This station has five different cards with word problems involving operations with polynomials. Students chose three to complete.

A—Alone Time—Complete a worksheet on repeated differences, operations, and binomial expansion.

T—Take a Chance—Thinking about polynomial division: What about factoring? Do I really need the variables? This station asks students to reason about the role of factoring based on their prior knowledge and leads students' thinking toward synthetic division. Both color tasks are the same.

H—Hmmmm—How would you answer the following challenging questions?

Figure 8.40 shows The T station: Take a Chance activity.

FIGURE 8.40

TAKE A CHANCE STATION

Take a Chance (Red, Blue, and Purple)

1. "Been There, Done That!" You have had experience factoring in your previous math classes.

   a. How would factoring relate to multiplication? How does it relate to division?

   b. Use factoring to find $(x^2 + x - 20) \div (x - 4)$

   c. Use factoring to find $(6x^2 + x - 2) \div (2x - 1)$

2. "Been There, Done That!" You have also learned to use long division to divide polynomials.

   a. Use long division to divide $(2x^5 + 5x^4 + 7x^3 + 2x^2 - x + 3)$ by $(x^2 + 2x + 3)$

   b. Notice the role of the variables in the long division. Do you think they are necessary? Could you use only the coefficients instead? Why or why not?

The T station worksheet can be downloaded at resources .corwin.com/everymathlearner6-12.

Figure 8.41 shows the red and blue H stations.

FIGURE 8.41

HMMMM STATION

Hmmmm . . . (Red)

1. If you know the degree of two different polynomials, how could you determine

   a. The degree of the sum of the polynomials?

   b. The degree of the product of the polynomials?

   c. The degree of the quotient of the polynomials if the greater degree polynomial is divided by the lesser degree polynomial?

2. What went wrong with the following binomial expansion? Correct the work please!

$$(2x^2 + 3)^3 =$$

$$(1 \bullet 2(x^2)^3) + (3 \bullet 2(x^2)^2(3)) + (3 \bullet 2(x^2)(3)^2) + 3^3 =$$

$$2x^5 + 18x^4 + 54x^2 + 27$$

3. Nancy says that the sum of two binomials will always be a binomial, and the product of two binomials will always be a trinomial. What do you think? What is the greatest and smallest number of terms that might be possible from adding or multiplying binomials? Explain how you know.

Hmmmm . . . (Blue)

1. Suppose you have a fourth-degree polynomial and a fifth-degree polynomial.

   a. What is the degree of the sum of the polynomials? Give an example to prove you are correct.

   b. What is the degree of the product of the polynomials? Give an example to prove you are correct.

   c. The degree of the quotient of the polynomials if the fifth degree polynomial is divided by the fourth degree polynomial? Give an example to prove you are correct.

2. What went wrong with the following binomial expansion? Correct the work please!

$$(2x^2 + 3)^3=$$

$$(1{\bullet}2(x^2)^3\,) + (3{\bullet}2(x^2)^2(3)\,) + (3{\bullet}2(x^2)\,(3)^2\,) + 3^3 =$$

$$2x^6 + 18x^4 + 54x^2 + 27$$

3. Nancy says that the sum of two binomials will always be a binomial, and the product of two binomials will always be a trinomial. What do you think? Defend why you agree or give counter-examples if you disagree.

The Hmmmm tasks can be downloaded at resources.corwin .com/everymathlearner6-12.

ADVICE FROM THE FIELD

The goal of sharing these two different weeks of differentiation is not to overwhelm you but to give you ideas on how to make adjustments for each day based on what you see in your students' learning from a previous day. Also bear in mind that not everything is differentiated. Many times, only one segment or one activity in a lesson will be differentiated, and often that will be a minor adjustment rather than separate activities.

Your practice in differentiating your classroom will build and grow over time, and anything you do *right now* to identify, acknowledge, and address your students' various learning needs will help them grow, succeed, and feel successful. The teachers you have seen throughout this book have been asked to share with you their best advice for getting started or continuing to grow in differentiation. Each teacher who differentiates begins in ways that make sense to him or her. What are your next steps?

WATCH IT!

As you watch Video 8.1, *Advice for Getting Started With Differentiation*, consider the following questions:

1. Which piece of advice motivates you to try or continue differentiation?

2. What will you do to take your next step in differentiation?

Video 8.1 Advice for Getting Started With Differentiation

CONCLUSION

One of my first years teaching, I had a mother come visit me at the end of the year. Her daughter was in my Algebra 1 class, and to say that she struggled would be one of the greatest understatements of my life. Kristen was a wonderful girl and tried very hard. She just was not able to grasp, understand, or remember much of anything. The mom asked me if there were any way I would consider giving her a D for the class so she could pass and graduate. Mind you, this was many years ago, before the state in which I taught had state testing, and any 2 years of mathematics was sufficient to graduate from high school. You see, Kristen already had a pre-algebra credit and would graduate if she had this Algebra 1 credit. I think back to so many students I have had over the years and wonder if I knew then what I know now, could I have reached Kristen? Perhaps, if I had known how to reach her artistic soul and taught more in pictures, it might have reached her and helped her learn math. Instead, I repeated what I had taught and tried to tutor her but had no way of thinking about teaching mathematics other than showing and repeating steps. And practice a lot.

It is even tougher for students today where expectations are more rigorous and high-stakes tests are prevalent. As secondary mathematics teachers, we probably all love math. We were probably good at it when we were students. There are a few secondary teachers out there who struggled to learn mathematics or had a later epiphany in understanding mathematics, but they are rare. The truth is, often we, as successful mathematicians, do not know why students have such a hard time learning math, yet we know they do. If you are like me and did not struggle as a student, please pause a moment to realize that it is probably your weakest link in being a mathematics teacher. If you are one of the teachers who went into secondary mathematics after struggling, we have much to learn from you and what turned you around! Learning to recognize how our students learn, and what they need to be successful, is a mark of artistry in teaching. That is what this book is about.

We have an added consideration when teaching mathematics to our students. As secondary students, they often come into our classrooms already shut down and convinced that they cannot do math. Yet we are able to change students' beliefs about themselves as learners, especially as learners of mathematics. If you have ever broken through with struggling students, you know the incredible joy of being a teacher.

As you have worked through this book, I hope you have new ideas about the teaching of mathematics and reaching our different learners. I trust that you understand the purposefulness of designing effective differentiation that is grounded in rigorous and conceptual standards and driven by individual students' needs. The fact that our students have very different needs, at the same time and in the same class, is incredibly challenging but critical to recognize and address if our students are to be successful. I have tried to equip you with a balance of the philosophy and reasoning of differentiation and practical application and examples.

Our goal in differentiation is to lift students up to their greatest potential in learning. By recognizing what is truly important in our content, where our students are as learners, and how they can best take their next steps in learning, we will reach that goal. It's not easy, but it is worth it. Think of all that is at stake with the best possible education of our children. I wish I could say that Kristen was my only example of my not being able to reach a student. She is not. Thankfully, there were many more years with understanding my students and differentiating than there were without. I hope you will start even now if you have never made addressing every mathematics learner in your classroom a priority. I encourage you to continue and grow in this very important profession of ours. Thank you for all you do for our students.

APPENDIX A

FURTHER READING ON THE TOPIC OF ENGLISH LANGUAGE LEARNERS

Throughout the text, there are suggestions for addressing English language learners (ELLs) that are specific to the topic of the text at the time. This does not begin to address the depth of research and knowledge in the area. We know that those struggling with language need very specific vocabulary instruction, both Tier 1 and Tier 2. Warning students in advance that they will be called on and allowing them to practice what they will say with a partner prior to having to speak will ease some of the stress of having to speak in class. Asking students to teach the class to count in their own language will help others understand the struggle to learn a new language, put the students in the role of the teacher, and help the students feel more a part of the classroom community. Pictures and motions help as well. These are just the beginnings of addressing our students who struggle with the language.

Following is a list to begin further reading.

Calderon, M. E., & Soto, I. (2016). *Academic language mastery: Vocabulary in context.* Thousand Oaks, CA: Corwin.

Coggins, D. S. (2014). *English learners in the mathematics classroom* (2nd ed.). Thousand Oaks, CA: Corwin.

Ellis, M., & Malloy, C. (2008). *Mathematics for every student: Responding to diversity, Grades 6–8.* Reston, VA: NCTM.

Freeman, D., Freeman, Y. S., & Soto, I. (2016). *Academic language mastery: Grammar and syntax in context.* Thousand Oaks, CA: Corwin.

Gottlieb, M. (2016). *Assessing English language learners* (2nd ed.). Thousand Oaks, CA: Corwin.

Gottlieb, M., & Ernst-Slavit, G. (2013). *Academic language in diverse classroom: Promoting content and language learning, mathematics Grades 6–8.* Thousand Oaks, CA: Corwin.

Gottlieb, M., & Ernst-Slavit, G. (2014). *Academic language, definitions and contexts.* Thousand Oaks, CA: Corwin.

LeMoyne, N., & Soto, I. (2016). *Academic language mastery: Culture in context.* Thousand Oaks, CA: Corwin.

Malloy, C. (2009). *Mathematics for every student: Responding to diversity, Grades 9–12.* Reston, VA: NCTM.

Moschkovich, J. N. (2013). Principles and guidelines for equitable mathematics teaching practices and materials for English language learners. *Journal of Urban Mathematics Education, 6*(1), 45–57.

Moschkovich, J. N. (2014). Building on student language resources during classroom discussions. In M. Civil & E. Turner (Eds.), *The Common Core State Standards in mathematics for English language learners: Grades K–8.* Alexandria, VA: TESOL International Association.

Ramirez, N. (2012). *Beyond good teaching: Advancing mathematics education for ELLs.* Reston, VA: NCTM.

Rodriguez, E. R., Bellanca, J., & Esparza, D. R. (2016). *What is it about me you can't teach? Culturally responsive instruction in deeper learning classrooms* (3rd ed.). Thousand Oaks, CA: Corwin.

Tellez, K., Moschkovich, J. N., & Civil, M. (Eds.). *Latinos/as and mathematics education: Research on learning and teaching in classrooms and communities.* Kansas City, MO: Information Age Publishing.

Zwiers, J., & Soto, I. (2016). *Academic language mastery: Conversational discourse in context.* Thousand Oaks, CA: Corwin.

APPENDIX B

FURTHER READING ON THE TOPIC OF SPECIAL EDUCATION

Students with diagnosed learning disabilities will benefit from the attention of differentiated tasks and lessons. This is not to imply that differentiation could, or should, replace special services. Certainly a student's Individual Education Plan (IEP) must be strictly followed. In addition, by differentiating appropriately for all students, mainstreamed students will often feel more a part of the learning community because they are not the only students doing something slightly different or with different pacing. In a differentiated math classroom, this is true of all students at various points of time.

The following is a partial list to continue reading in the field of special education.

Allsopp, D. H., Kyger, M. M., & Lovin, L. H. (2007). *Teaching mathematics meaningfully: Solutions for reaching struggling learners.* Baltimore: Brookes.

Berch, D. B., & Mazzocco, M. M. (2007). *Why is math so hard for some children?* Baltimore: Brooks.

Fattig, M. L., & Taylor, K. T. (2007). *Co-teaching in the differentiated classroom: Successful collaboration, lesson design and classroom management.* San Francisco: Jossey-Bass.

Fennell, F. (Ed.). (2011). *Achieving fluency: Special education and mathematics.* Reston, VA: NCTM.

Kurth, J. A., & Gross, M. (2015). *The inclusion toolbox: Strategies and techniques for all teachers.* Thousand Oaks, CA: Corwin.

Murawski, W. W., & Spencer, S. (2011). *Collaborate, communicate & differentiate! How to increase student learning in today's diverse schools.* Thousand Oaks, CA: Corwin.

Sousa, D. A. (2016). *How the special needs brain learns* (3rd ed.). Thousand Oaks, CA: Corwin.

Witzel, B. S., Riccomini, P. J., & Herlog, M. L. (2016). *Building number sense through the Common Core.* Thousand Oaks, CA: Corwin.

APPENDIX C

FURTHER READING ON THE TOPIC OF RICH PROBLEMS AND MATHEMATICAL DISCOURSE

This book has focused on the details of differentiating a mathematics classroom. I wish I had been able to include more information on choosing rich tasks and orchestrating productive mathematical discourse. Certainly the types of tasks that are chosen is of the utmost importance for learning. Mathematical discourse is the primary manner in which students make sense of learning and communicate thinking to both their peers and their teacher.

The following list is for further reading in these areas.

Kazemi, E. and Hintz, A. (2014). *Intentional talk: How to structure and lead productive mathematical discussions*. : Stenhouse.

Hull, T. H., Balka, D. S. & Miles, R. H. (2011). *Visible thinking in the K–8 mathematics classroom*. Thousand Oaks, CA: Corwin.

Schrock, C., Norris, K., Pugalee, D. K., Seitz, R. & Hollingshead, F. (2013). *NCSM Great tasks for mathematics: Engaging activities for effective instruction and assessment that integrate the content and practices of the common core state standards for mathematics, 6–12*. NCSM.

Sherin, M. Jacobs, V. & Philipp, R. (2011). *Mathematics teacher noticing: Seeing through teachers' eyes*. New York: Routledge.

Small, M. (2009). *Good questions: Great ways to differentiate mathematics instruction*. New York: Teachers College Press.

Small, M. and Lin, A. (2010). *More good questions: Great ways to differentiate secondary mathematics instruction*. New York: Teachers College Press.

Smith, M. S. & Stein, M.K. (2011). *5 Practices for orchestrating productive mathematics discussions*. Reston, VA: NCTM.

REFERENCES

Boaler, J. (2015). *Mathematical mindsets: Unleashing students' potential through creative math, inspiring messages and innovative teaching.* San Francisco: Jossey-Bass.

Cummings, C. B. (2000). *Winning strategies for classroom management.* Alexandria, VA: ASCD.

Dixon, J. K., Adams, T. L., & Nolan, E. C. (2015). *Beyond the Common Core: A handbook for mathematics in a PLC at work.* Bloomington, IN: Solution Tree.

Doubet, K. J. & Hockett, J. A. (2015). *Differentiation in middle & high school: Strategies to engage all learners.* Alexandria, VA: ASCD.

Dweck, C. S. (n.d.). AZQuotes.com. Retrieved January 1, 2016, from http://www.azquotes.com/quote/937595

Dweck, C. S. (2006). *Mindset: The new psychology of success.* New York: Random House.

Hattie, J. (2012). *Visible learning for teachers: Maximizing impact on learning.* New York: Routledge.

Hattie, J. (2013). Understanding learning: Lessons for learning, teaching and research. Retrieved from http://research.acer.edu.au/cgi/viewcontent.cgi?article=1207&context=research_conference

Jensen, E. (1998). *Teaching with the brain in mind.* Alexandria, VA: ASCD.

Kanold, T. D., & Larson, M. R. (2012). *Common Core mathematics in a PLC at work: Leader's guide.* Bloomington, IN: Solution Tree and NCTM.

Kanold, T.D. (2016), personal communication.

Kilpatrick, J., Swafford, J., & Findell, B. (Eds.). (2001). *Adding it up: Helping children learn mathematics.* Washington, DC: National Academies Press.

National Council of Teachers of Mathematics. (1989). *Curriculum and evaluation standards for school mathematics.* Reston, VA: Author.

National Council of Teachers of Mathematics. (1995). *Assessment standards for school mathematics.* Reston, VA: Author.

National Council of Teachers of Mathematics. (2000). *Principles and standards for school mathematics.* Reston, VA: Author.

National Council of Teachers of Mathematics. (2014). *Principles to actions: Ensuring mathematical success for all.* Reston: VA, Author.

Nisbet, R. E. (2009, February 8). Education is all in your mind. *New York Times.*

O'Connor, K. (2009). *How to grade for learning K–12* (3rd ed.). Thousand Oaks, CA: Corwin.

Popham, W. J. (2011). *Transformative assessment in action.* Alexandria, VA: ASCD.

Reeves, D. (2015). *Elements of grading.* Bloomington, IN: Solution Tree.

Smith, M. S., & Stein, M. K. (1998). Selecting and creating mathematical tasks: From research to practice. *Mathematics Teaching in the Middle School, 3*(5), 344–350.

Smith, N. N. (2017). *A mind for mathematics: Meaningful teaching and learning in elementary classrooms.* Bloomington, IN: Solution Tree.

Sousa, D. A. (2015). *How the brain learns mathematics* (2nd ed.). Thousand Oaks, CA: Corwin.

Sousa, D. A., & Tomlinson, C. A. (2011). *Differentiation and the brain: How neuroscience supports the learner-friendly classroom.* Bloomington, IN: Solution Tree.

Stein, M. K., Smith, M. S., Henningsen, M. A., & Silver, E. A. (2009). *Implementing standards-based mathematics instruction: A casebook for professional development* (2nd ed.). New York: Teachers College Press.

Sternberg, R. J. (2005). The theory of successful intelligence. *Interamerican Journal of Psychology, 39*(2), 189–202.

Styles, V. (2015, December 2). A primer for on personalized learning for Mark Zuckerberg—by Harvard's Howard Gardner. *Washington Post.* Retrieved from https://www.washingtonpost.com/news/answer-sheet/wp/2015/12/02/a-primer-for-mark-zuckerberg-on-personalized-learning-by-harvards-howard-gardner/

Tomlinson, C., & Imbeau, M. (2014). *A differentiated approach to the Common Core: How do I help a broad range of learners succeed with challenging curriculum?* Alexandria, VA: ASCD.

Tomlinson, C., & Moon, T. (2013). *Assessment and student success in a differentiated classroom.* Alexandria, VA: ASCD.

Tomlinson, C. A. (2001). *How to differentiate instruction in mixed-ability classrooms* (2nd ed.). Alexandria, VA: ASCD.

Tomlinson, C. A. (2014). *The differentiated classroom: Responding to the needs of all learners* (2nd ed.). Alexandria, VA: ASCD.

Tomlinson, C. A., & Imeau, M. B. (2010). *Leading and managing a differentiated classroom.* Alexandria, VA: ASCD.

Van de Walle, J. A. (2007). *Elementary and middle school mathematics: Teaching developmentally* (6th ed.). Boston: Pearson.

Walkington, C., Milan, S., & Howell, E. (2014). Personalized learning in algebra. *The Mathematics Teacher, 108*(4), 272–279.

Wiggins, G. (2012). Seven keys to effective feedback. *Educational Leadership, 70*(1), 10–16.

Wiliam, D. (2011). *Embedded formative assessment.* Bloomington, IN: Solution Tree.

Willis, J. (2006). *Research-based strategies to ignite student learning.* Alexandria: VA, ASCD.

INDEX

Supporting Teachers, Empowering Learners

Why Corwin Mathematics?

We've all heard this—"either you are a math person, or you are not." At Corwin Mathematics, we believe ALL students should have the opportunity to be successful in math! Trusted experts in math education such as Linda Gojak, Ruth Harbin Miles, John SanGiovanni, Skip Fennell, Gary Martin, and many more offer clear and practical guidance to help all students move from surface to deep mathematical understanding, from favoring procedural knowledge over conceptual learning, and from rote memorization to true comprehension. **We deliver research-based, high-quality content that is classroom-tested and ready to be used in your lessons**—today!

Through books, videos, consulting, and online tools, we offer a truly **blended learning experience that helps teachers demystify math for students.** The user-friendly design and format of our resources provides not only the best classroom-based professional guidance, but many activities, lesson plans, rubrics, and templates to help you implement changes at your own pace in order to sustain learning improvement over time. We are **committed to empowering every learner.** With our forward-thinking and practical offerings, Corwin Mathematics helps you enable all students to realize the power and beauty of math and its connection to everything they do.

Warm Regards,
The Corwin Mathematics Team

New titles from Corwin Mathematics!

The *what*, *when*, and *how* of teaching practices that evidence shows work best for student learning in mathematics.

Grades: K–12

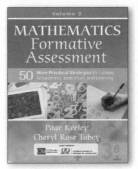

Everything you need to promote mathematical thinking and learning!

Grades: K–12

Move the needle on math instruction with these 5 assessment techniques!

Grades: K–8

See what's going on in your students' minds, plus get access to 340 rich tasks to use in instruction or assessment!

Grades: K–2 and 3–5

Students pursue problems they're curious about, not problems they're told to solve.

Grades: K–12

When it comes to math, standards-aligned is achievement-aligned...

A SAGE Publishing Company

Helping educators make the greatest impact

CORWIN HAS ONE MISSION: to enhance education through intentional professional learning.

We build long-term relationships with our authors, educators, clients, and associations who partner with us to develop and continuously improve the best evidence-based practices that establish and support lifelong learning.